# A Primer on Legal Reasoning

# A Primer on Legal Reasoning

Michael Evan Gold

ILR Press
AN IMPRINT OF
CORNELL UNIVERSITY PRESS
ITHACA AND LONDON

First published 2018 by Cornell University Press

Printed in the United States of America

Library of Congress Cataloging-in-Publication Data

Names: Gold, Michael Evan, author.
Title: A primer on legal reasoning / Michael Evan Gold.
Description: Ithaca [New York] : Cornell University Press, 2018. |
   Includes bibliographical references.
Identifiers: LCCN 2018011993 (print) | LCCN 2018012784 (ebook) |
   ISBN 9781501728600 (pdf) | ISBN 9781501728617 (epub/mobi) |
   ISBN 9781501730276 | ISBN 9781501730276 (cloth; alk. paper) |
   ISBN 9781501728594 (pbk.; alk. paper)
Subjects: LCSH: Law—Methodology. | Law—Interpretation and
   construction. | Reasoning.
Classification: LCC K213 (ebook) | LCC K213 .G65 2018 (print) |
   DDC 340/.19—dc23
LC record available at https://lccn.loc.gov/2018011993

# BRIEF CONTENTS

# Detailed Contents

# A Primer on Legal Reasoning

# Introduction

Lawyers, particularly law professors speaking to prospective or beginning law students, are fond of stating that thinking like a lawyer is something special, something that is powerful, esoteric, and unique. Such statements are partly true. Thinking like a lawyer—analytical thinking, as lawyers call it (everyone else calls it "critical thinking")—is a powerful tool because it allows one to understand and evaluate others' arguments and to make sound arguments of one's own. Further, analytical thinking is esoteric because most persons need advanced education to learn how to do it, and the subject matter to which it is applied is broad and complex. But the statements are partly false because analytical thinking is by no means unique. It is practiced in many disciplines, from engineering to economics, from statistics to philosophy. (For this reason, we wrote that learning analytical thinking requires advanced education, not law school.) The first premise of this book is that legal reasoning is simply rigorous thinking applied to the domain of law.

Legal reasoning is typically taught via the Socratic Method. In the early dialogues of Plato, the philosopher Socrates asked questions but gave no answers. Perhaps the questions he asked lacked good answers. Perhaps he wanted his interlocutors to figure out the answers for themselves. And perhaps (given that he was called a gadfly) he wanted to show them that they did not know as much as they thought they did. Most classes in law school resemble a dialogue with Socrates. The professor asks many questions and explains very little, either about the content of the law or about legal reasoning. A synonym for the "Socratic Method" as practiced in many law schools is "hide the ball."

The second premise of this book is that the ball need not be hidden, that analytical thinking can be taught in as transparent and orderly a manner as is mathematics or any other academic subject. Courses on critical thinking have precisely the same premise. Thus, this book is an introduction to critical thinking in the context of law. This book is not a shortcut to becoming a lawyer; it is not a substitute for law school. Rather, the book is a discussion of some of the most important techniques of reasoning used by lawyers—and by other rigorous thinkers.

The author believes that this book can be useful to two classes of reader. The first class comprises college students who are preparing to go to law school and law students who are in the first months of their legal education. Being familiar with the forms of legal argument will help students understand cases and respond to professors' hypothetical questions. The second class comprises anyone else who wants to understand and evaluate others' arguments and to make sound arguments of one's own. All citizens in a democracy need to be able to think critically about public issues, to cut through politicians' rhetoric and judge the validity of their assertions. Thinking analytically is a necessary step toward that end.

# § 1

# ISSUES

The purpose of this section is to introduce the student to the concept of issues. The student will learn how issues are created and how they are classified. In addition, the student will learn how to identify an issue.

## I. Definitions

Issues and resolutions go by various names, depending on the field of inquiry. In daily life, an issue is often called a "question," and the resolution of a question is an "answer."

QUESTION

Should Lennis and Phela paint the den pale blue, light green, or off white?

ANSWER

Pale blue.

In science, the resolution of an issue is a theory.

ISSUE

What is the mechanism of evolution?

THEORY

Changes in species are explained by natural selection.[1]

In law, the resolution of an issue by a tribunal such as a court or an administrative agency is a **finding** or a **holding**. Some holdings pertain to what the law should be.

ISSUE

Under the National Labor Relations Act, is an employer responsible for an unfair labor practice committed by a supervisor?

HOLDING

Yes.[2]

---

1. Before it is proved, a scientific theory is called a "hypothesis." When a scientific theory is well supported by evidence, the theory is often called a "law" or a "law of nature."

2. This book focuses on the interpretation of existing law, not the creation of new statutes. Nonetheless, it may be noted that the resolution of issues by a legislature is similar to resolution by a tribunal, though the terminology differs. When a legislature enacts a bill, the result is a **statute** or an **ordinance**. For example—

ISSUE

Should the legislature enact a statute that outlaws sending spam?

STATUTE

Sending spam shall be a felony punishable by thirty years of torture followed by death by kimchi.

As they consider whether to enact statutes, legislatures often make determinations about facts of the past, present, or future. Such determinations are called "findings." For example—

ISSUE

Is spam harmful?

FINDING

Spam costs America 666 gazillion dollars per day in lost productivity.

Other holdings pertain to facts.

ISSUE

> Did supervisor *S* of employer *ER* discharge worker *WR* because *WR* was soliciting coworkers to join a union?

HOLDING

> Yes.

Still other holdings pertain to the legal significance of facts.

ISSUE

> Is employer *ER* guilty of an unfair labor practice because supervisor *S* discharged worker *WR* for soliciting for a union?

HOLDING

> Yes.

A law case typically boils down to one or a small number of issues. When a tribunal makes holdings that resolve the issues, one party wins the case and the other party loses it.

As the foregoing illustrations demonstrate, issues and resolutions come in pairs. A resolution applies to the issue that generates the resolution, but not to other issues. Lennis and Phela's answer applies to the den in their house at this time; their answer does not apply to another time or another room. The theory of natural selection may explain evolution, but does not explain the orbit of the earth or the size of the gross domestic product. The holding that an employer is responsible for an unfair labor practice committed by a supervisor applies to the Labor Act, but not necessarily to other statutes.[3] The finding that *S* discharged *WR* for soliciting for a union applies to these persons at a particular moment, but not to other moments or to other persons.

An issue-and-resolution pair is often related to other issue-and-resolution pairs. For example, Lennis and Phela's decision about the color to paint their den relates to the issues of whether they should do anything to the den or leave it alone, whether they should paint the den or wallpaper it, whether they should do the work themselves or pay someone else to

---

3. For example, this holding does not tell us whether an employer is responsible under Title VII of the Civil Rights Act of 1964 for a supervisor's sexual harassment of a subordinate.

do it, whether they should remodel the den this year or next, and whether they should borrow the necessary money or take it from their savings. Of course, many other decisions that Lennis and Phela need to make are not related to these issues, for example, whether to eat Thanksgiving dinner with Lennis's family or Phela's, or whether to tell their daughter the truth about Santa Claus.

## II. Creation of Issues

If an issue is something that persons disagree about, issues are created by disagreements. But which aspect of a disagreement creates the issue? The answer is the **facts**. *Issues grow out of facts, and facts define issues.*

Lennis and Phela want to paint the den. Lennis prefers off white; Phela prefers pale blue. These facts generate the issue, which color should the den be painted? These facts do not generate the issue, should the den be painted or wall papered, nor the issue, should Lennis, Phela, or a professional painter paint the den? Of course, if the facts changed, these issues might arise. For example, suppose that after Lennis and Phela decide to paint the den pale blue, Lennis wants to paint the room himself and Phela prefers to hire a painter. From these facts arises the issue, who should paint the den?

Here is a legal example. Supervisor $S$ and worker $WR$ are employed by $ER$. $S$ discharges $WR$, who has been soliciting coworkers to join a union. When $WR$ asks why she is being discharged, $S$ replies that her job performance has become unsatisfactory, but $WR$ believes the true reason is her union activity. These facts generate the issue, did $S$ discharge $WR$ because of $WR$'s union activity? These facts do not generate the issue, is $ER$ in the class of employers to whom the Labor Act applies, nor the issue, is $ER$ responsible for $S$'s act? The reason is that nothing in the facts indicates that the parties disagree about whether the Labor Act covers $ER$ or whether $ER$ is responsible for $S$'s act. But the facts do show that the parties disagree about why $S$ fired $WR$: $ER$ asserts that the reason was $WR$'s poor job performance, and $WR$ asserts that the reason was her union activity.[4]

---

4. If the facts were different, other issues would arise. For example, suppose that $S$ privately supports unionization of the firm, and $S$ and $WR$ secretly conspire to manufacture an issue that would make $ER$ look bad in the eyes of the workers. These facts would generate the issue, is $ER$ responsible for $S$'s discharge of $WR$?

## III. Resolution of Issues

When parties cannot themselves settle a dispute or disagreement, and wish to settle it peaceably, they ask someone else to resolve it. The one who resolves the dispute may be a person such as a relative, a friend, or an arbitrator, or an institution such as a court or an administrative agency such as the National Labor Relations Board. In this book, the term **tribunal** will refer to any person or institution that parties ask to resolve a dispute.

A dispute is composed of one or more issues.[5] To resolve a dispute in a rational way is to resolve those issues. A tribunal must perform four functions in order to resolve an issue. The functions are—

- **Frame the issue in the dispute**
- **Find the facts that pertain to the issue**
- **Identify and interpret, or if necessary create, the authority that governs the issue**
- **Apply law to fact, i.e., use the authority to determine the legal consequences of the facts of the dispute**

Issues may be classified according to the function they perform.

A. FRAME THE ISSUE IN THE DISPUTE

The first function a tribunal performs in resolving a dispute is to identify the issue. Parties usually agree on the issue in a case. However, sometimes it is advantageous to one party to frame the issue in a particular way and advantageous to the other party to frame the issue in another way. For example, suppose the forensic society holds a debate over outlawing automatic firearms. The opponent of such a law might frame the issue as, may a state infringe on citizens' right to bear arms under the Second Amendment? The advocate of such a law might frame the issue as, may a state

---

5. This book deals only with disputes that can be settled in a rational way. Of course, not all disputes can be settled rationally. Many disputes are emotional. The issue in an emotional dispute may never be identified. Indeed, there may be no issue in the sense in which we are using the term. Even if one exists and is identified, the issue in an emotional dispute may be settled without resolving (and often without addressing) the issue. The parties decide to make up with one another and go on with life.

protect its citizens from mass murder? This disagreement generates an issue as to the issue in the debate.

Here is a legal example. In the late nineteenth century and first third of the twentieth century, the federal courts played an active role in reviewing federal and state statutes pertaining to employment, and the courts struck down as unconstitutional many (albeit not all) such statutes.[6] The basis of these decisions was the Fifth and Fourteenth Amendments to the Constitution, which prohibit state and federal government from "depriv[ing] any person of life, liberty, or property, without due process of law." The Supreme Court held that the word "liberty" in these amendments includes the right to enter contracts on any terms the parties may choose. The government may not limit liberty of contract, that is, may not prohibit certain terms in a contract, except when the limitation is justified by a strong public policy. The law regards employment as a contract between an employer and a worker. In *Holden v. Hardy* Utah enacted a statute limiting the workday of underground miners to eight hours. Although the statute infringed on the parties' liberty of contract by prohibiting them from agreeing to a workday longer than eight hours, the Court upheld the statute. The Court reasoned a state has a strong interest in protecting the safety of miners. Accidents increase with workers' fatigue; accordingly, Utah could reduce fatigue and, therefore, injuries by limiting hours at work. But in *Lochner v. New York* a state statute limited the workday of bakers to ten hours, and the Supreme Court invalidated this statute. The Court held that the statute interfered with employers' and workers' liberty to agree on the length of the workday, and New York had failed to demonstrate that a longer workday jeopardized the safety of bakers.[7]

---

6. Today the courts are much less active in this regard; they accept legislative judgments about the need for regulation of employment. Nonetheless, the example that follows in the text is still valid because legal reasoning has not changed.

7. The theory that the employment relationship is contractual is an accurate description when an employer and a worker actually negotiate (exchange offers) over the terms of employment (wages, hours, etc.). In the typical case, however, the employer dictates the terms of employment, and the worker accepts them or looks for another job. Seeming to ignore this fact, the law presumes that the employer makes an offer of a job to a worker. The offer contains terms of employment. If the worker takes the job, the worker accepts the employer's offer, and a contract results.

Now suppose that shortly after these cases were decided, a state promulgated a regulation requiring that a hair stylist must wear gloves when applying dye to a customer's hair and that the owner of the salon must supply gloves at no cost to stylists. The association of salon owners challenges the regulation, and the state defends it. The owners frame the issue as, does the regulation interfere with liberty of contract? They frame the issue this way because *Lochner v. New York* prohibits a state from interfering with liberty of contract, and the regulation restricts owners and stylists from agreeing that stylists need not wear gloves or that stylists will pay for their gloves. By contrast, the state frames the issue as, does the regulation protect the safety of workers? The state frames the issue this way because *Holden v. Hardy* held that a state may protect the safety of workers, and gloves protect stylists from chemicals in hair dye. Because the parties disagree on the issue, the tribunal will frame it.

## B. Find the Facts That Pertain to the Issue

A tribunal's second function in resolving an issue is to find the facts of the events involving the parties. Sometimes the parties agree on one or more facts; in this event, they **stipulate** to those facts, and no issue of fact regarding those facts arises. Other times the parties disagree about the facts.

"I didn't change the channel."
"Yes he did."

* * *

"You made a snarky remark behind my back."
"No, I didn't. It must have been some other girl."

* * *

"You did it on purpose."
"No, I didn't. It was an accident."[8]

* * *

---

8. Note that the fact in dispute in this example is a party's state of mind. State of mind—that is, what a party was thinking—can be crucial in a case. The student may be thinking

"You never told me what you were going to do."

"I told you, but you weren't listening."

Such disagreements give rise to **issues of fact**. When parties disagree about facts, the tribunal must determine what happened—or, as a lawyer would say, the tribunal must *find the facts*.

## C. Identify and Interpret, or If Necessary Create, the Authority That Governs the Issue

A tribunal's third function in resolving a dispute is to identify and interpret the authority (i.e., the law) that governs the issue. Authorities abound in daily life, but in law three types of authority predominate:

- An **authoritative text** such as a constitution or statute.
  The Internal Revenue Code provides that federal income taxes must be paid by April 15.

- A **precedent**, that is, a tribunal's previous resolution of an analogous dispute.[9]
  "When Johnny threw his broccoli at his sister, I told him that was naughty of him; and now you're doing the same thing."

- A principle of **public policy** or the common good.[10]
  "Protective tariffs are good for the economy of Lilliput."

---

that we can never know what goes on in another person's mind; but humans have made such judgments from time immemorial, and the law regards state of mind as a fact. For example, although the following statement is not recorded in the *Iliad*, it may well have occurred. Suppose Helen sued Hecuba for unkindness. (Unkindness is not a legal claim today, but let us suppose it was a legal claim in ancient Troy.) The basis of Helen's suit was that Hecuba had said to Helen, "You look awful today." Now, a good critic is one's best friend, but a malicious critic is an abomination. If Hecuba wanted Helen to look good in order to hearten Paris, the criticism was good; if Hecuba wanted to make Helen feel bad for causing the Trojan War, the criticism was bad. It all depended on Hecuba's state of mind. The tribunal deciding Helen's case would consider Hecuba's state of mind to be a fact that could be found as any other fact is found.

9. The word "precedent" is sometimes used to mean any prior decision. In better usage, "precedent" has a more limited meaning, namely, a prior decision that controls the present case. The difference between these meanings is apparent in the sentence, "*Up v. Down* was decided long ago and is not a precedent for the case at bar."

10. Synonyms for "public policy" include "social policy," "public welfare," and "social welfare."

Parties may disagree about which authority governs an issue. *A* says that authority α applies to the issue, and *B* says that authority β applies.

"This case is governed by Pennsylvania's law of contract."
"No, this case is governed by the National Labor Relations Act."

Parties may also disagree on how to interpret an authority. *A* and *B* agree that authority γ applies; but *A* says γ means this and that, whereas *B* says γ means the other thing.

"Thou shalt not kill."
"True, but what does 'kill' mean? Does it include self-defense?"

Both types of disagreement are **issues of law,** which a tribunal must resolve.

Sometimes no relevant authority exists. In this event, the tribunal's decision may become a new authority.

D. APPLY LAW TO FACT (i.e., use the authority to determine the legal
consequences of the facts of the dispute)

The fourth function in resolving a dispute is applying the governing authority to the facts of the dispute. After the tribunal has found the facts, and has identified and interpreted the governing authority, the question arises, what did the law require these parties to do in these circumstances? The parties may disagree about the answer to this question. *A* says that, under the authorities, he did the right thing. *B* says that, under the same authorities, *A* did the wrong thing.

"You were negligent to install a swimming pool without putting a fence
around it."
"I was not negligent. There was a fence around my yard, and the pool
was in the yard."

This sort of disagreement is an **issue of application of law to fact.** The tribunal determines the legal consequences of the parties' behavior.

## IV. Identifying Issues

Perhaps the most daunting task facing a beginning student of law is identifying or "spotting" issues. Curiously, we all are able to identify issues in daily life, but we do not know how we do it (or even realize that we are doing it). In fact, identifying issues is simple and, once the student understands how it is done and practices it, identifying legal issues will not be difficult.

A student needs to identify an issue in two different contexts. The first context is reading a document such as a law case, an article (whether in a magazine or a professional journal), or a statute. The student must know what issue(s) the author is addressing. The second context is listening to or reading a set of facts. The student must know what issue(s) the facts generate. Let us begin with the first context.

## A. IDENTIFYING ISSUES IN DOCUMENTS

Issues occur in various types of documents. For example, suppose one encounters the following editorial in a newspaper.

### The College Daily

An American is legally an adult at eighteen years of age. One may vote, run for political office, be conscripted into the armed forces, and be held fully accountable in a court of law for one's criminal behavior. One may leave home and be free of parental supervision. One may marry, divorce, obtain a credit card, and in general enter into binding legal relationships. One may even view or purchase pornography. But the law also provides that one may not consume alcoholic beverages until one turns twenty-one. Need anything more be said?

Doubtlessly, the student knows that the issue that this passage addresses is whether the drinking age should be reduced to eighteen. But how does one know this?

Identifying issues is essentially a matter of drawing analogies. Analogies and distinctions are discussed in detail in § 11 ANALOGIES AND PRECEDENTS and § 12 DISTINCTIONS, but the student's intuitive understanding of analogies will suffice for present purposes.

The student recognized the issue in the foregoing editorial because of an analogy. The student knew that people in the past have disagreed about what the minimum drinking age should be, or about whether there should be one at all. Knowing this history, the student (probably without realizing it) drew an analogy between the past and the present. The student found that the facts of the past and the present were similar; and knowing that the issue arose in the past, the student concluded that the same facts generated the same issue in the present. Therefore, the student knew what issue the author of the editorial was addressing.

One cannot draw an analogy between the past and the present without knowing the past. Thus, the student's first task is to learn what issues have arisen in the past.[11] Unfortunately, no book in the library contains lists of issues. The student will have to discover the issue(s) in a case. Fortunately, the student already has some ability to recognize disagreements, to sense when points of view clash; and a disagreement is another name for an issue. Accordingly, a student reading a case should make a list of each point of disagreement (issue) between the parties or the judges. The list should include the facts underlying the disagreement.

How can the student spot a disagreement? A disagreement may be explicit in an opinion. Blessed are the judges who write, "The issue is. . . ." Often, however, disagreements are implicit, and the student must learn to recognize signals. A common signal of a disagreement or issue is, "One party argues . . . ," followed by either, "The other party argues . . ." or "This argument is mistaken because . . ." But (too often!) the opinion gives no signals and merely presents the judge's reasoning. In this event, the student must dig beneath the surface of the opinion.

Perhaps the best tool for digging into an opinion is to ask—

- **What claim is the author trying to make?**

A claim (or point or position) is the resolution of an issue. Therefore, by changing a claim into a question, the student will identify an issue. For example, in the *The College Daily*, the editorial contains an implied claim that eighteen-year-olds should be allowed to consume alcohol. Accordingly, the issue was, should the law be changed to allow persons aged eighteen and older to consume alcohol?

Other useful tools for digging into an opinion are questions such as—

- **Why is the tribunal saying this? What obstacle is the tribunal is trying to surmount?**

---

11. Of course, new issues arise, but they are usually easy to recognize. Commonly, they are explicitly identified as questions. Does a woman have a constitutional right to an abortion? Should "intelligent design" be taught alongside of evolution in biology courses?

- What would the counterargument be? How might one disagree with this?
- If the tribunal wanted to reach the opposite result, what would the tribunal have said?
- Wherein might a reasonable person disagree with this opinion? Could the outcome be different?

Answers to these questions will lead to the issues that the tribunal was confronting.

Another useful tool for digging issues out of legal opinions is to list each rule of law stated in a case. Whenever the opinion announces a rule of law, the student knows that an issue lurks behind the rule: every rule of law represents the resolution of an issue over which parties, at one time or another, have disagreed. *Change a rule of law into a question, and it becomes an issue.* For example, the rule, "Thou shalt not steal" resolves the issue, "Should a commandment forbid stealing?" Or consider the following example:

### When Is an Offer Accepted?

On July 1, *S* sent letters to several friends, offering to sell her dining room furniture for $4,000. The letter stated, "If you want it and accept my price, mail me your check for $4,000 and tell me when you'd like to pick up the furniture." *B* found the letter in her mailbox when she came home from work in the evening of July 3. She immediately wrote a check, put it in a stamped envelope addressed to *S*, and deposited it in a mailbox at 6:00 p.m. Normally, the Post Office would have picked up the letter at 9:00 a.m. of the following morning, but, observing the Independence Day holiday, the Post Office collected the letter on July 5 and delivered it to *S* the following day. In the meantime, *S* held a party on July 4, and she mentioned to her guests that her dining room furniture was for sale. "How much do you want for it?" asked *X*. "Oh, I don't know, it's very nice, but really I don't know anything about these things," replied *S* coyly. "Will you take $5,000 for it?" offered *X*. "Yes, I will," answered *S*, and *X* immediately wrote a check. *B*, having always admired this furniture, was upset to learn that *S* had accepted *X*'s check, and she went to a lawyer. "That furniture belongs to me," said *B*. "I mailed my check on July 3, before *X* even knew the furniture was for sale. The lawyer told *B* that she was right. "The rule in this state," said the lawyer, "is that, when an offer contemplates that it will be accepted by mail, a contract is formed when the party accepting the offer [in legal parlance, the 'offeree'] deposits into a mailbox a properly stamped letter of acceptance addressed to the party who made the offer [the 'offeror']."

Like every rule, this rule resolves an issue, and the student knows the issue as soon as one knows the rule. The rule was that an offer is accepted when the offeree mails the acceptance. Therefore, the issue was, "At what point in time is a contract formed if the offer contemplates acceptance by mail?"

A problem with identifying the issue by listing each rule of law is that most rules that are mentioned in a case, or that are not mentioned but are conceptually necessary in order to decide the case, are not in dispute. The parties accept these rules as valid. For example, a rule of law that is necessary in every civil case is, the plaintiff must initiate the action by filing a complaint and serving it on the defendant. The beginning student's list of the rules of law in a case will probably contain some such "background" rules. These rules are surely worth learning for their own sake, but they will not lead to the issue in the case. How does a student distinguish between the background rules and the rules that lead to *the* issue(s) in a case? One way is to identify the claim (or point or position) that the tribunal is trying to make (or defend). Usually a claim is the resolution of a disputed issue in the case. Another way to distinguish between background rules and the issue in a case is to follow the action. Feel the heat. Look for the disagreement, the conflict, the clash of ideas—the legal reason why the case is in court.[12]

Identifying issues in statutes is similar to identifying issues in cases. One knows that a passage in a statute generates an issue because one knows that a similar passage in another statute generated that issue. For example, Title VII of the Civil Rights Act of 1964 uses the term "employee." Does this term generate any issues? The answer is yes, as we know because the term

---

12. The legal reason must be distinguished from the personal reason. Parties have their personal reasons with which the law is not concerned. *A*'s personal reason for suing *B* may be that *B* insulted *A*. The *legal* reason the case is in court must be that an issue that the law considers significant has arisen between the parties; for example, did *B* purposefully misrepresent material facts on which *A* reasonably relied and thereby lost money? The parties may be unaware of the legal reasons, but the lawyers and the judges know those reasons.

"employee" also appears in the National Labor Relations Act and generated issues under that act. Thus, under the Labor Act the issue arose, "Is a supervisor an 'employee'?" and the same issue later arose under Title VII.[13]

## B. IDENTIFYING ISSUES IN FACTS

So far this section has discussed identifying issues in a document. Now let us discuss identifying issues in a set of facts. The student must know which (if any) issues that a set of facts generates. Of course, a lawyer must identify the issue(s) in a story told by a client who asks for advice. Other persons also must identify the issue(s) in the situations that occur in daily life, as illustrated below.

Like identifying issues in a document, *identifying issues that lurk in facts requires drawing analogies*, and drawing analogies requires knowledge of the past. Consider the following summary of a tale that Jonathan Swift relates in chapter 4 of *Gulliver's Travels*.

> The inhabitants of Lilliput opened their soft-boiled eggs at the small end; the denizens of Blefuscu opened their eggs at the big end. Thousands of lives had been lost in battles, and another was about to commence, over which end of an egg should be opened. This issue had not arisen in England, and therefore Gulliver had no idea that the issue existed until he was informed about it. Had he been offered an egg to eat, he would not have known that cracking open one end or the other would involve him in a ferocious controversy.

Gulliver did not know the history that preceded the situation in which he found himself and, therefore, did not know the issue that was about to affect his life.

It follows that identifying the issues in a set of facts is essentially the same as identifying the issues in a reported case. The student asks oneself,

---

13. Under the Labor Act, a supervisor is not an "employee" and is not protected by the act. Under Title VII, a supervisor is an "employee" and is protected by the act. The resolutions of the issues are different because the purposes of the statutes are different, but the important point for present purposes is that the same issue arose under both statutes.

are the *facts* of this situation or case the same as, or similar to, the *facts* of issues with which I am familiar? The guiding principle is the same in both contexts:

• **Similar facts beget similar issues.**

When Ham and Shem came to a fork in the road, they disagreed about which was the better route to Zuzim. Ham said the left was shorter; Shem said the right was faster. When Meshech and Shadrach came to the same fork, the same issue may well have arisen.

Now consider these not entirely hypothetical cases:

### The Coconut Cases

### Case 1

A sophomore at an American university in New York State approaches the Coconut Bar, which is near the campus. A hefty bouncer standing near the entrance says, "Let me see your ID."

What is the issue generated by these facts? Is it whether the sophomore resides in the county in which the bar is located? Is it whether the sophomore meets minimum height and weight requirements? Of course not. The student knows that the issue in Case 1 is whether the sophomore is at least twenty-one years old, and the student knows this is the issue because the student (probably without realizing it) has drawn an analogy. The facts of Case 1 are analogous to Cases *A, B, C . . .* in the past in which bouncers were employed to check the identification of young persons who sought to enter bars. The student knows that the issue in Cases *A, B, C . . .* was whether the potential patrons were legally old enough to drink. Applying the principle that *similar facts beget similar issues*, the student has concluded that the issue that arose in Cases *A, B, C . . .* also arises in Case 1.

### Case 2

An octogenarian approaches the same bar. Without saying a word, the bouncer opens the door.

Why does the bouncer fail to check the octogenarian's identification? Is the bouncer negligent about his duty? Is the octogenarian a relative of the bouncer? Of course not. The student knows that the bouncer does not check the octogenarian's identification because Case 2 is analogous to Cases *R, S, T* . . . in which bouncers did not check the identification of elderly patrons. Like the elderly patrons in Cases *R, S, T* . . . , the octogenarian in Case 2 is obviously old enough to drink. Therefore, concludes the student, Cases *R, S, T* . . . and Case 2 are analogous. The octogenarian is plainly old enough to drink; the issue of minimum age does not arise, and the bouncer has no need to check the octogenarian's identification.

### Case 3

A twenty-two-year-old student from Denmark enrolls as a graduate student in an American university in New York State and wants to enter the Coconut Bar. The bouncer asks her for identification. She is not carrying satisfactory proof of age and is turned away. She asks, "What's going on here?" Recognizing a foreign accent and having experience with foreigners, the bouncer understands the question and explains.

The woman from Denmark does not carry proof of age because she has entered bars at home without having to prove her age. She draws an analogy between bars in Denmark and bars in America and concludes that she can enter an American bar without proof of age. The analogy is false, however, because Denmark has no minimum drinking age whereas America does.

### Case 4

Subsequently, the Danish student is preparing to accompany friends to the Palm Bar, a tavern popular among graduate students. She puts her passport in her purse.

Without consciously thinking it, she has drawn an analogy between Cases 3 and 4. The Palm and the Coconut are both bars, and they are both in America. Knowing that similar facts beget similar issues, she knows that she will need to prove her age in order to enter the Palm.

### Case 5

Our Dane plans to go to dinner in the Acorn, an upscale restaurant. Being a European, she wishes to order wine with her meal. She is unsure whether she needs to take her passport with her.[14]

She asks herself the question (probably consciously this time), "Are the facts of this situation analogous to my experience at the bars?" The answer is not obvious because she can think of arguments on both sides of the matter: "On the one hand, alcohol is alcohol, so perhaps the silly American rule applies to restaurants. [In other words, Case 5 is analogous to Cases 3 and 4.] On the other hand, alcohol consumed with a meal has a lesser effect than alcohol consumed on an empty stomach, and the environment of a restaurant is more controlled than the environment of a bar; so perhaps the rule does not apply to restaurants. [In other words, Case 5 is not analogous to Cases 3 and 4.]"

A lawyer is frequently in the same position as the Danish student in the foregoing cases. A client tells a story, and the lawyer must identify the issues raised by the facts of the story. The practicing lawyer draws analogies. The lawyer asks, "Are the facts of my client's story analogous to the facts of cases in the past or the facts contemplated by a statute?" As ever, the guiding principle is—

- **Similar facts beget similar issues.**

## V. Review

### Questions

More than one answer may be correct to questions 1–5.

1. An issue is—
   - ☐ (a) a flimsy piece of paper.
   - ☐ (b) a question with different reasonable answers.
   - ☐ (c) a point of contention between parties.
   - ☐ (d) the reason a case comes before a tribunal.
   - ☐ (e) generated by facts.

---

14. In this example, the question is trivial. Taking her passport with her costs nothing, so she may as well take it in the event she has to prove her age. But we are considering theoretical, not practical questions. Our question is, does she *need* to take her passport with her? To make the question important practically, let us assume that the Danish government charges ten thousand Krone to replace a lost or stolen passport, and our student carries it with her only when necessary.

2. In law the resolution of an issue is called—
   ☐ (a) the answer.
   ☐ (b) the theory.
   ☐ (c) the judgment.
   ☐ (d) the holding.

3. The steps in resolving any issue are—
   ☐ (a) identify the issue in the dispute.
   ☐ (b) find the facts that pertain to the issue.
   ☐ (c) identify and interpret the authority that governs the dispute.
   ☐ (d) apply the authority to the facts of the dispute.
   ☐ (e) prevent future injury.
   ☐ (f) determine which party is offering the larger bribe.

4. The guiding principle in recognizing an issue is—
   ☐ (a) anything can be an issue in any case.
   ☐ (b) look for words in italics or boldface.
   ☐ (c) similar facts beget similar issues.

5. One recognizes an issue by—
   ☐ (a) remembering (or finding) an analogous case in the past; an
       issue that arose in that case probably arises in the case at hand.
   ☐ (b) listing the points of disagreement between the parties or
       judges.
   ☐ (c) looking for phrases such as, "one party argues . . ." or "party
       A is mistaken because . . ."
   ☐ (d) asking, what claim is the author trying to establish?
   ☐ (e) asking, why did the judge write this?
   ☐ (f) asking, what is the counterargument?
   ☐ (g) asking, could a reasonable person disagree with this?
   ☐ (h) asking, could the law be different?
   ☐ (i) focusing on the footnotes, where everything important appears.
   ☐ (j) making a list of each rule of law in the case.
   ☐ (k) calling your mother.

6.

### Sally's Case

Sally transferred as a sophomore to First Choice U. She had spent her freshone year at Second Choice U., where she had rushed and was accepted

into membership in βΦΦ, a sorority. Upon enrolling in First Choice, she applied and was accepted into βΦΦ's chapter at First Choice without going through the chapter's usual initiation ritual.

Red is the primary color of First Choice's archrival. A bylaw of βΦΦ at First Choice states, "No member of this chapter shall wear red to an athletic event. Any sister who violates this bylaw shall wash dinner dishes for a week."

Sally attended the rally preceding the first game of the season. It was a chilly evening, and she decided to wear her warmest socks, which were red. The next day Sister accused Sally of violating the bylaw. Sally replied that she did not know about it. Sister read it to her. Sally replied that a rally is not an athletic event.

What issues must be addressed by the judicial committee of βΦΦ?

7.

### The Case of the Research Papers

TA:     Professor, I'm almost through grading the research assignment, but I think you should read two of the papers yourself.

PROF:     What's the problem?

TA:     They're pretty similar.

PROF:     Well, we did say the students could work together on the research, although each student had to write one's paper by oneself. So we can expect some similarities.

TA:     I think one copied from the other.

PROF:     What they actually did certainly matters. The punishment for copying is usually heavier than the punishment for writing together.

What issues must the professor resolve before deciding whether to file charges against the students with the Academic Standards Committee?

## VI. References

*Holden v. Hardy,* 169 U.S. 366 (1898).
*Lochner v. New York,* 198 U.S. 45 (1905).

# § 2

# Identifying the Governing Rule of Law

The **governing rule of law**—also called a **standard**, an **authority**, or a **governing authority**—is the law that a tribunal uses to decide an issue in the case at bar. The question naturally arises, how does a tribunal identify the governing rule? Commonly, the tribunal simply announces that law $\alpha$ applies; or if one party urges the tribunal to use law $\alpha$ and the other party urges law $\beta$, the tribunal will say why it chooses $\alpha$ over $\beta$, but not why $\alpha$ and $\beta$ are applicable. Evidently, the lawyers for the parties and the judges usually agree on which laws govern, or might govern, a case. And when they disagree, they still agree on the fundamental process for making the choice, a process which all persons trained in the common law are taught, a process to which all lawyers and judges subscribe. This section introduces the student to that process. The student will find that the process of identifying the governing rule, which is described in this section, closely resembles the process of identifying the issue, which is described in § 1 Issues.

## I. Definition of a Rule of Law

Before learning about the process of identifying the governing rule of law, the student needs a definition of the term "rule of law." A **rule of law** has two, and sometimes three parts:

(1) a determination that certain facts are legally significant
(2) a statement of the legal consequences of those facts, and
(3) a list of excuses (affirmative defenses) if any.[1]

For example—

It is a rule of law that the speed limit on the Interstate is 65 miles per hour.

LEGALLY SIGNIFICANT FACTS

Like every rule of law, this one makes certain facts legally significant. The legally significant facts in this example are where the vehicle is, and how fast it is going.

CONSEQUENCES OF THE LEGALLY SIGNIFICANT FACTS

Also, this rule of law states the consequences of the legally significant facts. If the vehicle's speed is 65 miles per hour or less, the vehicle is complying with the law; if the speed is above 65 miles per hour, the vehicle is violating the law.

AFFIRMATIVE DEFENSES

No excuse for speeding is recognized.

A rule of law (or standard or authority) may be found in an authoritative text like a statute or in a precedent. In the foregoing example, the rule of law that the speed limit is 65 miles per hour occurs in a statute.

---

1. Relief or remedy, e.g., damages or an injunction, may also be considered part of a rule of law, but relief is beyond the scope of this book.

A rule of law may also be thought of as one or more issue-and-resolution pairs:

ISSUE

What is the speed limit on the Interstate?

RULE OF LAW

The speed limit on the Interstate is 65 miles per hour.

* * *

ISSUE

Is hurrying to grandmother's house to save her from the big bad wolf an excuse for exceeding the speed limit?

RULE OF LAW

Nice try.

## II. Identifying an Existing Rule of Law

Rules of law are legion and protean. How does one know which rule of law applies to the facts of the case at bar? The answer lies in aspects of legal reasoning which the student has already learned. A rule of law is the resolution of an issue. Therefore, the appropriate rule of law for a case depends on the issue in the case. So now the question becomes, how does one know the issue in a case? The answer, which was addressed above in § 1 ISSUES, is that analogous facts generate the same issue. Accordingly, one identifies an issue in a case, in an article, in a statute, or in a set of facts, by reviewing the authorities (cases and authoritative texts). If the facts of an authority are analogous to the facts of the case at bar, the issue in the authority also arises in the case at bar. The rule of law that governed that issue in the authority is also the governing rule of law in the case at bar.

Therefore, identifying the rule of law that governs a case is a process in two steps:

- **Identify the issue in the case at bar by comparing its facts to the facts of an authority. If an analogy can be found, the issue that arose in the authority also arises in the case at bar.**

- If the same issue arises in the case at bar as arose in the authority, the rule of law that resolved the issue in the authority will be the governing rule of law on that issue in the case at bar.

This process may be observed at work in the following hypothetical case.

### The Refusal to Bargain Case

The leader of a local union goes to a regional office of the Labor Board. "I've got a complaint against my employer," he says to the receptionist.

"Please have a seat," she replies, "and I'll call the officer of the day."

A few minutes later, two persons approach the union leader. "My name is Ms. Cortes," says one of them; "I am the officer of the day. This is Mr. Burke. He is a new field representative in training."

"Hi, I'm Scott Melnick," says the local leader as he shakes hands with Cortes and Burke. "I'm president of Local 1 of the Tattlers, Chattelers, and Dawdlers of the World. We've got a complaint against our employer."

"Come this way," says Cortes, "and we'll discuss it." They walk to a small conference room and sit down. Cortes says, "Tell us what happened."

Melnick speaks animatedly: "Seven months ago, my union won an election to represent the workers in our shop. Our employer pulled a lot of dirty tricks during the election campaign, but we managed to win anyway. Ever since then, I've been trying to set up a bargaining session, but our employer is always too busy, or is out of town, or has another appointment. On top of that, we've just got this new superintendent who won't cut us any slack; I mean, we have to meet the production quotas every day. If you miss it even by one percent—even if you've been with the company for twenty years—you get in trouble. It never used to be like that."

"So you haven't met to bargain even once since the election?" asked Cortes.

"That's right," replied Melnick.

"I think I understand your complaint," says Cortes. "Do you have any questions, Mr. Burke?"

Burke says no.

"All right. Would you excuse us for a few moments, Mr. Melnick? We won't be long."

Cortes and Burke rise and walk to Cortes's office. "Well, what do you think?" she asks.

"It sounds to me like discrimination under § 8(a)(3)," replies Burke.

"Not a bad guess," Cortes responds. "If we only had the words of the statute to go by, that would be a plausible interpretation of discrimination. But the cases tell a different story. According to them, the prima facie case, or the legally significant facts, of § 8(a)(3) are, first, the employer disadvantaged (or discriminated against) a worker in the terms and conditions of her employment (maybe fired her or put her on the night shift) and, second, the employer's reason or intent was to discourage union activity. The second fact is true in this case: the employer was evading its duty to bargain with the union, which surely discourages union activity. But the first fact is not true: the employer has not discriminated against any workers."

"Yes, it has," says Burke. "The employer won't bargain. The workers lose money every day they can't bargain for a better contract."

"Maybe so," replies Cortes, "but they are not being disadvantaged in the ways recognized in the cases. Now, if the employer had fired Melnick because he requested bargaining, that would be the right kind of disadvantage for purposes of discrimination."

"Are you saying the union doesn't have a case?" asks Burke.

"No. It does have a case of refusal to bargain in good faith under §§ 8(a)(5) and 8(d). The Act specifically requires an employer to meet at reasonable times with the union that represents the workers. The legally significant facts are, first, the union requests a meeting; second, the employer refuses to meet; and third, the employer's refusal is unreasonable. All of these facts are present. The union requested a meeting. The employer refused to meet. Seven months is more than a reasonable period for a meeting to occur."

"What about the election campaign?" inquires Burke. "Some of those dirty tricks might've been unfair labor practices. Of course, it depends on what Mr. Melnick meant by 'dirty tricks.' I think I'll ask him about it."

"Don't bother," says Cortes. "Whatever they were, they probably don't matter because the union won the election in spite of them. Anyway, they occurred more than six months ago, so the statute of limitations has expired."

"What about the new superintendent? All of the sudden strictly enforcing production quotas sounds like discrimination or retaliation to me," opines Burke.

"Possibly discrimination for unionizing. Of course, on the face of it, nothing is wrong with enforcing production quotas. Even if the new super cracked down right after the election, an employer can usually make a pretty good case that the old super had been allowing production to slip. But you ought to find out more about it."

Cortes and Burke return to Melnick. "I think we can do something for you," says Cortes. "Mr. Burke will take your affidavit, and we'll go from there."

This example illustrates how an experienced person identifies the rule of law that governs a set of facts. The officer of the day, Cortes, was familiar with the authorities. She knew their legally significant facts, the issues generated by those facts, and the rules of law that resolved the issues. After hearing the facts related by the leader of the local, Melnick, she compared those facts to the legally significant facts of the authorities. She found one sound analogy, one unsound analogy, one possible analogy, and some irrelevant facts.

The sound analogy was between the facts contemplated by §§ 8(a)(5) and 8(d) of the Labor Act and the facts of the union's efforts to commence, and the employer's efforts to evade, collective bargaining. Section 8(a)(5) establishes the duty of an employer "to bargain collectively" with the workers' union, and § 8(d) defines the duty to bargain as the obligation "to meet at reasonable times and confer in good faith." If the facts as stated by Melnick were true, the employer committed this unfair labor practice: seven months is an unreasonable period to delay the start of collective bargaining.

The unsound analogy was to discrimination. Unlike Burke, who was a novice, Cortes was not misled by a partial analogy. Even though one of the legally significant facts of discrimination was present (the employer is motivated by animus against the union), she knew from the precedents that discrimination had not occurred because the other significant fact was missing (a worker is disadvantaged in the terms or conditions of employment).

The possible analogy—which, again, Cortes knew from the precedents—was also to discrimination. The element that was present was a disadvantage in the terms and conditions of employment, namely, the new superintendent's crackdown on production quotas. The element that was missing, but might be present, was the employer's motive. If the employer meant to punish the workers for having unionized, the crackdown was discriminatory; but if the employer meant only to improve production, the crackdown was lawful. More information was needed, and Cortes instructed Burke to pursue the matter.

The irrelevant facts pertained to the employer's dirty tricks during the election. As a practical matter, it was no longer important that the employer may have committed unfair labor practices during the election campaign, for in spite of them the union won the election. As a legal matter, the statute of limitations (an unfair labor practice charge must be filed within six months of the unlawful act) had expired.

Because choosing the governing rule of law is analogical, an analogy may be appropriate here. Cortes's mind is like a computer in which are stored the rules of law and the facts that those rules make legally significant. When she wants to know which law governs a transaction, she loads the program entitled "Match the Facts." Then she inputs the facts of the transaction at hand, and clicks on <run>. In a few seconds, the computer identifies any good matches; it also identifies any possible matches and recommends that more information be obtained.

## A. Identifying the Governing Rule of Law Using Precedents

Common law tribunals are never happier than when they can "follow a precedent on point," which means "find a governing rule of law in a precedent," which means "identify a prior case the legally significant facts of which are analogous to the facts of the case at bar." Examples are innumerable. In the *Refusal to Bargain Case*, Cortes knew that many precedents hold that an employer's unreasonable delays in setting up bargaining sessions constitute a refusal to bargain in good faith, a violation of § 8(a)(5) of the Labor Act. She also used precedents to conclude that the employer's refusal to meet with the union was not discrimination under the Labor Act. She reached this conclusion because the precedents established that discrimination has two elements—the employer disadvantaged (or discriminated against) a worker in the terms and conditions of employment, and the employer's reason or intent was to discourage union activity—and the first element was not true in the case before her. She used the same precedents to conclude that the new superintendent's crackdown on production quotas might be discrimination because the crackdown proved the first element and the second one might be true.

For an example in a reported case, consider one of the first American labor disputes to reach the courts, the *Philadelphia Cordwainers Case* of 1806. The defendants were journeymen cordwainers (bootmakers) who were members of a society of cordwainers (an early union). The rules of the society provided that its members must work only at the rates of pay set by the society (today such a rate is called "union scale") and that members must refuse to work in the same shop as anyone who accepted a lower rate. The cordwainers, many of whom worked at home, sold the boots they made to retail shops. When the owners of the shops reduced the rate they paid for boots, the members of the society threatened to strike: whereupon the cordwainers were prosecuted for the crime of criminal conspiracy.

As all parties and the judge agreed, the governing authority was the law of conspiracy. How did they identify this particular law? Why did they not identify another authority, such as the law of master and servant? They identified conspiracy by comparing the facts of the case at bar with the legally significant facts of the law against conspiracy. The parties did not choose the law of master and servant because it contemplates—that is, one of its legally significant facts is—that a servant is employed by a master; the cordwainers were not employees of the shops, but instead were independent journeymen who sold to various shops.

The parties identified the law of conspiracy because its legally significant facts were, at least arguably, similar to the facts of the case at bar. This law appeared in precedents that stated the legally significant facts of conspiracy: two or more persons either plan to commit an unlawful act, or plan to commit a lawful act by unlawful means, and take at least one step in furtherance of the plan. For example, *A* and *B* draw up a plan to forge documents in order to obtain a loan from a bank. The facts of the case at bar were similar to these facts. The society of cordwainers comprised two or more persons, and they planned to withhold their labor, not as individuals, but as a group. Although withholding labor as an individual was generally legal, withholding labor as a group was a crime at the time. Therefore, the cordwainers were planning to commit a crime, and such a plan is a conspiracy.

Thus, the parties and the judge identified the governing rule of law by looking for precedents with facts similar to the facts of the case at bar. The law that governed the precedents also governed the case at bar. (The jury convicted the cordwainers, and they were fined.)

The *Philadelphia Cordwainers Case* and the *Refusal to Bargain Case* illustrate that a tribunal can find the governing rule of law for a case at bar by finding prior cases with analogous facts. Because the facts are analogous, the same issue arises in both cases. Because of the doctrine of *stare decisi*s (Latin for "to stand by things that have been decided") the decision on an issue in a prior case becomes the governing rule of law when that issue arises in subsequent cases.

A tribunal follows the same process in finding the governing rule of law in authoritative texts.

## B. IDENTIFYING THE GOVERNING RULE OF LAW USING AUTHORITATIVE TEXTS

A tribunal often finds the rule of law that governs a case in an authoritative text such as a constitution, a statute, or a regulation. The relevant text is identified by an analogy between the facts contemplated by the text and the facts of the case at bar.

Let us take statutes as a typical example of authoritative texts. When a legislator proposes a bill, she contemplates a set of facts. She intends the bill to ameliorate a problem that arises from those facts or to promote a good that would affect those facts. To say the same thing, the bill is intended to change a set of facts in a particular way. The bill does not contemplate other facts; that is, the bill is not intended to affect other situations. If the bill is enacted, a party to a dispute may assert that the new statute is the governing rule of law for the dispute. The tribunal will examine the two sets of facts—the facts of the dispute and the facts which the statute contemplates. If the facts are analogous, the tribunal will hold that the statute governs the dispute. If the facts are not analogous, the tribunal will search for another governing rule of law.[2] For example—

### Two Cases of Second Thoughts

A legislature recently added § 99 to the Commercial Code of the State of Grace:

> Consumers shall have three days within which to rescind a contract for the purchase of an automobile from a licensed dealer.

---

2. The description in this paragraph of the legislative process is simplified. For example, it does not discuss the role that other legislators and committees play in delimiting the set of facts to which the bill would apply. Nonetheless, this description captures the essence of the process as it is viewed by a tribunal that is called upon to apply a statute.

The legislature contemplated the following facts:

a person
reaches an agreement
with a licensed dealer
to purchase
an automobile
from the dealer.

The law before § 99 was enacted provided that a contract for a consumer to purchase an automobile from a dealer bound both parties at the moment the contract was signed. Under § 99 the contract is binding at once on the dealer, but not on the purchaser until three days have elapsed. Like any law, § 99 does not contemplate other sets of facts; it is not intended to affect other situations. Thus, § 99 contemplates a purchaser who is a consumer, not a business. Accordingly, an automobile dealer who purchased an automobile from another dealer would not have three days to rescind the contract. Similarly, the bill contemplates the purchase of an automobile. Accordingly, even a consumer would not have three days to rescind a contract for the purchase of a boat.

### Diallo's Case

Shortly after § 99 was enacted, a case comes before Judge Janus in which Diallo, an individual, offered to sell her car to Jung. The latter was a vegan, and he asked Diallo, "Have any murdered animals been eaten or transported in this vehicle?" Diallo said no and, relying on this answer, Jung bought the car. In truth, however, Diallo was a carnivore; she had frequently used the car to carry raw meat from the grocery store, and sometimes she or a passenger ate a hamburger in the vehicle. The next day as Jung was cleaning the car, he detected scraps of meat in it. Covering his face with a surgical mask, he drove the car to Diallo, said that he rescinded the sale, and demanded the return of the purchase price. Diallo refused and Jung sued, invoking § 99. Judge Janus had to decide whether this section was the governing rule of law for this dispute. Comparing the facts contemplated by § 99 and the facts of the case at bar, the judge concluded that the section did not govern the case (the analogy was unsound). He ruled that § 99 contemplates a seller who is a dealer, whereas Diallo was a private party. (He suggested to Jung that the law of misrepresentation might be applicable.)

### Niner's Case

A few days after Judge Janus's ruling in *Diallo's Case*, another case about rescinding the sale of an automobile came to his court. Velarde, an individual, signed a contract to buy an automobile from Niner, a dealer. Two days later, Velarde lost his job, and he realized that he would be unable to make the payments on the vehicle. He informed Niner that he was rescinding the contract. Niner offered to reduce the price, but Velarde was adamant. When he asked Niner to return his deposit, Niner refused, and Velarde sued for it. He invoked § 99 as the governing rule of law, and once again the judge compared the facts contemplated by the section and the facts of the case at bar. The judge found that the facts matched well (the analogy was sound) and used § 99 to decide the case in Velarde's favor.

Here is an example from a reported case.

### Packard Motor Car Company

The United Auto Workers organized the supervisors of the Packard Motor Car Company and demanded that the company engage in collective bargaining. The company declined on the ground that the Labor Act does not apply to supervisors, and the union took the dispute to the Labor Board. The issue before the Board was whether supervisors are covered by the Labor Act. To resolve this issue, the Labor Board had to determine the governing rule of law. The Board turned to § 2(3) of the Act, which states, "The term 'employee' shall include any employee." The section contemplated the following facts:

an employer
employees of that employer
employees who wish to engage in collective bargaining.

These facts matched exactly the facts of the case at bar, so § 2(3) became the governing rule of law in the case.[3]

## III. Review

### *Exchange Parts*

In *Exchange Parts*, the Labor Board scheduled an election for a unit of workers to decide whether they wanted to be represented by a union. Shortly before the election, the employer announced a new birthday holiday and new overtime benefits for the workers in the hope of influencing them to reject the union. The strategy worked: the workers voted to reject unionization. The union filed an unfair labor practice charge, alleging that the employer violated § 8(a)(1) of the Labor Act, which prohibits interference with concerted activity, because the employer created the benefits for the purpose of influencing the outcome of the election.

Imagine that you are responsible for deciding *Exchange Parts*. In your research, you come across *Medo Photo Supply*, in which an employer recognized a union as the bargaining agent of its workers, and the union proposed a collective bargaining agreement. Perhaps dissatisfied with the union's proposal, a group of twelve workers, purporting to speak for the majority, approached the employer and said that they would abandon the union if they could obtain certain wage increases on their own. A few days later, the employer met with a committee of four of these workers, agreed to the increases, and then informed the union that, because it no longer represented a majority of the workers, the employer would not bargain with it. The union charged the employer with refusing to bargain in good faith. The Labor Board and the Supreme Court sustained the charge. They held that the majority of workers had not repudiated the union when the

---

3. Having determined that § 2(3) governed the dispute, the Board then had to determine the meaning of the section. The Board, as well as the Court of Appeals and the Supreme Court, all held that supervisors are employees and, therefore, are covered by the Labor Act and have the right to organize and bargain collectively. Subsequently, Congress amended the section specifically to exclude supervisors from the protection of the Act.

group of twelve met with the employer; rather, the workers said that they would repudiate the union *if* the employer met their demands. Thus, the wage increase induced the workers to repudiate the union. The Court wrote, "There could be no more obvious way of interfering with [the] rights of employees than by grants of wage increases upon the understanding that they would leave the union in return. The action of employees with respect to the choice of their bargaining agents may be induced by favors bestowed by the employer as well as by his threats or domination."

Is *Medo Photo Supply* the governing rule of law for *Exchange Parts*? State your analysis.

## References

*Medo Photo Supply v. NLRB*, 321 U.S. 678, 686 (1944).
*NLRB v. Exchange Parts*, 375 U.S. 405 (1964).
*Packard Motor Car Co.*, 64 NLRB 1212 (1945); *Packard Motor Car Co.*, 157 F.2d 80 (6th Cir. 1946); *Packard Motor Co. v. NLRB*, 330 485 (1947).
*Philadelphia Cordwainers* case, 3 John Rogers Commons and Eugene Allen Gilmore, *A Documentary History of American Industrial Society* 55ff. (Cleveland: A. H. Clark Company, 1806).

# LEVELS OF ABSTRACTION

## I. Levels of Abstraction: The Basic Idea

Imagine a late-night conversation among friends in a college dormitory.

### A Conversation in a Dormitory

A: I'm doing a paper on the pay gap in my Feminist Studies class. In the twenty-first century, a woman still gets paid only 72 cents for every dollar a man gets. That's sex discrimination pure and simple, and we have to do something about it.

B: I'm taking the New American Workforce this semester, and we've just covered the effect of education on compensation. Workers with college degrees earn a ton more than workers without degrees. You have to control for education. I suggest comparing men and women with college degrees.

C: Last semester in Labor Economics I learned that full-time workers are paid more than part-time workers, and more women than men hold part-time jobs. You have to choose one of these categories in order to make a true comparison. I recommend comparing male and female full-time workers with college degrees.

D: Besides that, experience in the labor market matters. We were talking in Elder Studies about how much people make, and it turns out that experience is monetized, at least up to a point; and it's a fact that men have more paid-work experience than women have. A fair comparison evens out for experience as well as education and hours per week.

E: You're all missing the most important thing. Some occupations pay better than others. I learned in the Gendered Workplace that women typically enter lower-paying occupations like teaching and social service. You're comparing apples and oranges unless the men and the women are in the same or very similar occupations, even if they have equal education and experience and work weeks.

Facts operate at various levels of abstraction or generality, that is, apply to various numbers of persons and situations. The more persons of whom, and situations of which, the facts are true, the higher the level of abstraction. The data (facts) mentioned by the students are ordered from the more general to the more particular, from higher to lower levels of abstraction. At each successive step, fewer persons were involved. Thus, *A* wanted to compare the average compensation of all men to that of all women. *B* factored in education, believing that a proper comparison would be men versus women among workers with equal education. *C*, knowing that full-time workers earn more than part-time workers, recommended that *A* eliminate part-time workers and narrow the comparison to men versus women among full-time workers with equal education. Because experience also affects compensation, *D* urged *A* to narrow the comparison still further to men versus women among full-time workers with college degrees and equal experience on the job. Finally, *E* pointed out that compensation varies across occupations, and so *A* should be comparing men versus women among full-time workers with college degrees and equal experience in the same or similar occupations.

Note that *B, C, D,* and *E* each added to the discussion a new fact that was relevant or significant. Education, experience, etc. should be taken into account because each of those facts affects compensation. To make this point clear, suppose *G* had said, "Why don't you also control for whether they prefer dogs or cats as pets?" The appropriate response would have been, "That fact is not significant. No evidence exists that dog lovers earn more than cat lovers or vice versa."

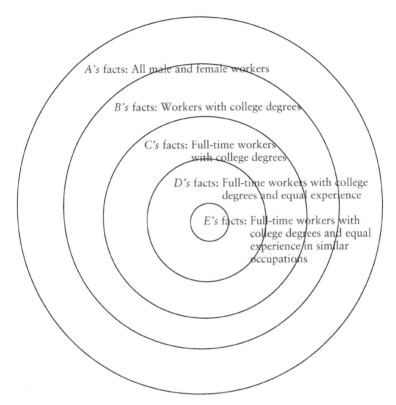

**Figure 3.1**

Facts generate issues. An issue operates on the same level of abstraction as the facts out of which the issue arises. Issues cry for resolution. The resolution of an issue operates on the same level of abstraction as the issue. The issues and resolutions that correspond to the students' facts are—

Table 3.1

| | Facts | Issue | Resolution |
|---|---|---|---|
| A | Women earn 72 cents for every dollar that men earn. | Does a gap exist between the average compensation of all men and women? | A gap exists between the average compensation of all men and women. |

*(Continued)*

**Table 3.1** (Continued)

| | Facts | Issue | Resolution |
|---|---|---|---|
| B | Workers with college degrees earn more than workers without degrees. | Is there a gap between the average compensation of men and women with college degrees? | The gap between the average compensation of men and women with college degrees is less than the gap between the average compensation of all men and women. |
| C | Full-time workers earn more than part-time workers earn. | Does a gap exist between the average compensation of men and women who hold college degrees and work full time? | The gap between the average compensation of men and women who hold college degrees and work full time is less than the gap between the average compensation of men and women who hold degrees. |
| D | Experience increases compensation. | Does a gap exist between the average compensation of men and women who hold college degrees, work full time, and have equal years of experience? | The gap between the average compensation of men and women who hold college degrees, work full time, and have equal years of experience is less than the gap between the average compensation of men and women who hold college degrees and work full time. |
| E | Compensation varies across occupations. | Does a gap exist between the average compensation of men and women who hold college degrees, work full time in similar occupations, and have equal years of experience? | The gap between the average compensation of men and women who hold college degrees, work full time in similar occupations, and have equal years of experience is less than the gap between the compensation of men and women who hold college degrees, work full time, and have equal experience. |

In this table, the facts, the issues that these facts generate, and the resolutions of those issues, are ordered from higher to lower levels of abstraction.

These examples demonstrate that a problem may be considered at various levels of abstraction. The more facts that are taken into account, the lower the level of abstraction. At the most general level (A), the only fact is the average compensation of all male and female workers. Adding (B) education lowers the level of abstraction. Adding (C) the difference in male and female participation in full-time and part-time jobs lowers the level again, and adding (D) experience and (E) occupations lowers the level still further. As the number of facts increases, the level of abstraction of the facts decreases; and as the level of abstraction of the facts decreases, so do the level of abstraction of the issue and of the resolution of the issue.

The level of abstraction on which one considers an issue is often a matter of choice.[1] That is, the same set of facts can generate issues on different levels of abstraction. By focusing on more or fewer facts, one can move the analysis and argument to a different level. The preceding example reveals that one can reasonably choose to consider the earnings gap between men and women at several different levels of abstraction. Here is another example. At this writing a controversy exists over the use of drugs by professional baseball players. One could frame the issue at a high level of abstraction: (A) Should the government regulate private behavior that does not injure other persons? By adding facts, one could frame the issue at a low level of abstraction: (F) Should Major League Baseball and the players' union add a clause in their collective bargaining agreement prohibiting the use of anabolic steroids? Or one could frame the issue at any one of several intermediate

**Table 3.2**

**An issue at varying levels of abstraction**

| Level of Abstraction: | |
| --- | --- |
| Higher | |
| A | Should the government regulate private behavior that does not injure other persons? |
| B | Should the government regulate professional sports? |
| C | Should the government regulate drugs in professional sports? |
| D | Should the government regulate drugs in professional baseball? |
| E | Should the government prohibit professional baseball players from using anabolic steroids? |
| F | Should Major League Baseball and the players' union add a clause in their collective bargaining agreement prohibiting the use of anabolic steroids? |
| Lower | |

---

1. We say "often" instead of "always" because sometimes one has no choice about the facts. One may be constrained to use certain facts, or additional facts may be unavailable. For example, when a precedent has resolved an issue at a particular level of abstraction, one may be constrained to address the issue (or a closely related one) at the same level.

levels of abstraction: (B) Should the government regulate professional sports? (C) Should the government regulate drugs in professional sports? (D) Should the government regulate drugs in professional baseball? (E) Should the government prohibit professional baseball players from using anabolic steroids?

One reason that the level of abstraction of an issue and its resolution matters is that a question which is conceived at one level of abstraction may be quite a different question if it is conceived at another level of abstraction, even though the two questions grow out of the same situation. Thus, suppose that you are a United States Senator, and Morality for All, a vocal interest group in your state, demands action on the problem of the use of drugs in sports. The issue could be framed at any of the six levels mentioned above. Imagine the debate that would occur if the issue were framed at the highest level of abstraction (should the government regulate private behavior that does not injure other persons?) and contrast it with the debate that would occur if the issue were framed at a lower level of abstraction (should Major League Baseball and the players' union add a clause in their collective bargaining agreement prohibiting the use of anabolic steroids?).

## II. The Definition of "Level of Abstraction"

The scope of facts/issue/resolution may be broad, narrow, or anything in between. Scope has two dimensions: the number of persons and the number of situations.

*Number of persons:* The resolution of an issue may affect everyone in the society; for example, should the defense of America be entrusted to a military of volunteers, or should conscription be revived? Or the resolution may affect only the parties to a specific case; for example, does *A* have a good excuse for failing to register with the Selective Service? Or the resolution of an issue may affect some number of persons in between these extremes; for example, should women be required to register with the Selective Service?

*Number of situations:* The resolution of an issue may apply to many situations; for example, should the Second Amendment be interpreted according to the intent of the Founders, or should the interpretation of the Amendment change with the times? The resolution of an issue may apply to one situation; for example, under the Second Amendment, may a city or state prohibit civilians from keeping firearms in their homes? Or the resolution of an issue may apply to some number of situations in between these extremes; for example, does the Second Amendment apply only to state militias, or does it apply to all individual citizens?

These two dimensions are independent of one another. An issue and its resolution may affect everyone but in only one situation; for example, should there be a sales tax on water? Or an issue and its resolution may affect only the parties to one case but in all of their transactions; for example, should a court issue an order of protection prohibiting *A* from approaching or speaking to *B*?

The term **level of abstraction** refers to the scope of an issue and its resolution. The broader the scope of an issue, the higher its level of abstraction. A handy metaphor is the **abstraction ladder.** The higher one climbs on a ladder, the more one can see: the higher the level of abstraction, the more persons and situations to which the issue and resolution apply. An issue and resolution that have broad scope occupy a high rung on the abstraction ladder; an issue and resolution that have narrow scope occupy a low rung on the abstraction ladder. An abstraction ladder exists for each universe of issues and resolutions.

Let us place on the abstraction ladder some of the issues and resolutions mentioned in § 1 Issues.

QUESTION

Should Lennis and Phela paint the den pale blue, light green, or off white?

ANSWER

Pale blue.

This issue and resolution occur at a low level of abstraction (stand on the bottom rung of the abstraction ladder). The reason is that their scope is narrow: they apply to two persons regarding one room in one house at one moment of time. The decision will apply to no other persons, to no other room in that house, to no other house in the world, and at no other time in history. By way of contrast, an issue occurring at a higher level of abstraction in the same universe is, should Lennis and Phela paint the den or leave it alone? An issue occurring at a lower level of abstraction in the same universe is, having decided on pale blue, do Lennis and Phela want shade No. 123 or No. 124 on the color chart of the Dripless Paint Company?

ISSUE

What is the mechanism of evolution?

THEORY

Natural selection.

This issue and resolution occur at a fairly high level of abstraction. Many things evolve; and if natural selection is the theory that explains evolution, natural selection applies to just as many things. Within the same universe, an issue that occupies a higher rung on the abstraction ladder is, which is the better explanation of the diversity of life forms, natural selection plus evolution or intelligent design? Within the same universe, an issue that occupies a lower rung on the abstraction ladder is, do Homo sapiens and gorillas have a common ancestor?

ISSUE

Should labor law require a union to win an election supervised by the Labor Board before the union may bargain with an employer, or should a union and an employer be allowed to bargain without an election if the majority of the workers desire union representation?

HOLDING

An election is unnecessary if the majority of workers desire union representation.

Within the universe of the National Labor Relations Act, this issue and its resolution stand high on the abstraction ladder. The issue pertains to every employer who is covered by the Labor Act and to every union that wishes to organize workers. By contrast, an issue on a higher level of abstraction in this universe is, should the Labor Act be repealed? An issue on a lower level of abstraction in the same universe is, do the majority of workers of ABC Company desire the union to bargain on their behalf?

ISSUE

> Did Δ punch π in the nose at 1:30 a.m. on August 12 in O'Leary's Bar after π accused Δ of cooking with molasses?

HOLDING

> Yes.

This issue and resolution occupy a low rung on the abstraction ladder. They apply only to two persons at one time and place. Within the same universe, an issue on a higher rung of the abstraction ladder is, "Is π's accusation that Δ cooks with molasses sufficient provocation to justify Δ's assault on π?" This issue stands higher on the abstraction ladder than the preceding one because the resolution will apply, not only to π and Δ in the wee hours of August 12, but also to anyone else who is accused of cooking with molasses. An issue on a still higher level of abstraction is, "May one person assault another if the latter has seriously provoked the former?" The resolution of this issue will affect many persons and apply to many different provocations.

## A. Unrelated Issues and Levels of Abstraction

A single legal proceeding can involve two or more issues. Such issues are "related" when the resolution of one issue affects the resolution of another issue. Related issues may operate on the same or on different levels of abstraction.

Let us first examine issues that are not related. Here follow two issues that might arise in the same legal proceeding, are not related, and occur on the same level of abstraction:

> Did the tenant pay the rent each month?
> Did the tenant damage the landlord's property?

Whether the tenant paid the rent has no connection to whether the tenant damaged the landlord's property. It is possible that the tenant paid the rent and damaged property, paid the rent and did not damage property, failed to pay the rent and also damaged property, or failed to pay the rent and did not damage property. These issues occur on the same level of abstraction because each issue involves the same number of persons and transactions.

Here follow two other issues, which (like the previous issues) might arise in the same legal proceeding and are not related, but (unlike the preceding issues) occur on different levels of abstraction:

> If the landlord does not pay the utility bill, may the tenant pay the bill and deduct the cost from the rent?
>
> When the furnace failed last February, did the landlord repair it within a reasonable period of time?

These issues are not related to one another (they exist in different universes of issues) because the resolution of one of them does not affect the resolution of the other; whether a tenant may, or may not, pay an unpaid utility bill and credit it against the rent, tells us nothing about whether this landlord repaired the furnace last February in a timely manner, and vice versa. These issues occur on different levels of abstraction; the first issue stands at a moderate level on the ladder, and the second issue is at a low level: whether a tenant may pay a utility bill that the landlord has failed to pay, and then credit the payment against the rent, is likely to arise from time to time, whereas whether a specific landlord repaired the furnace within a reasonable time last February applies only to one transaction and involves only two parties.

### B. Related Issues and Levels of Abstraction

Now let us examine issues and resolutions that are related to one another. One type of relationship among issues is conceptual priority. One issue is **conceptually prior** to another if the former must be resolved before the latter is addressed. Such issues commonly occur on different levels of abstraction. For example, suppose a firm is considering whether to create a new supervisory position. The following issues arise:

> Is it necessary that the new supervisor have prior supervisory experience?
>
> If so, what is the minimum number of years of experience that should be required?

The first issue is the more abstract, for it applies to all candidates for the job. The second issue ranks lower on the abstraction ladder; the issue applies only to the group of candidates who have supervisory experience.

Also, the first issue is conceptually prior to the second. If we decide that supervisory experience is not necessary for the job, we will not need to decide how many years of experience to demand. But if we decide that supervisory experience is necessary, we will also need to decide on a minimum number of years.[2]

Sometimes either of two issues may be considered conceptually prior to the other. Suppose a lease provides, "Tenant shall keep no pets on the premises." A tenant keeps a goldfish in a bowl, and the landlord seeks to evict the tenant. Two issues arise:

> Is a goldfish a pet?
> May the landlord evict the tenant for violating the clause in the lease concerning pets?

These issues occur on different levels of abstraction. The second issue is the more abstract because whether the landlord may evict the tenant for keeping a pet applies to the entire length of the lease and to every nonhuman creature that the tenant might care to keep on the premises. The first issue is the less abstract because whether a goldfish is a pet applies to only one sort of nonhuman creature. The issues are related because the resolution of one determines whether it is necessary to resolve the other, but one may reasonably argue that either issue is conceptually prior. The first issue is arguably prior because, if a goldfish is not a pet, the tenant has not violated the lease and we need not consider whether violating the pet clause is cause for eviction. But the second issue is also arguably prior because, if the landlord may not evict a tenant for violating the pet clause in the lease, we need not consider whether a goldfish is a pet.

In order to reinforce the student's understanding of levels of abstraction, and in keeping with our belief about the similarity of good legal and non-legal reasoning, here is a homely example in which a single set of events gives rise to related and unrelated issues at various levels of abstraction.

---

2. One might argue that we need not decide on a minimum number of years: for example, we might say that more experience is better than less experience. But a convincing counterargument exists. Suppose an applicant had one day of supervisory experience. Would we not ignore this amount of experience? Therefore, a minimum amount of experience must be determined.

The counterargument takes the form of a reductio ad absurdum. We will study this form in § 14 REDUCTIOS AD ABSURDUM.

### Ben and Gerrie's Case

Ben and Gerrie have a son aged two years. As they are adopting their second child, they are happy to learn that it will be a girl. They feel they need a separate bedroom for each child as well as one for themselves, but their house has only two bedrooms. Instead of adding a room to their present house, they decide to buy a house with at least three bedrooms. They read some books and talk to friends and family, and decide that each bedroom must measure at least 150 square feet. They also want to live within one mile of an elementary school, to have off-street parking for two cars, and to be able to drive to work in less than half an hour. Finally, they want to buy the house for the lowest possible price, but in no event more than $500,000. A realtor shows them many houses over the course of two months.

The issues and resolutions that Ben and Gerrie address occur on various levels of abstraction. Consider an issue at a high level in this particular universe.

QUESTION

Should Ben and Gerrie add a bedroom to their present house, or should they buy a new house?

ANSWER

They should buy a new house.

Within the universe of Ben and Gerrie's situation, this issue and resolution pair occurs at a high level of abstraction and is conceptually prior to nearly every other issue.

Consider now an issue at an intermediate level of abstraction in this universe.

QUESTION

How close to an elementary school must the new house be?

ANSWER

The house must be within one mile of an elementary school.

Having determined to buy a new house (a conceptually prior issue), Ben and Gerrie need to decide on the criteria they want the house to satisfy. One criterion is its distance from an elementary school. They decide they want the house to be within a mile of an elementary school.

A realtor shows Ben and Gerrie many houses to which they apply their criteria. Each criterion generates an issue of application of law to fact: does this house satisfy this criterion? (The criterion plays the role that the law plays in application of law to fact.[3]) For example, suppose the realtor shows Ben and Gerrie the house at 123 Bygone Alley. One of their criteria is whether the house has off-street parking. This criterion generates the following issue and resolution pair:

CRITERION

The house must have off-street parking for two cars.

ISSUE

Does the house at 123 Bygone Alley have off-street parking for two cars?

FACTS

The house at 123 Bygone Alley has off-street parking for two cars.

CONCLUSION

The house 123 Bygone Alley satisfies this criterion.

This issue and resolution pair occurs at a low level of abstraction. Whether a particular house has off-street parking for two cars pertains to no other house. In addition, this issue and resolution are unrelated to other issues and resolutions at the same level of abstraction; the resolution of one has no effect on the resolution of another. For example, that 123 Bygone Alley has off-street parking for two cars has no effect on whether this house is located within a mile of an elementary school, and vice versa.

---

3. See § 18 APPLICATION OF LAW TO FACT below.

Although most of the low-level issues in Ben and Gerrie's search for a house were unrelated to one another, one such issue was related to all of the others.

QUESTION

How much should we offer for this house?

This issue is low on the abstraction ladder because it applies to one house at one moment in time. The issue is related to the other low-level issues because, ceteris paribus, a house with large rooms is more valuable than a house with small rooms; a house nearer a school is more valuable than a house farther from a school; et cetera.

## III. Why the Level of Abstraction Matters

In the foregoing discussion and examples of issues at various levels of abstraction, we identified an abstraction ladder within each universe of issues and resolutions. We did not indicate, however, why it is important to know that one issue is more or less abstract than another.

One reason for knowing whether one issue is more or less abstract than another is that

- in making arguments about how an issue should be resolved,
- in replying to an adversary's arguments about how an issue should be resolved, and
- in reaching decisions about how an issue should be resolved,

one must use and take into account the appropriate sort of evidence and arguments.

- **As a rule, evidence and arguments must operate on the same level of abstraction as the issue to which they pertain.**

The reason is that the resolution of an issue necessarily applies to the same level of abstraction as the issue. When an issue occurs high on the abstraction ladder, its resolution will apply to a large number of persons and transactions. It is reasonable that

- *if an issue applies to many persons and transactions, the evidence and arguments that lead to resolving the issue should pertain to all (or at least most) of those persons and transactions.*

A law usually applies to everyone in a jurisdiction. An argument for or against a new law should be based, therefore, on facts that are generally true in the jurisdiction. Professor Kenneth Culp Davis used the term **legislative facts** to refer such facts, which operate at a high level of abstraction and are appropriately used in making law.

By contrast, when an issue occurs low on the abstraction ladder, the resolution of the issue will apply to a small number of persons and transactions; and so it is reasonable that

- *if an issue applies to a small number of persons and transactions, the evidence and arguments that lead to resolving the issue should pertain to those specific persons and transactions.*

The issues in most lawsuits pertain only to the parties to the suit. The parties do not disagree over the relevant law; instead, they disagree over the facts or over how the law should be applied to the facts. For example, suppose buyer *B* expects to receive 100 chattels from seller *S* on June 1st, but the chattels never come, and a lawsuit results. *B* and *S* agree that the law of contract controls the case. Their disagreements pertain only to their transaction. Did *S* promise to deliver 100 chattels on June 1? Did *S* fail to deliver the chattels? Did *B* make a reasonable effort to obtain 100 chattels from another source? What economic loss did *B* suffer? Professor Davis used the term **adjudicative facts** to refer to facts at a low level of abstraction that are appropriately used in adjudicating particular disputes.

One exception exists to the rule that facts and arguments must match the level of abstraction of the issue that they address. The exception is—

- **Evidence from a higher level of abstraction may help to prove a fact on a lower level of abstraction, provided the evidence is used with care.**

The reason is that what is true in general is probably true in a given case. For example, suppose the issue is whether John gave Abigail correct change in Filene's Basement in Boston at 10:30 a.m. on July 5. The resolution of this issue will stand at the lowest level on the abstraction ladder. Nevertheless, evidence that clerks in Filene's usually give correct change to customers, or that John has never previously been accused of short-changing a customer, is relevant. This evidence is higher up the abstraction ladder than the issue between John and Abigail because the evidence applies to many clerks and many transactions, yet the evidence is relevant to John and Abigail—relevant, but far from determinative. General evidence can only suggest the truth in a specific case. The best evidence, of course, is what happened between John and Abigail at 10:30 a.m. on July 5.

By contrast—

- **Evidence of a few facts at a lower level of abstraction may never prove a fact on a higher level of abstraction.**

The reason is that a generalization must not be based on a small number of facts. Politicians commonly commit this error. Senator Sounder holds a press conference and declares, "We need a law against walking a dog on a leash that attaches to a collar around the dog's neck. I know of a case where a woman was walking her beloved dog on a leash attached to a collar, and the leash slipped out of the woman's hand. The dog ran away and fell into a utility hole that happened to be open. The leash got caught on the lip of the hole, and the poor dog choked to death." The misfortune of one dog is not sufficient reason to outlaw leashes attached to collars. (Of course, evidence of many facts at a lower level of abstraction may combine to create a generalization that is relevant to an issue on a higher level of abstraction. A law against leashes attached to collars might be justified if thousands of dogs per year choked to death.)

In many situations, common sense leads us naturally to match the level of abstraction of the evidence and arguments to the level of abstraction of the issue. As Ben and Gerrie decided how much they could pay for a new house, they thought about their income, their savings, and their plans for the future, not about the average income, savings, or future plans of all young families. But if a state legislature were deliberating on a bill to provide low-interest financing for first-time home buyers, a legislator would properly be concerned, not with the finances of Ben and Gerrie, but with the finances of many families that were trying to purchase their first houses. In formal argument, however, common sense sometimes fails us (or our adversary tries to mislead the tribunal), and we may fail to appreciate the need to match the generality of evidence to the generality of an issue. For this reason, it is necessary to make explicit the concept of levels of abstraction and to practice applying it.

A second reason that level of abstraction matters is—

- **A precedent at a higher level of abstraction may support a proposition at a lower level, but not vice versa, except that many precedents** at a lower level may, taken together, support a proposition at a higher level.

A precedent that operates at a higher level of abstraction may support a proposition that would operate at a lower level. For example, consider a divorce proceeding, *W v. H*. The couple has two children, a boy and a girl. The issue is, which parent shall have custody of the children? *H* argues for the proposition that he take custody of the boy and *W* take custody of the girl. *W* argues for the proposition that the children stay together, regardless of which parent takes custody. Both of these propositions operate at a low level of abstraction because they apply only to the parties to this case. In support of her proposition, *W* cites a precedent which holds that children should be kept together absent special circumstances. This precedent operates at a high level of abstraction because it was intended to apply to all cases; therefore, the precedent supports *W*'s proposition.

A case at a lower level of abstraction does not support a proposition at a higher level of abstraction. In the divorce case of *W v. H*, suppose the couple owns a house, which *H* has vacated and *W* continues to occupy. *W* demonstrates that *H* has threatened to burn down the house rather than let *W* have it. Based on this evidence, the judge issues an injunction restraining *H* from going within a mile of the house. This precedent operates at a low level of abstraction, applying only to the circumstances of these parties at a particular time. The precedent would not support the proposition at a high level of abstraction that a restraining order should be issued against any spouse who moves out of a house during a divorce proceeding.

Nonetheless, many cases at a low level of abstraction may together support a proposition at a higher level. Suppose judges in dozens of divorce cases issue orders that, pending final settlement of the case, the spouse with the greater income must make the mortgage payments and pay the taxes on the couple's house. These cases would support the general proposition that the spouse with the greater income must make such payments.

A third reason that level of abstraction matters is—

- **The outcome of a dispute can vary with the level of abstraction of the issue.**

If the issue is, "Should the government regulate private behavior that does not injure other persons?" one might be strongly inclined to answer no. But if the issue is, "Should the collective bargaining agreement between Major League Baseball and the players' union prohibit major league baseball players from using anabolic steroids?" one might be inclined to answer yes. Or think again of Lennis and Phela, who are deciding what to do with their den. Suppose Lennis says, "The question is, what is the best possible color for a den?" and Phela says, "No, the question is, what is the best color for our den, which has tan curtains and dark brown upholstered furniture, which I like and want to keep?" Of all possible colors for any den (Lennis's issue), the best color might be a restful shade of blue, but the best color for a den that has tan curtains and dark brown furnishings (Phela's issue) might be a light shade of green. Or think of a case in which a supervisor may have violated a worker's legal rights. The worker might say, "The issue is whether an employer is responsible for an unfair labor practice committed by a supervisor." At this level of abstraction, the argument for an answer of no is hardly worth discussing: if employers were not responsible for the acts of supervisors, unfair labor practices would be all but uncontrollable. But the employer might say, "The issue in this case is whether an employer is responsible for a supervisor's discharge of a worker in department 1 when the supervisor had supervisory authority only in department 2 and disobeyed explicit instructions (a) not to deal in any way with workers in department 1 and (b) not to discharge any workers during the union's organizing campaign without consulting the company's attorney." At this level of abstraction, the argument for an answer of no is more forcible. When parties disagree about the issue, the disagreement often occurs over the level of abstraction at which the issue should be framed; and a good advocate will address arguments to this issue.

A fourth reason that level of abstraction matters is—

- **One's purpose may dictate a particular level of abstraction.**

The issue one wishes to resolve may dictate the level of abstraction at which to address the issue. For example, suppose you are an advisor to a candidate in an American presidential election. The candidate wants to know how well she is doing vis-à-vis the other candidate. You might say to her, "Based on the latest polls, you are four points ahead of your opponent." This answer assumes that the issue is, who will win the popular vote? But as a knowledgeable advisor, you know this issue is not the correct one. You know that the president is not elected by the popular vote. Rather, the president is elected by the majority of votes in the Electoral College; votes in the Electoral College are determined state by state, and a candidate can win the popular vote and lose the election.[4] Therefore, the correct issue is, if the election were held today, which candidate would get the majority of votes in the Electoral College? A proper answer would indicate which candidate is leading in each state, how many votes in the Electoral College the state has, and the totals. Thus, you might say, "We are leading in California, which has 55 votes, in New York, which has 29 votes . . . and we are trailing in Texas, which has 38 votes, in Florida, which has 29 votes . . . and the total is that we are leading in states with 300 Electoral College votes, while our opponent is leading in states with 238 votes." In short, to determine which candidate is leading in the race, the correct level of abstraction is the state, not the nation.

### Guenevere v. Arthur

The following statute took effect on January 1 of this year:

An employer of four or more employees in this State shall test any of the employer's employees for use of alcohol or illegal drugs whenever the employer has a reasonable belief that the employee is under the influence of alcohol or illegal drugs on the job. The employer shall discharge any such employee who refuses to be tested. An employer may not test an employee for alcohol or illegal drugs in any other circumstances.

Guenevere enjoyed a good income from assets she had inherited, but she liked to work from time to time to avoid boredom. She was registered with Camelot Services, Inc., which dispatches workers to short-term jobs. Her job duties and methods of performance were controlled by the firms to which she was referred; her paychecks, however, came from Camelot.

---

4. Candidates won the popular vote and lost the election in 1824, 1876, 1888, 2000, and 2016.

Guenevere accepted an assignment at Arthur's Company on December 15 of last year. She performed tasks that Arthur assigned to her. On January 2 of this year, Arthur approached Guenevere and said, "You look a little funny. Do you feel all right?"

"I'm fine," replied Guenevere.

"Give me a urine sample," Arthur instructed.

"What for?" Guenevere asked.

"What's the difference?" replied Arthur. "The law says we have to test everybody."

"I don't think that's right. I don't want to do that," said Guenevere.

"I guess you'll have to go then," Arthur said.

Guenevere went to Lancelot the lawyer, who told her the statute was an unconstitutional invasion of privacy, and, even if it were constitutional, Arthur had no reason to require her to submit to the test. Guenevere then sued Arthur.

Which of the following—IN LANCELOT'S OPINION—is the *issue of law* in *Guenevere v. Arthur*, and on what level of abstraction does the issue operate?

- ☐ (a) May a new statute be applied to a worker who was on the job when the statute took effect?
- ☐ (b) Was Arthur wrong to instruct Guenevere to submit to the test because she was an employee of Camelot, not of Arthur?
- ☐ (c) Does the statute interfere with the privacy of workers?
- ☐ (d) Does the statute authorize an employer to test all workers for alcohol or illegal drugs?

(a) is incorrect. You are looking for an issue of law, and this is an issue of law because it operates at a high level of abstraction, the answer to which will apply to many persons and situations. Nonetheless, although this issue might arise in another case, it does not arise in this case because Lancelot, as Guenevere's lawyer, did not assert that the statute should not apply to workers already on the job. For something to be an issue, the parties must disagree about it, and nothing in the facts of this case suggests that the parties disagree about the application of a new statute to a worker already on the job.

(b) is incorrect. If (b) were the issue (i) Guenevere would be arguing for a particular interpretation of the statute, namely, that it requires an employer to test only one's own employees. An argument on how a statute should be interpreted raises an issue of law. Then (ii) based on this interpretation, Guenevere would be arguing that, because she was an employee of Camelot, not of Arthur, he had no right to test her. Such an argument is application of law to fact. Law: an employer must test only one's own employees. Fact: Guenevere was not Arthur's employee. Conclusion: the law did not require Arthur to test Guenevere. These arguments may be interesting, and Lancelot should think about them; however, nothing in the facts indicates that he did.

(c) is the issue. Lancelot told Guenevere that the statute was an unconstitutional invasion of privacy. Whether a statute is constitutional is an issue of law at a high level of abstraction.

(d) is incorrect. It calls for an interpretation of the statute. Interpretation of a statute is an issue of law, and perhaps Lancelot should have raised it; but in this case he said nothing about testing all workers. Instead, he said the statute is unconstitutional.

Which of the following are *issues of fact* in *Guenevere v. Arthur*?

☐ (a) Did Guenevere refuse to be tested, or did she merely express her disapproval of the statute?

☐ (b) Was Guenevere an employee of Arthur, of Camelot, or of both?

☐ (c) Did the statute require Arthur to test everybody?

☐ (d) Did Arthur have sufficient reason to test Guenevere?

(a) is an issue of fact. To determine whether Guenevere refused to be tested, or merely expressed her disapproval of the statute, we need to know what she said, what she intended (was thinking), and perhaps what a reasonable person observing her would have thought that she intended. What she said, intended, and appeared to intend are plainly facts. Because the law considers state of mind to be a fact, what she intended is also a fact.

(b) is an issue of application of law to fact. The student may have thought that whether one is an employee is a fact, but it is not a fact because it cannot be perceived by the senses. (Remember that, in law, all facts except state of mind and reasonableness can be observed empirically.) It is true that, in determining whether someone is an employee, a number of genuine facts are pertinent, such as, in this case, that Arthur assigned tasks to Guenevere and that Camelot wrote her paychecks. But these facts have no legal significance by themselves. They are significant only in light of the law.

Therefore, the first step in resolving this issue is to ask, what is the legal definition of "employee"? The second step is to apply this definition to the facts of the case. The legal definition of "employee" has several elements, two of which are performing tasks at another person's direction and receiving money for one's labor. These elements can be applied to Guenevere: Arthur directed her tasks (indicating she was his employee) but she received her paychecks from Camelot (indicating that she was an employee of Camelot). The legal definition of "employee" includes additional elements, and more facts would be necessary to determine whether Guenevere was an employee of Arthur, Camelot, or both. Making this determination—determining the legal consequences of the facts—is application of law to fact.

(c) raises an issue of law. What a statute requires is an issue of law because it calls for interpretation of a statute.

(d) is an issue of fact. Actually, (d) raises two issues. The statute says that an employer shall test any employee if the employer has a reasonable belief that the employee is under the influence of drugs or alcohol on the job. The first issue is, did Arthur believe that Guenevere might be under the influence? (It is possible that he did not believe she was under the influence, but was looking for an excuse to fire her.) Assuming that Arthur did believe that Guenevere might be under the influence, the second issue is, was his belief reasonable? (It is possible that his belief was unreasonable. Suppose she had dreadlocks and tattoos, and he held the irrational belief that anyone with dreadlocks and tattoos uses drugs.) Whether something is reasonable usually depends on what the average person, informed of the facts, would think. The law considers reasonableness to be a fact.

Suppose *Guenevere v. Arthur* goes to trial, and witnesses testify to the following facts. Identify the issue to which each fact is relevant, and classify the fact as legislative or adjudicative.

A testifies that the use of drugs or alcohol is a minor problem in most American workplaces.

☐ Legislative
☐ Adjudicative

A testifies to a legislative fact. It pertains to all workplaces, not Arthur's; thus, the fact operates at a high level of abstraction. The fact helps us decide the issue of law, namely, whether the statute is constitutional, because individual rights must be balanced against social interests. An individual right such as privacy may have to give way in order to solve a serious social problem, but not to solve a minor problem

*B* testifies that Arthur was out to get Guenevere for refusing to date him.

☐ Legislative
☐ Adjudicative

*B* testifies to an adjudicative fact. It pertains only to this case and helps us decide the issue of application of law to fact, namely, whether Arthur had a reasonable belief that Guenevere was under the influence of drugs or alcohol. If the fact is true, Arthur may have been retaliating against Guenevere and lying about whether she appeared to be intoxicated.

*C* testifies that use of alcohol or drugs on the job impairs job performance.

☐ Legislative
☐ Adjudicative

*C* testifies to a legislative fact. It pertains to all workplaces, and it helps us to decide the issue of law (whether the statute is constitutional), because individual rights must be balanced against social interests. If drugs and alcohol do not impair job performance, they would be less important as a problem than if they do impair job performance. Also, if they do not impair job performance, attacking their use on the job could be irrational.

*D* testifies that Guenevere had an ear infection.

☐ Legislative
☐ Adjudicative

*D* testifies to an adjudicative fact. It applies only to these parties in this case and helps us to decide the issue of application of law to fact, namely, whether Arthur had a reasonable belief that Guenevere was under the influence of drugs or alcohol. An ear infection can make a person dizzy; dizziness can make a person appear disoriented, as though from drugs or alcohol.

*E* testifies that drug testing is valid and reliable.

    ☐ Legislative
    ☐ Adjudicative

*E* testifies to a legislative fact. It pertains to the issue of law, namely, whether the statute is constitutional. A law requiring an employer to discharge a worker based on the result of an unreliable or invalid test would be irrational.

*F* testifies that Guenevere did not report having an ear infection, nor did she file a medical insurance claim for a visit to a doctor about an ear infection.

    ☐ Legislative
    ☐ Adjudicative

*F* testifies to an adjudicative fact. It pertains only to this case and helps us decide the issue of application of law to fact, namely, whether Arthur reasonably believed that Guenevere was intoxicated. Guenevere offers the testimony of *F* because she wants us to believe that she did not have an ear infection because, if she had one, she might have been dizzy and appeared disoriented and, thus, Arthur might have reasonably believed that she was intoxicated. Guenevere will argue that ear infections are painful, and people usually go to a doctor for medication. That she did not report an infection or file an insurance claim suggests that she did not have an infection (and, therefore, did not appear disoriented because of one).

*G* testifies that use of drugs and alcohol on the job is increasing at a rapid rate.

    ☐ Legislative
    ☐ Adjudicative

*G* testifies to a legislative fact. It helps us to decide the issue of law, namely, whether the statute is constitutional. If use of drugs and alcohol on the job is increasing, it is a serious problem and the right to privacy might have to be curtailed to solve the problem.

*H* testifies that Guenevere appeared to be disoriented and unstable as she walked around the shop.

☐ Legislative
☐ Adjudicative

*H* testifies to an adjudicative fact. Arthur introduces this testimony in order to substantiate his assertion that he had a reasonable belief that Guenevere appeared to be under the influence of drugs or alcohol. The testimony applies only to the parties to this case on a particular date at a particular time and, therefore, is adjudicative.

*I* testifies that Guenevere appeared normal at all times

☐ Legislative
☐ Adjudicative

*I* testifies to an adjudicative fact. Guenevere introduces the testimony because, if she looked normal, Arthur could not have held a reasonable belief that she was intoxicated by drugs or alcohol. Applying only to the parties to this case at this place and time, the fact is adjudicative.

*J* testifies that many employers test job applicants for drugs and alcohol, and few workers object.

☐ Legislative
☐ Adjudicative

*J* testifies to a legislative fact. It pertains to the issue of law, namely, the constitutionality of the statute. If many employers test applicants and few applicants object, workers do not have an expectation of privacy with regard to drug testing or do not consider drug testing to be a serious invasion of their privacy.

## IV. Review

### Questions

1. The term "level of abstraction" refers to the scope of an issue or its resolution. The more persons and transactions to which an issue and resolution apply, the lower their level of abstraction.
   ☐ True
   ☐ False

2. Issues and resolutions come in pairs. The resolution applies to the issue, but not to other issues.
   ☐ True
   ☐ False

3. At which level of abstraction does the following issue occur: is a statute prohibiting abortion constitutional?
   ☐ High
   ☐ Low

4. At which level of abstraction does the following issue occur: did Mary know she was pregnant when she took birth control pills that caused her to abort her embryo?
   ☐ High
   ☐ Low

5. The level of abstraction of an issue and its resolution matters because (more than one answer may be correct)—
   ☐ (a) the level of abstraction of evidence and arguments must match the level of abstraction of the issue and its resolution.
   ☐ (b) an authority which is used as a precedent and the issue to which the authority applies should generally be on the same level of abstraction.
   ☐ (c) the same set of facts can often generate issues at different levels of abstraction, and the resolution of those issue can vary.
   ☐ (d) notwithstanding other principles, evidence at a high level of abstraction can be helpful, though is rarely dispositive, of an issue at a lower level.

6. The term "legislative fact" refers to (more than one answer may be correct)—
   ☐ (a) a fact at a high level of abstraction.
   ☐ (b) a fact at a low level of abstraction.
   ☐ (c) a fact often used in making laws.
   ☐ (d) a fact often used to decide a particular dispute.

7. The term "adjudicative fact" refers to (more than one answer may be correct)—

    ☐ (a)  a fact at a high level of abstraction.

    ☐ (b)  a fact at a low level of abstraction.

    ☐ (c)  a fact often used in making laws.

    ☐ (d)  a fact often used to decide a particular dispute.

### Mary's Case

Mary is a sixteen-year-old junior in high school. Her parents died when she was ten and her older sister, Magda, was seventeen. Mary and Magda went to live with an uncle. After Magda was graduated from high school, she went to college and became a nurse. Mary and her uncle never got along well. As soon as Magda got a job, Mary moved in with her. They have lived together for a year. Because Magda works the afternoon shift, plus as many extra shifts as possible in order to earn more money, she and Mary do not spend much time together.

Shortly after moving in with Magda, Mary meets a man, Joe, who is in his early fifties and married; he and his wife have no children. Joe buys meals and clothes for Mary and treats her very well. Mary does not tell Magda about Joe.

On New Year's Eve, Mary and Joe have sexual intercourse; it is Mary's first coitus, and she becomes pregnant. Toward the end of January, Mary begins to experience spells of nausea, usually in the morning. On February 5 she mentions the nausea to Magda. The latter asks Mary whether she has ever had sex, and Mary answers truthfully. Magda then asks a few specific questions about Mary's experience on New Year's Eve. The next day, when Magda returns from work, she offers Mary a small tablet. "This will take care of everything," Magda says. The tablet is Cytotec, a drug that is made for treating ulcers but is also an abortifacient, and Mary soon aborts. Joe happens to telephone that afternoon.

"I've just miscarried," she tells him.

"What!" he exclaims. "I didn't know you were pregnant. Why didn't you tell me? I wanted that baby. You know I have no children."

"I couldn't have a baby now," replies Mary. "I have no money."

"I would have given you all the money you needed," says Joe.

"But how could I finish high school if I was pregnant?"

"I would have been happy to take care of the baby for you."

"But everyone would know I was pregnant and not married."

"Mary, what you did is wrong. Abortion is murder. Don't you remember? We had several long conversations about that. You always said you thought the zygote was alive from conception."

"Yes, I still do."

"Then you shouldn't have murdered my baby!"

"I didn't murder it. I didn't know the pill would make me miscarry. I didn't even know I was pregnant. Magda told me the pill would help my nausea."

Joe tries to see Mary again, but she refuses several times. He then reports her to the district attorney. Their state has no statute regarding abortion and no judicial precedents on point. Nevertheless, the district attorney (after granting Joe immunity from prosecution for statutory rape) decides to prosecute Mary for the crime of murder

*Mary's Case* raises two issues. The first is (assuming it is constitutional for a state to outlaw abortion), should intentional abortion be considered murder in the State of Confusion? This is an issue of law; the answer to it will apply to everyone in the state. Legislative facts are appropriate to deciding this issue. Assuming the court decides that intentional abortion is murder, the second issue in *Mary's Case* is, did Mary intentionally have an abortion? This is an issue of fact; it raises the question of what Mary intended to do.

### Hints for the Following Questions

Regarding adjudicative facts, state only facts that could be observed empirically. (Imagine that you are a video camera.) Exception: the law considers intent (or, more generally, state of mind) to be a fact. Intent may be proved by inferences from statements that a subject makes and by inferences based on what a reasonable person in the subject's place would have intended.

Do not characterize an adjudicative fact. An example of a correctly stated fact: Mary occasionally felt nauseated in the morning. An example of a characterized fact: Mary had morning sickness.

Do not invent any facts. NEVER INVENT FACTS. An example of an actual fact: Mary and Joe had sex. An example of an invented fact: Joe seduced Mary.

## Questions

8(a). State two adjudicative facts in *Mary's Case* that tend to prove that she did intentionally abort. Regarding each fact, indicate why (i.e., state an argument that) each fact tends to prove that Mary intentionally aborted.

8(b). State two adjudicative facts in *Mary's Case* that tend to prove that she did not intentionally abort. Regarding each fact, indicate why (i.e., state an argument that) each fact tends to prove that Mary did not intentionally abort.

8(c). State one or more legislative facts and use the fact(s) in an argument that intentional abortion should be illegal.

8(d). State one or more legislative facts and use the fact(s) in an argument that intentional abortion should not be illegal.

### Wimp v. Bully

After class one day, Wimp and Bully were walking in front of Rich Guy Hall. They were discussing the undergraduate course they were taking, Introduction to Law.

"I love it!" exclaimed Wimp.

"It sucks!" muttered Bully.

"It's my favorite class," added Wimp. "I go to the library and read cases just for fun."

"People like you make life miserable for the rest of us," declared Bully.

"I've been working thirty hours a week on my briefs. I can't get enough of it. When we get the research assignment next week, I plan to work twice as hard. I've already finished all the assignments in my other courses, so I'll have the time. Then I'll get a great recommendation from Professor Kingsfield and get into a great law school."

"Because of curve busters like you, I'll probably flunk the course."

Suddenly Bully thrust out his arm and screeched, "Look! It's Professor Kingsfield, right in front of Rich Guy Hall!"

But Wimp did not see Professor Kingsfield because Wimp had fallen to the ground, his nose bleeding profusely because Bully's elbow had struck Wimp in the face.

"You meanie!" cried Wimp. "You did that on purpose."

"What do you mean?" replied Bully. "It was an accident. I was pointing out Professor Kingsfield to you. Weren't we just discussing his class?"

Wimp sued Bully for battery in small claims court. The only contested issue was whether Bully had struck Wimp intentionally or accidentally.

### Hints for the Following Questions

Same as in *Mary's Case*.

### Questions

9(a). Write an argument that Bully struck Wimp intentionally. Use both legislative and adjudicative facts. Label each element of the argument.

9(b). Write an argument that Bully struck Wimp accidentally. Use both legislative and adjudicative facts. Label each element of the argument.

### *The Spat*

H:  "What'cha doin'?"

w:  "Lea' me alone. Can't you see I'm busy right now?"

H:  "You complain when I don't pay attention to you, and you complain when I do."

### Question

10. Analyze this exchange in terms of levels of abstraction.

## V. References

Aristotle, *Nicomachean Ethics*, bk. I, ch. 7, 1098a15 (W. D. Ross, trans., 1908).

Kenneth Culp Davis, "An Approach to Problems of Evidence in the Administrative Process," 55 HARVARD LAW REVIEW 364, 402–410 (1942), and ADMINISTRATIVE LAW AND GOVERNMENT 149–151, 283–288 (1960).

# § 4

# DEDUCTION

## I. In General

For more than two millennia, in both legal and nonlegal discourses, one of
the dominant modes of secular reasoning and argument in the Western world
has been deduction. Anyone who makes or listens to arguments, whether
a politician, a lawyer, or a citizen, must understand the basic principles of
deduction. This section, the briefest of introductions to deduction, provides
a few examples that are frequently encountered in legal reasoning, with the
hope that they will suffice to apprise the student of the importance of deduction and to motivate the student to pursue the subject further, for example,
by taking a course or studying a text on logic[1] or on critical thinking.[2]

---

1. Although not texts on logic, two introductions to sound argument, from which some
of the examples in this section have been adapted, are Ruggero Aldisert, *Logic for Lawyers: A
Guide to Clear Legal Thinking* (Clark Boardman, 1989) and Bruce N. Waller, *Critical Thinking: Consider the Verdict* (Prentice-Hall, 1998).

2. Critical thinking, which we believe should be required in every undergraduate curriculum, encompasses not only deduction, but also induction, causation, proof (and more). A

The etymology of the word "deduction" and its cognates is—

DE = away from
DUCERE = to lead.

So deduction means to lead away from something, namely, a generalization. In deduction, the argument leads away from a generalization to a conclusion about the existence of something particular. One begins with a general statement, and then deduces that a particular thing exists. Here follow the form of deduction and an example.

DEDUCTION

| THE FORM | AN EXAMPLE |
|---|---|
| GENERALIZATION | GENERALIZATION |
| *A* is a *B*. | A polygon with three sides is a triangle. |
| PARTICULAR | PARTICULAR |
| *C* is an *A*. | Figure α is a polygon with three sides. |
| CONCLUSION | CONCLUSION |
| ∴ *C* is a *B*. | Figure α is a triangle. |

Deduction is "analytic"; it is not synthesized by human beings, but is an aspect of the nature of rationality (or perhaps the structure of our brains). If the rules of reasoning are followed, deduction leads to certainty. In a sense, the conclusion of deductive reasoning is already contained within the general statement. To say that all *A*'s are *B*'s is to say that anything that is an *A* (such as *C*) is also a *B*. For example, to say that a triangle is a polygon with three sides is to say that the particular polygon with three sides that you happen to be observing—and, indeed, any other polygon with three sides—is a triangle.

---

useful introduction to critical thinking is Merrilee Salmon, *Introduction to Logic and Critical Thinking* (Thomson Wadsworth, fifth or later edition).

## A. SYLLOGISMS

The example above expresses deduction in the form of a **syllogism,** and much deductive reasoning can be analyzed into this form. The word "syllogism" derives from ancient Greek, in which the word meant "a putting together of ideas." Today a syllogism is an argument that moves from premises (typically two, but more are possible) to a conclusion.

> If *A*, and
> If *B*,
> ∴ *C*.

In this book, two types of syllogism are discussed, deductive and inductive. This section focuses on the former type, and §5 INDUCTION, on the latter type.

The power of a deductive syllogism derives from its form. If the premises and the conclusion obey the rules of logic—that is, if the deductive syllogism is **valid**—its conclusion is indisputable. Anyone who disagrees is uneducated or behaving irrationally.

## B. ENTHYMEMES

Many arguments that one hears daily (and may not even think of as arguments) are actually syllogisms that have been truncated. Aristotle, who wrote the first great text on logic, called a truncated syllogism an **enthymeme,** which is a syllogism in which at least one element is not stated. Sometimes, one of the premises is omitted and, other times, the conclusion is omitted. For instance, the example above concerning a triangle might be expressed in ordinary conversation as an enthymeme: "α is a triangle because it has three sides."

It is crucial for the student to identify and articulate the missing element(s) of an enthymeme so that its validity can be verified. Fallacious reasoning is easily disguised by omitting the faulty element. Consider, for example, the argument, "Joe is religious. We can trust him." This argument is an enthymeme in which the generalization is omitted. If the generalization is included, the fallacy becomes evident:

GENERALIZATION

All persons who are religious are trustworthy.

PARTICULAR

Joe is religious.

CONCLUSION

Joe is trustworthy.

The statement is faulty because the generalization is false. Some persons who are religious are not trustworthy.[3]

### Exercise

1. Supply the missing premise in the enthymeme, "$\alpha$ is a triangle because a polygon with three sides is a triangle"?

## II. Categorical Syllogisms and Quasi Syllogisms

Two common types of deductive syllogism are the categorical syllogism and the quasi syllogism. In a **categorical syllogism** the major premise, the minor premise, and the conclusion all refer to categories or classes of things:

CATEGORICAL SYLLOGISM

| THE FORM | AN EXAMPLE |
|---|---|
| MAJOR PREMISE | MAJOR PREMISE |
| All $A$'s are $B$'s. | All cows eat grass. |
| MINOR PREMISE | MINOR PREMISE |
| All $C$'s are $A$'s. | All Jerseys are cows. |
| CONCLUSION | CONCLUSION |
| ∴ All $C$'s are $B$'s. | ∴ All Jerseys eat grass. |

---

3. Not all enthymemes are meretricious; they often serve rhetorical purposes. For example, omitting the conclusion (assuming it is obvious) may be a useful rhetorical move because it prompts the audient to supply the conclusion in one's own mind, thereby becoming more likely to accept the conclusion because it feels like one's own.

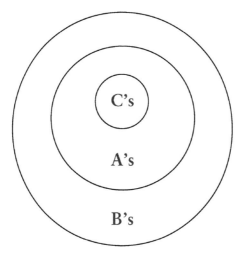

**Figure 4.1** Categorical syllogism

A **quasi syllogism** is like a categorical syllogism except that in a quasi syllogism one of the premises concerns a specific thing (as opposed to a class of things):

QUASI SYLLOGISM

| THE FORM | AN EXAMPLE |
|---|---|
| MAJOR PREMISE | MAJOR PREMISE |
| All *A*'s are *B*'s. | All men are mortal. |
| MINOR PREMISE | MINOR PREMISE |
| *C* is an *A*. | Socrates is a man. |
| CONCLUSION | CONCLUSION |
| ∴ *C* is a *B*.[4] | ∴ Socrates is mortal. |

---

4. It is customary to label the general premise of a quasi syllogism the "major premise" and the specific premise the "minor premise." The order of the premises, however, is not important; the meaning of the syllogism would not be changed if the minor premise or the conclusion were stated first.

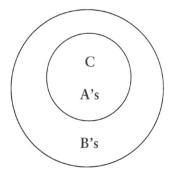

**Figure 4.2** Quasi syllogism in which the major and minor premises are affirmative

The quasi syllogism is the type more commonly used in legal reasoning (and the same may be true of daily life as well). Nonetheless, for the purposes of this book, the properties of categorical and quasi syllogisms are similar, and whatever is asserted about the one is also true of the other mutatis mutandis.

## A. THE MAJOR AND MINOR PREMISES ARE AFFIRMATIVE

### 1. The Valid Form

In the example above of a quasi syllogism, the major and minor premises were affirmative, and the syllogism was valid. It is obvious that if all men are in the category of mortals, and Socrates is in the category of men, Socrates is within the category of mortals.

A valid syllogism of this form is often expressed as an enthymeme. For example, "Socrates is mortal because he is a man" or "Every man is mortal, and Socrates is a man."

### 2. The Fallacy of the Undistributed Middle

A common fallacy associated with the quasi syllogism that has two affirmative premises is called the **fallacy of the undistributed middle**:

| THE FORM | AN EXAMPLE |
|---|---|
| MAJOR PREMISE | MAJOR PREMISE |
| All A's are B's. | All men are mortal. |
| MINOR PREMISE | MINOR PREMISE |
| C is a B. | Lassie is mortal. |
| CONCLUSION | CONCLUSION |
| ∴ C is a A. | Lassie is a man. |

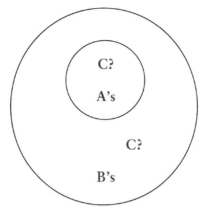

**Figure 4.3** Fallacy of the undistributed middle

This reasoning is fallacious because, whereas the conclusion of a valid syllogism is dictated by its premises, the conclusion of an invalid syllogism is *not* dictated by its premises. Thus, the major premise of the fallacy of the undistributed middle says that all *A*'s are *B*'s. Notice that the major premise does not say that no other *B*'s exist; therefore, as far as the major premise is concerned, *B*'s that are not *A*'s could exist. The minor premise says that *C* is a *B*. Notice that the minor premise does not say whether *C* is one of the *B*'s that is an *A*, or one of the *B*'s that is not an *A*. Accordingly, we cannot know whether *C* is, or is not, an *A*. The fallacy of the undistributed middle does not rule out the latter possibility and, for this reason, is invalid.

It is important to realize that a logical fallacy, be it the fallacy of the undistributed middle or any other fallacy (others are discussed below), remains a fallacy even if the conclusion happens to be true. For example:

MAJOR PREMISE

All birds are animals.

MINOR PREMISE

Chickens are animals.

CONCLUSION

Chickens are birds.

In this example, which we have borrowed from Prof. Judith Grabiner, both premises are true, and so is the conclusion. Nevertheless, the reasoning is fallacious. It happens to be true that chickens are birds, but this syllogism does not prove that proposition.

### Exercise

2(a). Supply the missing premise for the enthymeme, "This fruit is juicy. It must be a watermelon."

2(b). Using the missing premise plus the two express statements, write an invalid quasi syllogism in which both premises are affirmative.

### B. THE MAJOR PREMISE IS AFFIRMATIVE AND THE MINOR PREMISE IS NEGATIVE

#### 1. The Valid Form

In another type of quasi syllogism, the major premise is affirmative and the minor premise is negative:

| THE FORM | AN EXAMPLE |
|---|---|
| MAJOR PREMISE | MAJOR PREMISE |
| All A's are B's. | All pies are tasty. |
| MINOR PREMISE | MINOR PREMISE |
| C is not a B. | This dish is not tasty. |
| CONCLUSION | CONCLUSION |
| ∴ C is not an A. | This dish is not a pie. |

In ordinary discourse, this syllogism might become an enthymeme, for example, "This dish is not a pie because pies are tasty."

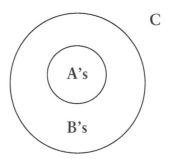

**Figure 4.4** Quasi syllogism in which the major premise is affirmative and the minor premise is negative

### Exercise

3(a). Supply the missing premise for the enthymeme, "This beast is not a puppy because it is not adorable."

3(b). Using the missing premise plus the two express statements, write a valid quasi syllogism in which the major premise is affirmative and the minor premise is negative.

### 2. *The Fallacy of the Illicit Major*

A common fallacy associated with the quasi syllogism that has an affirmative major premise and a negative minor premise is called the **fallacy of the illicit major**:

| THE FORM | AN EXAMPLE |
|---|---|
| MAJOR PREMISE | MAJOR PREMISE |
| All *A*'s are *B*'s. | All butlers are polite. |
| MINOR PREMISE | MINOR PREMISE |
| *C* is not an *A*. | Chester is not a butler. |
| CONCLUSION | CONCLUSION |
| ∴ *C* is not a *B*. | Chester is not polite. |

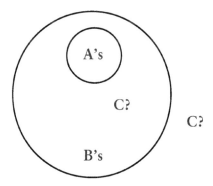

**Figure 4.5** Fallacy of the illicit major.

The reason this is a fallacy is that we do not know anything about *C* except that it is not an *A*; thus, *C* could be either a *B* or not a *B*. In the example, Chester (*C*) could be either one of the polite persons who is not a butler (*B* but not *A*), or he could be a person who is not polite (not *B*).

## Exercise

4(a). Supply the missing element for the enthymeme, "Olympic athletes train hard, but Annika Sörenstam was not an Olympic athlete."

4(b). Using the missing premise plus the two express statements, write an invalid quasi syllogism in which the major premise is affirmative and the minor premise is negative.

## III. Hypothetical Syllogisms

Deductive syllogisms come in another variety, the **hypothetical syllogism**. Like a quasi syllogism, a valid hypothetical syllogism—that is, one that obeys the rules of logic—reaches an indisputable conclusion.

### A. Modus Ponens

#### 1. The Valid Form

One type of hypothetical syllogism is the **modus ponens**. The first clause of the major premise of a modus ponens, which begins with "if," is called the **antecedent,** and the second clause of the major premise, which begins with "then," is called the **consequent**. In a valid modus ponens, the minor premise affirms the antecedent (i.e., the minor premise states that the antecedent in the major premise is true of someone or something).

| THE FORM | AN EXAMPLE |
|---|---|
| MAJOR PREMISE | MAJOR PREMISE |
| If $p$, then $q$. | If one studies Biology for eight hours per day, one will pass the course. |
| MINOR PREMISE | MINOR PREMISE |
| $p$. | Harlan studies Biology for at least eight hours per day. |
| CONCLUSION | CONCLUSION |
| $\therefore q$. | $\therefore$ Harlan will pass Biology. |

A modus ponens expresses the idea of sufficient causation. $P$ suffices to cause $q$. Studying Biology for eight hours per day suffices for a student to pass the course.

## 2. *The Fallacy of Denying the Antecedent*

A valid modus ponens *affirms* the antecedent. The **fallacy of denying the antecedent** *denies* the antecedent (i.e., the minor premise denies that the antecedent in the major premise is true of someone or something).

| THE FORM | AN EXAMPLE |
|---|---|
| MAJOR PREMISE | MAJOR PREMISE |
| If $p$, then $q$. | If one studies Biology for eight hours per day, one will pass the course. |
| MINOR PREMISE | MINOR PREMISE |
| Not $p$. | Marshall foolishly studies Biology only five hours per day. |
| CONCLUSION | CONCLUSION |
| ∴ Not $q$. | ∴ Marshall will not pass the course. |

One can understand why denying the antecedent is a fallacy in terms of the difference between a necessary cause and a sufficient cause. A **necessary cause** must exist in order for the effect to occur; if a necessary cause does not occur, the effect cannot occur. Submitting an application is a necessary cause of being admitted to a college: no application, no admission. A **sufficient cause** by itself can produce an effect. In some cases, a sufficient cause is the only cause that can produce the effect (in which event the cause is also necessary); in other cases, one or more other causes can also produce the effect. Snoring in class is one way to draw (is a sufficient cause of) a professor's ire, but other ways exist.

The reason denying the antecedent is a fallacy is that we know only that $p$ is a sufficient cause of $q$; we do not know whether $p$ is a necessary cause of $q$. Accordingly, $q$ may have causes other than $p$. Therefore, the nonexistence (falsity) of $p$ does not demonstrate the nonexistence (falsity) of $q$, for $q$ may have other causes. If he studies efficiently, Marshall will pass Biology.

### Exercise

5(a). Supply the missing element for the enthymeme, "I won't get rich because the stock market won't go up."

5(b). Using the missing premise plus the two express statements, write a modus ponens that commits the fallacy of denying the antecedent.

## B. Modus Tollens

### 1. The Valid Form

Another type of hypothetical syllogism is the **modus tollens**. The first clause of the major premise of a modus tollens, which begins with "if," is called the **antecedent,** and the second clause of the major premise, which begins with "then," is called the **consequent.** In a valid modus tollens, the minor premise denies the consequent (i.e., the minor premise denies that the consequent in the major premise is true of someone or something).

| THE FORM | AN EXAMPLE |
|---|---|
| MAJOR PREMISE | MAJOR PREMISE |
| If $p$, then $q$. | If the university had increased tuition, some students would have transferred to other schools. |
| MINOR PREMISE | MINOR PREMISE |
| Not $q$. | No students transferred to other schools. |
| CONCLUSION | CONCLUSION |
| ∴ Not $p$. | ∴ The university did not increase tuition. |

As an enthymeme in daily speech: "I know the university has not increased tuition because no student has transferred to another school."

### Exercise

6. Which element does the foregoing enthymeme omit?

A modus tollens expresses the idea of sufficient causation. $P$ suffices to cause $q$. Therefore, if $q$ does not exist (is false), $p$ also does not exist (is false): for if $p$ existed (were true), it would cause $q$ to exist (be true).

Modus tollens is proof by contradiction. The hypothesis is that $p$ exists. We know that if $p$ exists, $q$ must also exist. But we also know that $q$ does not exist and, therefore, we know that $p$ does not exist. Accordingly, our hypothesis that $p$ exists is contradicted. This form of reasoning is widely used in mathematics and the sciences, and is also the logical form of reductios ad absurdum, which are discussed in § 14.

## 2. The Fallacy of Affirming the Consequent

A valid modus tollens *denies* the consequent. The **fallacy of affirming the consequent** *affirms* the consequent (i.e., the minor premise states that the consequent in the major premise is true of someone or something):

| THE FORM | AN EXAMPLE |
|---|---|
| MAJOR PREMISE | MAJOR PREMISE |
| If $p$, then $q$. | If a person is insane, one's will is invalid. |
| MINOR PREMISE | MINOR PREMISE |
| $q$. | Anita's will is invalid. |
| CONCLUSION | CONCLUSION |
| ∴ $p$. | ∴ Anita is insane. |

The reason that affirming the consequent is a fallacy is that we know only that $p$ is a sufficient cause of $q$, but we do not know whether $p$ is a necessary cause of $q$; accordingly, $q$ may or may not have causes other than $p$. Therefore, the existence of $q$ does not demonstrate the existence of $p$, for another cause of $q$ may be accountable. Anita might be perfectly sane, but her will might be invalid for another reason, for example, her failure to sign it in front of sufficient witnesses.

### Exercise

7(a). Supply the missing element for the enthymeme, "The dorms are empty. The Greeks must be having a party."

7(b). Using the missing premise plus the two express statements, write an invalid modus tollens that commits the fallacy of denying the antecedent.

## IV. The Soundness of Syllogisms

A syllogism is **sound** if its premises are true and they lead logically to its conclusion. If a syllogism is sound, it proves its conclusion. (These statements are equally true of any other type of argument.)

An *invalid* syllogism—whether categorical, quasi, or hypothetical—cannot be sound because its premises do not lead logically to its conclusion. Thus, an invalid syllogism proves nothing. Curiously, the conclusion of an invalid syllogism might happen to be true, but the invalid syllogism does not prove its truth. Anita might actually be insane, but the invalidity of her will does not prove that she is insane. See also Prof. Grabiner's example in II.A.2 above of chickens and birds.

Is the conclusion of a *valid* syllogism always true? The answer is no. A syllogism may be logically valid, yet untrue. Here is an example of a valid but unsound hypothetical syllogism:

MAJOR PREMISE

If prices rise, war must have been declared.

MINOR PREMISE

War has not been declared.

CONCLUSION

Prices have not risen.

This syllogism is a valid modus tollens, yet it is unsound because the major premise is false. Prices may rise for reasons other than war. Therefore, this syllogism does not prove that prices have not risen—and this statement is correct even if the conclusion happens to be true: even if prices actually have risen, *this syllogism* does not prove that they have risen.

Here is an example of a valid but unsound quasi syllogism:

MAJOR PREMISE

All college students abide by the Code of Academic Integrity.

MINOR PREMISE

Rosalind is a college student.

CONCLUSION

Rosalind abides by the Code of Academic Integrity.

We have it on good information that the major premise in this example is false. Therefore, although this is a valid quasi syllogism, it does not prove the conclusion. But suppose the conclusion is true. Suppose Rosalind does abide by the Code. Even so, this syllogism does not prove that she does.

Perhaps even more dangerous than a premise that is always false is a premise that is partially true, but happens to be false in this case. Such a premise is often hidden. Consider—

(1)

MAJOR PREMISE

Drinking water is good for you.

MINOR PREMISE

Water ($H_2O$) has oxygen in it.

CONCLUSION

Drinking oxygen is good for you.

(2)

MAJOR PREMISE

Drinking oxygen is good for you.

MINOR PREMISE

Hydrogen peroxide ($H_2O_2$) has even more oxygen in it than water does.

CONCLUSION

Drinking hydrogen peroxide is better for you than drinking water.

A hidden premise of the second syllogism is, more of a good thing is better. This premise is only partially true, and it is false in this case.[5]

Thus, validity is not the same as truth. A logically valid syllogism does not necessarily reach a true conclusion. An argument is **sound** only if all of the following criteria are satisfied:

- **the argument is valid** (the conclusion follows logically from the premises)
- **both the premises are true,** and
- **no hidden premise is false.**

Even though it follows the rules of logic, an argument in the form of a syllogism is not sound—fails to prove its conclusion—if either premise is false (or both are false).

---

5. A hidden premise of both syllogisms is that an element in a compound operates independently of the other elements of the compound. This premise is false.

### V. Moral Syllogisms and Legal Syllogisms

#### A. MORAL SYLLOGISMS

A **moral syllogism** argues that one has done something moral or immoral. A moral syllogism may take the form of any valid syllogism. For example, suppose Melinda spoke unkindly to Michael without good cause.

QUASI SYLLOGISM

MAJOR PREMISE

It is immoral to speak unkindly to another without good cause.

MINOR PREMISE

Melinda spoke unkindly to Michael without good cause.

CONCLUSION

∴ Melinda behaved immorally.

This syllogism is expressed in the way we ordinarily speak, and it may not appear to be a valid quasi syllogism. However, with no change in meaning, the major premise can be reworded so that the argument is a valid quasi syllogism: "All persons who speak unkindly to another person without good cause behave immorally."

The argument can also be expressed as a modus ponens—

MODUS PONENS

IF $p$, THEN q.

If one speaks unkindly to another without good cause, one behaves immorally.

$p$.

Melinda spoke unkindly to Michael without good cause.

∴ $q$.

∴ Melinda behaved immorally.

A common moral syllogism pertains to the violation of a rule. For example—

### Deflategate

A rule of the National Football League is that footballs in games must be inflated to a pressure between 12.5 and 13.5 pounds per square inch. Scofflaw, the quarterback of the Chauvinists, knowingly used a football that was inflated to less than 12.5 psi in a game, and thereby broke the rule.

#### QUASI SYLLOGISM

MAJOR PREMISE

A rule of the league stipulates that a football in a game must be inflated to a pressure between 12.5 and 13.5 psi, and no player may knowingly use a football that is over- or under-inflated.

MINOR PREMISE

Scofflaw knowingly used in a game a football that was inflated to less than 12.5 psi.

CONCLUSION

∴ Scofflaw violated the rule.

Again, this argument is expressed in normal speech and does not appear to be a valid syllogism, but the major premise can be reworded, with no change in meaning, so that the argument is a valid quasi syllogism.

### Exercise

8. Reword the major premise of the argument in *Deflategate* so that it is a valid quasi syllogism.

In many cases, an argument in the form of a quasi syllogism can also be expressed in the form of a hypothetical syllogism. Thus, the argument in *Deflategate* can also be expressed as a modus ponens—

#### MODUS PONENS

MAJOR PREMISE

IF $p$, THEN $q$.

If one knowingly uses a football that is inflated to less than 12.5 psi or more than 13.5 psi in a game, one violates the rule.

MINOR PREMISE

    *p.*

       Scofflaw knowingly used a football that was inflated to less than 12.5 psi.

CONCLUSION

    *q.*

       ∴ Scofflaw violated the rule.

## B. LEGAL SYLLOGISMS

A legal syllogism is much like a moral syllogism.[6] A **legal syllogism** argues that one has behaved lawfully or unlawfully. A legal syllogism may take the form of any valid syllogism. For example, consider—

### Willie Sutton's Case

The crime of theft is taking property that one does not own, with the intent of making it one's own, without the owner's consent. Suppose Willie Sutton robs a bank. Is he guilty of theft?

QUASI SYLLOGISM

MAJOR PREMISE

    Theft is taking property that one does not own, with the intent of making it one's own, without the owner's consent.

MINOR PREMISE

    Sutton took money that he did not own from a bank, with the intent of making the money his own, without the bank's consent.

CONCLUSION

    ∴ Sutton is guilty of theft.

This syllogism appears to commit the fallacy of undistributed middle, but, with no change in meaning, the major premise can be rewritten to make the syllogism valid.

---

6. One might plausibly believe that legal syllogisms are a subset of moral syllogisms.

## Exercise

9. Reword the major premise of the argument in *Willie Sutton's Case* so that it is a valid quasi syllogism.

The argument in *Willie Sutton's Case* can also be expressed as a modus ponens—

MODUS PONENS

MAJOR PREMISE

IF $p$, THEN $q$.

If one takes property that one does not own, with the intent of making it one's own, without the owner's consent, one is guilty of theft.

MINOR PREMISE

$p$.

Sutton took money that he did not own from a bank, with the intent of making the money his own, without the bank's consent.

CONCLUSION

$q$.

∴ Sutton is guilty of theft.

## Exercise

10. A rule of the fraternity ΔβT is that no member may serve an alcoholic beverage to a guest who is under the age of twenty-one. Senior serves beer to Freshone, who is nineteen. Express the argument that Senior has violated the fraternity's rule (a) as a valid quasi syllogism and (b) as a valid modus ponens.

## VI. The Value of Syllogisms

The value of analyzing arguments into syllogisms is that errors become obvious, especially when the argument is an enthymeme. Sometimes a logical error is revealed. For example, suppose your enemy says, "I'll get into medical school because I have straight A's, but you won't get in because you only got a B+ in Etruscan Archeology." The argument may seem forcible when it is expressed in ordinary English, but analysis reveals its error. It is an enthymeme, and so the first step is to supply the missing element. The missing element is the major premise. In a hypothetical syllogism, the major premise would be, "If you apply to medical school and have straight A's, you will get in." The second step is to fit the premises and conclusion into a syllogism—

MAJOR PREMISE

If you apply to medical school and have straight A's, you will get in.

MINOR PREMISE

You don't have straight A's.

CONCLUSION

You won't get into medical school.

This argument commits the fallacy of denying the antecedent. Having straight A's may be a sufficient cause of admission to medical school, but is not a necessary cause. Some applicants without straight A's are admitted.[7]

Other times, the logic of the argument is valid, but analysis reveals that a premise of the argument is false and so the argument unsound. For example, suppose someone says, "Nixon wasn't a crook; he didn't participate in the Watergate cover up." This argument being an enthymeme, the first step is to supply the missing element. The missing element is the major premise, "If Nixon didn't participate in the Watergate cover up, he wasn't a crook." The second step is to fit the premises and conclusion into a syllogism—

MAJOR PREMISE

If Nixon didn't participate in the Watergate cover up, he wasn't a crook.

---

7. The argument may also be expressed as a quasi syllogism—

MAJOR PREMISE

All applicants who are admitted to medical school have straight A's.

MINOR PREMISE

You don't have straight A's.

CONCLUSION

You won't get into medical school.

This syllogism is valid, but the major premise is false.

MINOR PREMISE

Nixon didn't participate in the cover up.

CONCLUSION

Nixon wasn't a crook.

This argument is a valid modus ponens. However, the major premise is doubtful (Nixon could have been a crook for other reasons), and the minor premise is false (he did participate in the cover up).[8]

- **An advocate must analyze as many arguments as possible, especially enthymemes, into syllogisms and evaluate them for validity and soundness.**

## VII. Review

### Exercises

Exercises 1–10 are in the text above.

11.

MAJOR PREMISE

A creature that is half man and half bull is a Minotaur.

---

8. The argument may also be expressed as a quasi syllogism—

MAJOR PREMISE

Anyone who didn't participate in the Watergate cover up wasn't a crook.

MINOR PREMISE

Nixon didn't participate in the cover up.

CONCLUSION

Nixon wasn't a crook.

This argument is a valid quasi syllogism, but the major premise is doubtful (one might be a crook for other reasons) and the minor premise is false (Nixon did participate in the cover up).

MINOR PREMISE

Minny is half man and half bull.

CONCLUSION

∴ Minny is a Minotaur.

This syllogism is—

    ☐ (a) valid and sound.
    ☐ (b) valid and unsound.
    ☐ (c) invalid because it commits the fallacy of the undistributed middle.
    ☐ (d) invalid because it commits the fallacy of illicit major.

12.

MAJOR PREMISE

If a vertebrate nourishes its young with milk, that vertebrate is a mammal.

MINOR PREMISE

Goats, which are vertebrates, do not nourish their kids with milk.

CONCLUSION

∴ Goats are not mammals.

    ☐ (a) valid and sound
    ☐ (b) valid and unsound.
    ☐ (c) invalid because it commits the fallacy of affirming the consequent.
    ☐ (d) invalid because it commits the fallacy of denying the antecedent.

13.

### The Sly Dancer

HE:    Will you come to the dance with me?

SHE:    I wouldn't go out with you if you were the last man on earth.

HE:    Great! I'm not the last man on earth, so I'll pick you up at 7:00

Express his argument as a hypothetical syllogism. Is it—

- ☐ (a) valid and sound.
- ☐ (b) valid and unsound.
- ☐ (c) invalid because it commits the fallacy of affirming the consequent.
- ☐ (d) invalid because it commits the fallacy of denying the antecedent.

14.

### The Tired Student

"You're tired. You've studied enough to pass the test."

Express this argument as a valid categorical syllogism. Is it—

- ☐ (a) sound.
- ☐ (b) unsound because the major premise is false.
- ☐ (c) unsound because the minor premise is false.

# § 5

# INDUCTION

## I. Inductive Generalizations

### A. THE NATURE OF INDUCTION

The etymology of the word "induction" and its cognates is—

IN = into
DECURE = to lead.

So "induction" means "to lead into a conclusion." Induction is reasoning that begins with one or more particulars and leads to a conclusion about one or more particulars.

The student is likely to be familiar with the type of induction that leads from particular observations to a generalization about those observations. This type of reasoning is called **inductive generalization**. It is commonly used in science. For example—

PARTICULAR OBSERVATIONS

The sun has risen in the east every day of which we know.

GENERALIZATION

The sun rises in the east.

An abstract representation of inductive generalization looks like this—

particulars 1, 2, 3 . . . → generalization

↑

inductive leap

The move from particulars to generalization is called "inductive leap" because it is a leap of faith. We can never be fully certain that the move is right.

## B. PROBABILITY OF CONCLUSIONS

Whereas deduction is analytic, induction is synthetic; that is, induction is synthesized by human beings. Its conclusion is not necessarily true. It leads only to a probable conclusion. In the case of inductive generalization, no matter how many instances of a phenomenon one may observe, it is always possible that one did not observe a previous instance that was different or that one's next observation will be different. The sun may not have risen in the east every day in the past (perhaps the earth in its early days did not rotate, or rotated in the opposite direction, and five billion years in the future the sun will probably not rise at all because it will have expanded to envelop the earth. Thus, it is not appropriate to say that an inductive argument is valid in the same sense that a deductive argument is valid. An inductive argument may be strong or weak; but however strong it is, it is not necessarily true.

To express the same idea in formal terms: the form of inductive reasoning may be correct and its premises may be true, yet its conclusion may be false.[1] For example:

The forecasts of the National Weather Service are usually correct.
The forecast for tomorrow is a 90 percent chance of rain.
It will rain tomorrow.

---

1. Contrast deduction, in which, if the form is correct and its premises are true, the conclusion must be true.

The premises may be true, but it might not rain tomorrow.

Nonetheless, inductive arguments can be convincing. In inductive generalization, the more particulars we observe, the greater our confidence in the generalization that we infer from them. The conclusion that the sun will rise in the east tomorrow is strong.

We use inductive generalization often in our daily lives without realizing that we are using it. For example, you take your seat in Rhetoric and cease talking by 10:00 because you have observed that Prof. Curmudgeon starts the class on time, rarely wastes a minute, and scowls at latecomers and chatterboxes. But who knows? He might change his ways tomorrow and tell a joke.

## C. ANALYSIS OF ARGUMENTS IN THE FORM OF INDUCTIVE GENERALIZATION

We can analyze an inductive generalization into the following elements:

- PARTICULAR(S): the events observed
- GENERALIZATION: what is true of the particulars
- INFERENCE: an additional particular that is true based on the generalization
- ARGUMENT: why the generalization and the inference are plausible

The argument is commonly omitted, but the generalization is much better supported when the argument is stated.

Hint: although this analysis presents an inductive argument as moving from particulars to generalization, it is often more useful to analyze an argument in the reverse of this order, that is, to identify the generalization and the inference first, then to search for the particulars, and finally to state the other elements of the argument.

## D. SOME ERRORS ASSOCIATED WITH INDUCTIVE GENERALIZATION

The following are common errors of inductive reasoning.[2] Such errors are not fallacies of logic, which are always mistakes. The following errors are

---

2. Such mistakes are often called "fallacies," but, in order to facilitate distinguishing mistakes of induction from mistakes of deduction, the term "errors" is used herein to refer to mistakes of induction and the term "fallacies" is reserved for a mistakes of deduction.

not always mistakes, but are more like risks of mistake. For example, "post hoc ergo propter hoc" refers to the mistake of assuming that $X$ caused $Y$ merely because $X$ occurred before $Y$. In many cases, $X$ and $Y$ are altogether unrelated. And yet (outside of the quantum world) every cause does precede its effect, and one would be considered mad if one argued that $X$ occurred after $Y$ but caused it. The following errors, therefore, are warnings of the need for careful thinking. An advocate should never commit such errors.

### 1. Hasty Generalization

A common error of induction is the **hasty generalization,** in which too few particular facts support the generalization. For example, suppose you get sick to your stomach after eating at Super Fast Foods. If you conclude that Super Fast Foods serves tainted food, you would be jumping to a hasty conclusion. Your upset stomach might have another cause. Naturally, if fifty persons sickened after eating at Super Fast Foods in one day, you would have better evidence that it served tainted food.

### 2. Unrepresentative Sample

Another common error of induction is an **unrepresentative sample**. A famous example occurred during the presidential campaign of 1936, in which Franklin Roosevelt, a Democrat, ran against "Alf" Landon, a Republican. Shortly before the election, the *Literary Digest* conducted a poll by mail of millions of Americans. Respondents favored Landon, and the magazine predicted that he would win; but he received less than 40 percent of the popular vote and carried only Maine and Vermont. How could a poll based on such a large sample have been so wrong? The problem was that telephone books were the primary source of addresses. In 1936 telephones were still a luxury, and only 11 million American households had them. The wealthy supported Landon, but the common folk elected Roosevelt.

### 3. Vivid Counterexample

You plan to purchase a new television set. Naturally, you want the best picture and sound; you also want high reliability and prompt but inexpensive repairs. You gather opinions from the internet, and you consult *Consumer Reports*. You settle on a model made by Sayonara that has prompted many positive testimonials, is highly rated by the experts, and has a good repair history. But before you make your purchase, you happen to be talking to your older sister, and you mention that you plan to buy a Sayonara. She tells you that her roommate bought one six months ago and has had nothing but trouble with it. The picture is blurry, and the sound is unclear. She complained to the retailer, which referred her to the manufacturer, which sent a technician who said nothing was wrong with the set. You decide to buy a Konichiwa instead.

You have succumbed to the error of the **vivid counterexample**. The one case of the experience of your sister's roommate should not overwhelm the conclusion you drew based on hundreds or thousands of cases. Even the best manufacturer occasionally produces a lemon. You should choose the product with the highest probability of satisfying your criteria.

### 4. Argument Ad Hominem

An **argument ad hominem** is an argument pertaining to a person, as distinguished from an argument pertaining to an issue. For example, suppose at a public meeting *A* argues in favor of a law against abortion on the ground that human life begins at conception. The next speaker, *B*, attempts to discredit *A* by pointing out that *A* herself has had an abortion. *B* is not criticizing the merits of *A*'s argument about when life begins, but is attacking *A* as a person. *A* might be an even worse person than *B* says. *A* might have formerly performed back alley abortions! Yet nothing about *A*'s character is relevant to the issue of when life begins.

Nonetheless, in some situations, arguments ad hominem are appropriate. For example, suppose the issue is the effects on human health of hydrofracking. *C*, a medical researcher at a university, asserts that he has studied the health data and concluded that hydrofracking has no significant effect on human health. It would be appropriate for *D* to point out that *C*'s research was funded by Dastardly Drilling, Inc., for one who takes money from an interested party might not be objective about the data. A political campaign is another situation in which an argument ad hominem is appropriate. It is impossible to foresee the multitude of problems that an elected official will confront; thus, a candidate cannot take a stand on every issue that will arise during one's term in office. For this reason, a candidate's character is important: character is an indication of how the candidate would behave in office, and arguments about a candidate's character, though ad hominem, are appropriate.

## 5. *Post Hoc Ergo Propter Hoc*

**Post hoc ergo propter hoc** translates from Latin as "after this, therefore because of this." As mentioned above, it refers to the error of believing that $X$ causes $Y$ merely because $X$ occurs before $Y$. For example, you take your car to Crook's Car Care for an oil change. As you are driving home, the car's muffler, which had not attracted your attention previously, begins to emit a loud noise. If you blame Crook's for the noise, you would commit the error of post hoc ergo propter hoc. All mechanical systems fail eventually, and your muffler could have been gradually failing for several weeks without your noticing it. That you noticed it immediately after entrusting your car to Crook's might be merely a coincidence.

And yet, cause does precede effect. It is possible that Crook's did damage your muffler. To establish causation in this instance, you need to identify the specific cause of the muffler's failure. If you inspect the muffler and find a substantial area of rust and thinning metal surrounding an irregular hole, you cannot say that Crook's caused the muffler to fail. If, instead, you find several smalls dent at the centers of which are holes in the shape of the tip of a flat-blade screwdriver, you have reason to suspect Crook's of villainy.

## 6. *Failure to Falsify Alternative Hypotheses*

A crucial step in inductive reasoning is to falsify alternative hypotheses that seem to explain the observations. For example, suppose a freshone on the fraternity circuit drinks bourbon and ginger ale and awakens the next morning with a hangover. The next night he drinks gin and ginger ale and awakens with a hangover. The third night he drinks vodka and ginger ale and awakens with a hangover. He concludes, "I've got to stop drinking ginger ale!"[3]

Our freshone's hypothesis does explain his observations; however, he has paid no heed to alternative explanations. He should have thought along the following lines. "Two hypotheses fit the data: the cause of my hangovers was ginger ale, or the cause was alcohol. I cannot infer from these data which factor was the true cause, so I need more data. Tonight I will drink only ginger ale, and tomorrow night I will drink only alcohol. Then I will know the cause."

---

3. We have borrowed this example from a lecture by Prof. Judith Grabiner.

### *Excerpt from the* Phaedo *by Plato*

In the *Metaphysics*, Aristotle credited Socrates with inventing induction. A fine example occurs in the following excerpt from the *Phaedo* by Plato. Socrates asserts that he does not fear death because he knows that his soul will be reincarnated, and then he convinces his interlocutors of the truth of reincarnation. His argument begins with a description of several particular instances of "generation" (or the changing of conditions, such as the generation of hot from cold or less from more). Based on these instances, he formulates a generalization, and then locates the death and rebirth of human souls within the generalization.

[A jury in Athens has condemned Socrates to death. Several of his friends visit him on the day he must drink the hemlock. The conversation focuses on what happens after death.]

I reckon, said Socrates, that no one who heard me now, not even if he were one of my old enemies, the comic poets,[4] could accuse me of idle talking about matters in which I have no concern:—If you please, then, we will proceed with the inquiry.

Suppose we consider the question whether the souls of men after death are or are not in the world below.[5] There comes into my mind an ancient doctrine which affirms that they go from hence into the other world, and returning hither, are born again from the dead. Now if it be true that the living come from the dead, then our souls must exist in the other world, for if not, how could they have been born again? And this would be conclusive, if there were any real evidence that the living are only born from the dead; but if this is not so, then other arguments will have to be adduced.

Very true, replied Cebes.

Then let us consider the whole question, not in relation to man only, but in relation to animals generally, and to plants, and to everything of which there is generation, and the proof will be easier. Are not all things which have opposites generated out of their opposites? I mean such things as good and evil, just and unjust—and there are innumerable other

---

4. Athenian poets wrote publicly performed plays that lampooned Socrates, for example, the "Clouds" by Aristophanes.

5. Greek mythology held that, after death, all properly buried souls, whether good or bad, went to Hades, the underworld.

opposites which are generated out of opposites. And I want to show that in all opposites there is of necessity a similar alternation; I mean to say, for example, that anything which becomes greater must become greater after being less.

True.

And that which becomes less must have been once greater and then have become less.

Yes.

And the weaker is generated from the stronger, and the swifter from the slower.

Very true.

And the worse is from the better, and the more just is from the more unjust.

Of course.

And is this true of all opposites? and are we convinced that all of them are generated out of opposites?

Yes.

And in this universal opposition of all things, are there not also two intermediate processes which are ever going on, from one to the other opposite, and back again; where there is a greater and a less there is also an intermediate process of increase and diminution, and that which grows is said to wax, and that which decays to wane?

Yes, he said.

And there are many other processes, such as division and composition, cooling and heating, which equally involve a passage into and out of one another. And this necessarily holds of all opposites, even though not always expressed in words—they are really generated out of one another, and there is a passing or process from one to the other of them?

Very true, he replied.

Well, and is there not an opposite of life, as sleep is the opposite of waking?

True, he said.

And what is it?

Death, he answered.

And these, if they are opposites, are generated the one from the other, and have there their two intermediate processes also?

Of course.

Now, said Socrates, I will analyze one of the two pairs of opposites which I have mentioned to you, and also its intermediate processes, and you shall analyze the other to me. One of them I term sleep, the other waking. The state of sleep is opposed to the state of waking, and out of sleeping waking is generated, and out of waking, sleeping; and the process of generation is in the one case falling asleep, and in the other waking up. Do you agree?

I entirely agree.

Then, suppose that you analyze life and death to me in the same manner. Is not death opposed to life?

Yes.

And they are generated one from the other?

Yes.

What is generated from the living?

The dead.

And what from the dead?

I can only say in answer—the living.

Then the living, whether things or persons, Cebes, are generated from the dead?

That is clear, he replied.

Then the inference is that our souls exist in the world below?

That is true.

And one of the two processes or generations is visible—for surely the act of dying is visible?

Surely, he said.

What then is to be the result? Shall we exclude the opposite process? And shall we suppose nature to walk on one leg only? Must we not rather assign to death some corresponding process of generation?

Certainly, he replied.

And what is that process?

Return to life.

And return to life, if there be such a thing, is the birth of the dead into the world of the living?

Quite true.

Then here is a new way by which we arrive at the conclusion that the living come from the dead, just as the dead come from the living; and this, if true, affords a most certain proof that the souls of the dead exist in some place out of which they come again.

Yes, Socrates, he said; the conclusion seems to flow necessarily out of our previous admissions.

And that these admissions were not unfair, Cebes, he said, may be shown, I think, as follows: If generation were in a straight line only, and there were no compensation or circle in nature, no turn or return of elements into their opposites, then you know that all things would at last have the same form and pass into the same state, and there would be no more generation of them.

What do you mean? he said.

A simple thing enough, which I will illustrate by the case of sleep, he replied. You know that if there were no alternation of sleeping and waking, the tale of the sleeping Endymion would in the end have no meaning, because all other things would be asleep, too, and he would not be distinguishable from the rest.[6] Or if there were composition only, and no division of substances, then the chaos of Anaxagoras would come again.[7] And in like manner, my dear Cebes, if all things which partook of life were to die, and after they were dead remained in the form of death, and did not come to life again, all would at last die, and nothing would be alive— what other result could there be? For if the living spring from any other things, and they too die, must not all things at last be swallowed up in death?

There is no escape, Socrates, said Cebes; and to me your argument seems to be absolutely true.

Yes, he said, Cebes, it is and must be so, in my opinion; and we have not been deluded in making these admissions; but I am confident that there truly is such a thing as living again, and that the living spring from the dead, and that the souls of the dead are in existence, and that the good souls have a better portion than the evil.

---

6. A reference to the myth in which the goddess of the Moon, Selene, so loved the beautiful youth Endymion that she asked Zeus to keep Endymion young forever. Zeus granted her wish by putting Endymion into an eternal sleep. The rest of the story, or one version of it, is that Selene visited Endymion every night and bore him fifty daughters, the Minea, each of whom became the goddess of one of the fifty months in the Olympic cycle.

7. A reference to the early Greek philosopher Anaxagoras (d. 428 BCE), who maintained that the universe was initially a formless mass of infinitesimally small particles. They combined (thus bringing order out of chaos) and now continually recombine (thus explaining change).

### Exercise

1. Analyze Socrates's argument into the elements of an inductive generalization. Is the argument convincing?

## II. Statistical Syllogisms

### A. THE NATURE OF A STATISTICAL SYLLOGISM

Another form of induction is the **statistical syllogism**. The major premise of a statistical syllogism is an inductive generalization, and the minor premise is a particular observation. For example, we stated an inductive generalization above:

PARTICULAR OBSERVATIONS

The sun has risen in the east every day of which we know.

GENERALIZATION

The sun rises in the east.

The generalization of this reasoning can become the major premise of a statistical syllogism—

MAJOR PREMISE

The sun rises in the east.

MINOR PREMISE

According to Bishop Ussher, the first day of the earth was October 23, 4004 BCE.

CONCLUSION

The sun rose in the east on October 23, 4004 BCE.

It is apparent from this example that a statistical syllogism resembles in some ways the quasi syllogism that is used in deduction. Here are further examples of each:

| QUASI SYLLOGISM | STATISTICAL SYLLOGISM |
|:---:|:---:|
| MAJOR PREMISE | MAJOR PREMISE |
| All cats have whiskers. | Most men can grow whiskers. |
| MINOR PREMISE | MINOR PREMISE |
| Jennyanydots is a cat. | Oliver is a man. |
| CONCLUSION | CONCLUSION |
| ∴ Jennyanydots has whiskers. | ∴ Oliver can grow whiskers. |

As these examples make apparent, the form of a statistical syllogism is the same as the form of a quasi syllogism: each is composed of three elements, namely, a major premise, a minor premise, and a conclusion. (Thus, a statistical syllogism, like deduction, proceeds from the general to the particular.) Also, the content of the minor premise of each of these syllogisms is similar: each minor premise is a statement of a particular fact.

Nonetheless, a statistical syllogism differs from a quasi syllogism in important ways. First, the contents of the major premises differ. The major premise of a statistical syllogism is a statement of *statistical probability*, whereas the major premise of a quasi syllogism is a statement of *universal truth*. "Most men can grow whiskers" is a statement of probability. "All cats have whiskers" purports to state a universal truth.[8]

Second, the contents of the conclusions differ. The conclusion of a statistical syllogism is a statement of *probable truth*, whereas the conclusion of a quasi syllogism is a statement of *necessary truth*. If all cats have whiskers and Jennyanydots is a cat, it is necessarily true that Jennyanydots has whiskers. But if most men can grow whiskers and Oliver is a man, it is only probably true that Oliver can grow whiskers.

This difference is obscured because the conclusion of a statistical syllogism is customarily stated as though it were a necessary truth; conforming to this custom, the conclusion of the example above says, "∴ Oliver can grow whiskers." Nonetheless, it would be better to state the conclusion of a statistical syllogism in probabilistic terms, in which case the conclusion

---

8. We write "purports to state" because the statement might be false. This possibility is irrelevant for present purposes because we are discussing the validity, that is, the formal characteristics, of a quasi syllogism. (If we were discussing the soundness of a quasi syllogism, the truth of the major premise would be important.)

of the example would be, " ∴ Oliver probably can grow whiskers." This suggestion is unlikely to change the custom, however, and the student will need to bear in mind that probability is implied in the conclusion of statistical syllogism.

At the cost of repetition, it bears emphasis that the conclusion of a statistical syllogism may be probably true, but cannot be necessarily true. A conclusion may not exceed its premises. The major premise of a statistical syllogism is a statement of probability; therefore, the conclusion of a statistical syllogism, which is based on the major premise, can only be a statement of probability. Thus, it can be true that most men can grow whiskers, but it remains possible that a given man, such as Oliver, is unable to grow whiskers. To say the same thing, a statistical syllogism cannot be valid; its truth does not flow from its form.

## B. THE FORCE OF A STATISTICAL SYLLOGISM

Although a statistical syllogism cannot be valid, it can be convincing. For example—

MAJOR PREMISE

Every judge who has served on the Supreme Court has been a lawyer.

MINOR PREMISE

The President has nominated Snoozalot to the Supreme Court.

CONCLUSION

∴ Snoozalot is a lawyer.

This example shows that the persuasive force of a statistical syllogism depends on the degree of probability of the major premise.[9] A major premise that is true of 98 percent of the class it describes has more force than a major premise that is true of 55 percent of the class. Compare the force of these examples:

---

9. Other factors also influence the persuasive force of a statistical syllogism. Again we admonish the student to take a course or read a book on critical thinking.

(1)

MAJOR PREMISE

Nearly every freshone in Walden College has a high school degree.

MINOR PREMISE

BD is a freshone in Walden College.

CONCLUSION

∴ BD has a high school degree.

(2)

MAJOR PREMISE

The majority of freshone males in Walden College want to rush a fraternity.

MINOR PREMISE

Zonker is a freshone male in Walden College.

CONCLUSION

∴ Zonker wants to rush a fraternity.

## C. STATISTICAL SYLLOGISMS IN ORDINARY SPEECH

We mentioned above that inductive generalization is used often in daily life and that a statistical syllogism applies an inductive generalization to a particular case. It follows that we should be able to examine inductive arguments as stated in ordinary speech and analyze many of them into statistical syllogisms. For example—

You take your seat in Rhetoric and cease talking by 10:00 because you have observed that Prof. Curmudgeon starts the class on time, rarely wastes a minute, and scowls at latecomers and chatterboxes.

becomes—

MAJOR PREMISE

> So far this semester, Prof. Curmudgeon has started the class on time, rarely wasted a minute (problems with technology aside), and scowled at latecomers and chatterboxes.

MINOR PREMISE

> Prof. Curmudgeon's next class will start at 10:00.

CONCLUSION

> Prof. Curmudgeon will behave as he has behaved in the past, and a student is well advised to be seated quietly by 10:00.

The value of expressing an inductive generalization as a statistical syllogism is that the premises become apparent, the force of the argument can be judged, and one can adjust one's beliefs and behavior accordingly. If Prof. Curmudgeon's average of starting on time is forty-three of forty-five classes per term, the student may devote more effort to being punctual and quiet than if the professor's average is twenty-five of forty-five.

## III. Practical Syllogisms

Most of us are familiar with a third type of induction, which Aristotle called a **practical syllogism**. It is a syllogism in which the conclusion is an act rather than a proposition. In *De Anima* he wrote, "The [major] premise or judgment is universal and the [minor premise] deals with the particular (for the first tells us that such and such a kind of man should do such and such a kind of act, and the second, that this is an act of the kind meant and I am a person of the type indicated)." He provides illustrations in other works—

> I need a covering.
> A cloak is a covering.
> I need a cloak

* * *

I ought to make what I need.
I need a cloak.
I ought to make a cloak.

\*\*\*

Everything sweet should be tasted.
This thing is sweet.
[I should taste it.]

One use of practical syllogisms is particularly important to lawyers: *a practical syllogism is the frame of every argument based on precedent.*

Like cases should be decided alike.
*Right v. Wrong* is like *Now v. Then.*
∴ *Right v. Wrong* should be decided as *Now v. Then* was decided.

## IV. Review

### Questions

Question 1 is in the text above.

2. The following conversation is drawn from an example devised by Prof. Edward Corbett.

α:  O'Malley is probably Catholic.
β:  Why do you say that?
α:  He is Irish and was born in southern Ireland.
β:  So what?
α:  Most such people are Catholic.

3. Express this conversation as a statistical syllogism.

Beatrix is driving to campus after summer vacation. Her friend, Barbara, is sitting next to her. Bea's smart phone beeps. A glance at the screen informs her that she has just received a message from her best friend, Betty.

"Just got a message from Bob," it says. "He's breaking up with me. ☹"

Bea commences to type a reply. Barb says, "You shouldn't do that. You could get a ticket."

"No, I won't," says Bea. "I saw a study that found that the cops cite only about 1 percent of people who text while driving."

Bea makes an argument. It is composed of a statistical syllogism in which one of the premises is an inductive generalization. (a) State the inductive generalization. (b) Analyze Bea's statistical syllogism into the elements of a statistical syllogism.

## V. References

Aristotle, *De Anima* 434a15–20, reproduced in Alexander Broadie, "The Practical Syllogism," 29 *Analysis* 26 at 26, Oct. 1968.

Aristotle, *De Motu Animalium* 701a28–33, in Broadie.

Aristotle, *Metaphysics* 1078b25–30 (W. D. Ross, trans.).

Aristotle, *Nicomachean Ethics* 1147a25–30.

Plato, *Phaedo* (Benjamin Jowett, trans.), http://www.gutenberg.org/files/1658/1658-h/1658-h.htm.

# § 6

# ARGUMENTS IN GENERAL

The purpose of this section is to introduce the student to reasoned arguments in general. The discussion applies to reasoned arguments in any field. Sections 7–12 discuss specific types of arguments.

## I. Definition of an Argument

An argument can be a dispute, a disagreement, a quarrel. For example, "My parents got into an argument over last month's credit card bill." This definition emphasizes the emotional aspect of an argument, and in this sense the word has a negative connotation. Such an argument is not a good thing.

An **argument** can also be—

reasons given as proof; a series of statements leading to the resolution of an issue.

The latter definition emphasizes the rational aspect of an argument, and in this sense the word has a positive connotation. This sort of argument is a good thing, and many disciplines besides law, such as the physical sciences, history, and philosophy, use the word in this way. For instance, "Galileo clashed with the Church over his argument in favor of heliocentrism." Although lawyers get into plenty of arguments in the former sense, the law uses "argument" in the latter sense.

## II. Elements of an Argument

Having read § 1 ISSUES, the student is already familiar with three of the elements of a reasoned argument:

- ISSUE
  A point of disagreement between the parties. An issue is expressed as a question.

- FACTS
  The events that generated the dispute between the parties.

- RESOLUTION
  The answer to the question in the issue.

The remaining element, which usually falls between the facts and the resolution, is—

- REASONING
  The rationale a party offers to convince the tribunal how to resolve the dispute.[1]

Here follow some examples of arguments taken from daily life.

ISSUE

Should I carry my umbrella today?

FACTS

The weather forecast indicates a 70 percent chance of rain.

---

1. The word "argument" may be used to refer to the four elements in the text taken together, or to the reasoning alone. The rationale may include deductive or inductive arguments.

I dislike getting wet in the rain.

My umbrella is not heavy and fits easily into my backpack.

REASONING

It is no trouble to carry my umbrella, and the risk of getting wet is not trivial for me.

RESOLUTION

I should carry my umbrella today.

\* \* \*

ISSUE

Is one morally free to discriminate on the basis of where another's ancestors lived?

FACTS

America is a land of immigrants and their descendants.

REASONING

All humans are created equal.

RESOLUTION

Discrimination on the basis of national origin is unjustified.

## Should Use of Marijuana Be Legal?

### YES

ISSUE

Should the law against use of marijuana be repealed?

FACTS

Marijuana is no more harmful than alcohol.

Violence associated with the illegal importation of marijuana causes the deaths of thousands of persons every year in Latin America and hundreds in the United States.

Drug cartels dominate and all but supplant legitimate governments in many areas of Latin America.

Taxes on the sale of legal marijuana would add significant revenue to state budgets.

Laws in the United States against use of drugs, including marijuana, are enforced more aggressively against people of color.

The law against marijuana is widely ignored.

REASONING

The cost of the law against marijuana is high: thousands of people die violently every year because of the drug trade; governments in Latin America are weakened; the law is enforced discriminatorily in the United States; the war on drugs is expensive; potential tax revenue is lost; and the law is widely disobeyed. The benefit of repealing the law against marijuana would be great: deaths from the illegal drug trade would diminish; the cost of the war on drugs would be saved; marijuana could be taxed, thereby raising revenue for the government; and citizens would no longer have to break the law in order to enjoy a harmless pleasure.

RESOLUTION

The law against use of marijuana should be repealed.

## NO

FACTS

Marijuana typically has numerous bad short-term effects, including—

impairment of short-term memory
impairment of concentration
impairment of attention
impairment of physical coordination
impairment of balance
increased heart rate
dry mouth
increased appetite.

Marijuana can also have numerous bad long-term effects, including—

damage to the corpus callosum of the brain
psychological addiction
gateway to physically addictive drugs
paranoia
persistent anxiety

impaired learning skills
impairment of long-term memory
personality changes
apathy
loss of motivation
slowed reaction time
decreased physical coordination
permanent drop in IQ.

REASONING

On the one hand, marijuana is far more harmful to individuals than its advocates admit. The nation as a whole is also harmed. In an era when America must compete with the whole world, we cannot afford the diminished productivity that results from the apathy, mental diseases, and diminished IQ that marijuana causes, not to mention the harm resulting from even more dangerous drugs to which marijuana is the gateway. On the other hand, the benefits of marijuana are more imaginary than real. Legalizing marijuana would not improve the politics or economies of Latin American nations because the cartels would continue to traffic in other drugs like cocaine. If we want to help Latin America, we should eliminate the demand for marijuana and thereby substantially diminish the demand for even worse drugs. Although it is true that a tax on marijuana would raise some money for the government, so would a tax on blood diamonds or ivory.

RESOLUTION

The law against use of marijuana should not be repealed.

The resolution of one argument may be a part of another argument. For example, suppose the resolution of the issue "Should the law against marijuana be repealed?" is yes. This resolution can become an element of an argument on another issue.

## Katzenjammer for Congress

ISSUE

For whom should you vote in the election?

FACTS

Katzenjammer supports repeal of the law against use of marijuana.

REASONING

The law against use of marijuana should be repealed, and Katzen-jammer will work to repeal it.

RESOLUTION

You should vote for Katzenjammer.

The resolution of an argument is often stated, not at the end, but at the beginning of the argument—

Studies of identical twins can yield important medical information. Identical twins share all the same genes. If we find that, when one identical twin develops a certain disease, the other identical twin is more likely to develop the same disease than is a random member of the population of the same age, sex, and socioeconomic class, then we have evidence that the disease is genetic. Conversely, if we find that, when one identical twin develops a certain disease, the other identical twin is no more likely to develop the same disease than is a random member of the population of the same age, sex, and socioeconomic class, then we have evidence that the disease is not genetic.

In fact, a resolution may be stated anywhere in an argument—before the facts and argument, after them, before *and* after them (which is often the best practice), and even in the middle of them.

## III. Recognizing Arguments

Arguments influence our beliefs and our actions. Therefore, the student must learn to recognize an argument in order to be able to evaluate it. Sometimes an advocate gives a clear signal that an argument is coming—

I contend that . . .
It is my position that . . .

Individual words can also signal an argument—

> therefore
> consequently
> hence
> thus
> and so
> because
> since
> for
> reason.

Words or phrases such as the foregoing do not always signal an argument, however, because a word may have other meanings—

> I haven't been home since Christmas.
> My reason for running fifty miles last week was to get ready for the marathon.

Sometimes an advocate states an argument without signaling it. In this case, the student should ask oneself—

- **What point is the advocate trying to make?**
- **What does the advocate want me to believe or do?**
- **What evidence does the advocate provide?**

## IV. Incomplete Arguments

Often an advocate omits (or implies) a premise that is logically necessary for a complete argument (as in an enthymeme). Sometimes the reason for the omission is legitimate. The premise may seem so obvious that the advocate thinks that it need not be stated, or that one's audience would feel patronized if the premise were stated. Indeed, the premise may be so obvious, so completely taken for granted, that the advocate is unaware that it is part of the argument. Other times, the reason for the omission is illegitimate. An advocate may prefer that the audience not reflect seriously on a premise. Whatever the reason for the omission, the student should be alert for it and reconstruct the argument so that the omitted premise is explicit. Otherwise, the student will be unable to evaluate the argument.

## V. Issues, Arguments, and Rhetoric

Whenever one encounters an argument, one should always ask oneself two questions:

- **What issue does this argument address?**
- **Is the issue that the argument addresses the same issue that is under consideration?**

The answer to the second question may well be no: the argument might not address the issue under consideration. A subtle technique of rhetoric is to present a convincing argument that seems to address the issue at hand, but in fact addresses another issue, in the hope of swaying the unwary. For example, consider this argument, which appeared on bumper stickers shortly before a referendum on whether to approve a school budget:

If you think education is expensive, think of the cost of ignorance.

The idea was that the cost of ignorance can be enormous; what we do not know truly can hurt us. Should the voters have been persuaded by this argument to approve the budget? Not if they asked themselves the right questions! They should have asked—

*What issue does this argument address?*

> The argument addressed the issue, should we have public education? On that issue, the cost of ignorance was certainly relevant.

*Is the issue that the argument addresses the same issue that is under consideration?*

> The community had long since decided to maintain public education, and so this issue was not the one under consideration. Instead, the issue before the voters was, should we spend $x on education? Opponents of the budget argued that $x–y was the appropriate level of spending. In economic terms, the issue was, would the benefit of spending $y exceed the cost? The answer might have been one thing if $y was to be spent on a new science laboratory and another thing if $y was to be spent on additional salary for the football coach. In either case, the issue was clearly not whether to have

public education and, therefore, the bumper sticker was a piece of misleading rhetoric.

This section has introduced the student to arguments in general. The following section classifies arguments by the function they perform.

## VI. Review

### Questions

More than one answer to the following questions may be correct.

1. In law, an argument is—
   - ☐ (a) a disagreement between the parties.
   - ☐ (b) a reason to resolve an issue in a particular way.
   - ☐ (c) statements that lead from a premise to a conclusion.
   - ☐ (d) the step between an issue and its resolution.

2. The elements of a legal argument include—
   - ☐ (a) the issue.
   - ☐ (b) the premises.
   - ☐ (c) the resolution.
   - ☐ (d) the facts.
   - ☐ (e) the fist fight.

3. Words that signal an argument include—
   - ☐ (a) "therefore."
   - ☐ (b) "Get a load o' this!"
   - ☐ (c) "because."
   - ☐ (d) "a reason."

# § 7

# ARGUMENTS CLASSIFIED BY FUNCTION

The preceding section pertained to all arguments. This and succeeding sections pertain to legal arguments.

An advocate should understand the functions that arguments perform and the bases on which arguments rest. The advocate who has this understanding will present better arguments, and will detect errors in the arguments of one's adversaries, better than the advocate who lacks it. This section discusses the functions of arguments. Sections 8–12 discuss the bases of arguments.

Issues can arise as a tribunal performs each of the four functions of resolving a dispute, and parties present arguments on those issues. Thus arguments, like issues, can be classified by their function.

## I. Arguments as to the Issue in a Case

If the parties disagree over the issue in a case, they will present arguments, each party trying to persuade the tribunal to frame the issue as the party

desires. Such arguments may be called **arguments as to the issue in a case.**
For example—

### Clinics v. Hospitals

A new statute requires abortion clinics to meet the same standards as hospitals. The statute is challenged as unconstitutional. One party argues: Few abortion clinics in this state can meet these standards. As a result, the statute will force most clinics to close, making it very difficult for most women to obtain a safe abortion. Therefore, the issue in this case is, does the statute infringe on a woman's constitutional right to have an abortion?

The other party argues: Many things can go wrong during an abortion. A woman's health, indeed, her life may depend on having procedures performed in a facility that can handle any unfortunate complications that may occur. Therefore, the issue in this case is, may a state protect a woman's health by requiring that medical procedures be performed in facilities that are equipped to deal with possible complications?

## II. Arguments as to the Facts

**Arguments as to the facts** address the question, what happened between the parties?

*Issue:*      Did X do the deed?
*W says:*    "I know you did it because I saw you do it."
*X says:*    "Five witnesses have testified that I was in Pango Pango that day."

* * *

*Issue:*      Did H tell W that he was going to buy a boat?
*W says:*    "You didn't tell me you were going to do that. You never tell me anything."
*H says:*    "I know I have neglected to tell you things in the past. I regret that, and this time I was very careful to tell you everything. I remember the baby was crying. You were probably distracted and not paying attention to me."

Once the facts are found, they will play a role in the tribunal's other functions. Nonetheless, arguments as to the facts pertain only to the function of finding the facts.

## III. Arguments as to the Law

Identifying the authority that governs a case requires two steps. The first step is to choose which law governs the case.[1] The second step is to interpret the governing law. Parties can disagree at each of these steps and, when they do, they present **arguments as to the law**. Here are examples of arguments on the first step.

### A. Arguments as to Which Authority Governs the Case

#### *Here v. There*

On the surface, both regulations 123 and 789 seem to apply to the case at bar. The evidence shows that if this tribunal applies regulation 789, birds will no longer sing, and husbands and wives will fight endlessly. But if this tribunal applies regulation 123 to the case, children will go to bed on time without protest and peace will come to the Middle East. Accordingly, this tribunal should apply regulation 123 to the case at bar.

#### *Round v. About*

The defendant argues that regulation 789 should be applied to the case at bar. The argument is mistaken. The facts of *Here v. There*, 123 Conf. 456 (1987), are analogous to the facts of the case at bar, and in *Here v. There* the Supreme Court applied regulation 123. Therefore, this court must also apply regulation 123.

### B. Arguments as to How to Interpret the Governing Authority

The second step is to interpret the governing law. Laws commonly require interpretation or "construction" (from the verb "construe"), and various constructions of a text or a precedent are often plausible. Here are two examples of arguments as to how a law should be interpreted.

---

1. If a case is not governed by any existing law, the parties will present arguments as to the law which the tribunal should create to govern the case.

### Scarpia v. Sky

Ordinance 1 of Tiny Town states, "Any dog in Tiny Town must have a license." Δ lived in the Village of Small Potatoes, which is near Tiny Town. His dog, Sky, was licensed only in Small Potatoes. He brought Sky to play in a park in Tiny Town. The town dog catcher, Scarpia, cited Sky for violating Ordinance 1. In court, Δ, speaking for Sky, argued that the ordinance means that a dog in the town must have a license, but not necessarily a license issued by Tiny Town. Scarpia argued that the ordinance means that any dog in the town must have a license issued by the town. The issue of law was, which interpretation of the ordinance is correct? Judge Janus resolved the issue:

> The discussion in the town council before it enacted the license law shows that the law was intended to apply to dogs whose owners reside in the town, not to require visitors from Small Potatoes or elsewhere to obtain a license here. Councilman *A* feared that, if the ordinance were passed, visitors with dogs would not come to the town; businesses would lose customers, and sales tax revenue would decline. Councilwoman *B*, the sponsor of the ordinance, replied that *A*'s fears were ungrounded because the law would not apply to visitors provided their dogs were licensed where they lived. We conclude, therefore, that a dog may visit Tiny Town if it is licensed in its hometown.

### Puss v. Boots

Ordinance 2 of Tiny Town states, "Any cat in Tiny Town must have a license." C, a resident of Big City, visited Tiny Town with a cat, Puss, which was licensed only in Big City. Boots, the town catcher of cats, cited Puss for violating Ordinance 2. In court Puss, speaking for herself, argued that she was not required to have a license from Tiny Town. She relied on *Dog Catcher v. Sky* and argued that the texts of the dog and cat license ordinances are the same, mutatis mutandis, and therefore so are their meanings. Judge Grizabella, relying on her memory of *Dog Catcher v. Sky*, ruled that a cat may grace Tiny Town with its presence if it is licensed in its hometown.

## IV. Arguments Applying Law to Fact

Once a law is chosen and interpreted, the fourth function which a tribunal must perform is to determine what the law required the parties to do, or, as lawyers would say, to apply the law to the facts so as to reach the holding of the case. To say the same thing, application of law to fact is determining the legal consequences of the facts of a case. All of us are familiar with application of law to fact because we all apply rules and precedents to specific cases in our daily lives. For example, suppose Mother's rule is, no snacks before dinner. Dinner is usually served at 6:00 p.m. It is now 5:30, you are hungry, and the cookie jar is on the kitchen counter. You apply Mother's rule to the facts and walk out of the kitchen. Or you break the rule, stuff yourself with cookies, get caught, and Mother denies you dessert.

Here is a legal example of application of law to fact—

### *Don Juan in Hell*

Juan is accused of bigamy because Winifred and Winona claim to be married to him. In order to decide the case, Judge Devorah must apply law to fact four times. (1) Did Juan marry Winifred? The evidence shows that Juan and Winifred secured a marriage license and took vows before a justice of the peace. Judge Devorah applies the law of marriage formation to these facts and concludes that Juan married Winifred. (2) Ditto for Winona. (3) Juan defends himself on the ground that he divorced Winifred before he married Winona. Judge Devorah must apply the law regarding the termination of a marriage to Juan and Winifred. The evidence shows that Juan obtained a divorce decree online from Yoknapatawpha County, where neither Juan nor Winifred had ever set foot, for a fee of fifty dollars. Judge Devorah applies the law of divorce to this decree and holds it to be invalid. (4) Now the judge applies the law of bigamy to Juan, finds he is married to two women at the same time, and sentences him to live with both of them for the rest of his natural life.

This section has discussed classification of arguments by function or purpose. Arguments are also classified by basis, namely, legal doctrine and public policy. Policy arguments are discussed in § 9, and doctrinal documents in §§ 10, 11, and 12.

# V. Review

### *Jefferson Standard Broadcasting Company*

The heart of the Labor Act is section 7. The central idea of section 7 is to give workers the legal right to negotiate with their employer as a group instead of as individuals. Congress created this right because individuals have little bargaining power when they deal with employers, particularly large corporations. The result of this lack of power is that workers can be forced to accept low wages and poor working conditions. But if workers can band together and, as a group—usually, through a union—negotiate with their employer, they have a better chance to achieve a living wage and decent working conditions.

To reach these goals, section 7 guarantees employees the right to engage in **concerted activity**, which means the right to act together to improve their working lives.[2] The right to concerted activity includes the rights to assist and to join labor unions. Employers are forbidden to interfere with these activities. For example, it would be an unfair labor practice for an employer to fire a worker for talking to a union representative.[3]

The Labor Board has often heard cases that turned on whether the workers were engaged in concerted activity. For example, in *Washington Aluminum* the workers in a plant were not represented by a union. The furnace failed on an unusually cold day, and the workers walked out: whereupon the employer discharged them. The walkout was concerted activity, and the discharges were illegal, because the walkout was two or more workers reacting together to their conditions of employment. Now suppose a union supports the Pro Choice Fund. When the workers learn that

---

2. Usage of the word "concerted" has changed in recent years. Today its primary meaning is something focused and strong, as in, "Jennifer made a concerted effort to be on time for her 8:00 a.m. class." By contrast, when the Labor Act was passed, the word meant acting together, deriving from its root, "concert," as in, "The seniors on the team made a concerted effort to improve the play of the freshones." Thus, "concerted activity" in the Labor Act refers to action by two or more persons.

3. Congress recognized that some workers prefer not to engage in concerted activity. Accordingly, § 7 also guarantees employees the right to refrain from assisting and joining unions. Unions and employers are forbidden to interfere with this right as well. For example, it would be an unfair labor practice for a union to threaten to retaliate against a worker who refused to support the union in a representation election.

the employer plans to donate money to the Pro Life Fund, the union goes on strike. The strike would not be concerted activity, and the employer would be free to discharge the workers, because the issue is not the workers' conditions of employment.

Other cases involving the scope of concerted activity are not so clear. In *Jefferson Standard Broadcasting Company*, a television station in Charlotte, North Carolina and a union of the station's technicians reached an impasse in collective bargaining over the union's request for a grievance arbitration clause.[4] The union then picketed the station and distributed a handbill to passersby. The handbill accused the station of treating Charlotte like a second-class city because the station broadcast old films and programs instead of live programs such as local sporting and cultural events. The station discharged the workers who distributed the handbill, and the union accused the station of interfering with concerted activity.

The Board rule against the workers. It recognized that not all joint action by workers in regard to their working conditions is concerted activity. Suppose, for example, several workers become dissatisfied with how their supervisor is enforcing certain work rules and, to motivate him to change his ways, they beat him up in the parking lot. The employer discharges the assailants. Their action might seem to fall within the scope of concerted activity because several of them acted together regarding the conditions of their employment. Nonetheless, Congress certainly did not intend the Labor Act to protect unlawful behavior.

Regarding the handbill in *Jefferson Standard*, the Board conceded that the facts in it were true and its purpose (to extract concessions from the station) was lawful. But in order to be protected by the Labor Act, the workers must be engaged in concerted activity. The handbill urged the public to boycott the station because of its shoddy programming, not because of its labor policies. Thus, the handbill was disloyal and indefensible. By attacking the employer's product, the handbill was tantamount to physical sabotage.

One member of the Board dissented. He maintained that concerted activity is protected as long as its means and ends are legal. Congress,

---

4. "Impasse" means that the parties have not reached an agreement, and further negotiations would be futile. Impasses can be broken, however.

he asserted, did not intend to vest the Board with discretion to determine whether joint action by workers pertaining to the conditions of their employment is defensible or loyal. The means of the handbill were legal: it was a traditional form of labor protest, and it contained only truthful statements. The end of the handbill was also legal: it was intended to put pressure on the employer to agree to an arbitration procedure. Accordingly, the dissent concluded, the handbill was concerted activity, and the employer illegally discharged the workers.[5]

## Question

State the issue in the case and the level of abstraction of the issue. Then classify the issue, and the arguments that pertain to the issue, by their function.

## VI. References

*Jefferson Standard Broadcasting Company,* 94 NLRB 1507 (1951).
*National Labor Relations Board v. Local Union No. 1229 (Jefferson Standard),* 346 U.S. 464 (1953).
*Washington Aluminum v. National Labor Relations Board,* 370 U.S. 9 (1962).

---

5. The Supreme Court affirmed the Board's decision, albeit with a somewhat different rationale.

# ARGUMENTS BASED ON EVIDENCE

Section 7 classified arguments according to the function they perform. This section and §§ 9 and 10 classify arguments according to the basis on which they rest or, to say the same thing, according to the source from which they are drawn. This brief section pertains to arguments based on evidence.

## I. Varieties of Evidence

**Evidence** comes in four varieties—

> *testimony*
> *documents*
> *facts in a precedent*
> *judicial notice (i.e., indisputable knowledge)*

**Testimony** is an oral statement, under oath, from a witness with personal knowledge of the facts, or from an expert.

I observed the accused running from the crime scene with a gun in his hand.

As an optometrist, I know that a person with 20/200 vision who is not wearing his glasses could not recognize a human face at a distance of 50 yards.

**Documents** include (but are by no means limited to) contracts, wills, and business records.

On page 7, lines 3 to 9, the contract between the parties provides . . .

The ledger of the firm shows that it received a payment of 75,000 dollars to plaintiff's account on March 31.

**A fact found in a precedent** is sometimes adopted in a subsequent case. Commonly, such facts operate at a high level of abstraction and pertain to many persons or events.

As the Supreme Court found in *United Steelworkers of America v. Warrior & Gulf,* "arbitration is the substitute for industrial strife." This fact is important in the case at bar because . . .

Some facts are so indisputable that a tribunal may find them itself without evidence from the parties. Lawyers call this taking **judicial notice** of a fact.

The sun rose in Ithaca, New York, on December 8, 2013 at 7:23 a.m.

The Declaration of Independence of the United States of America was signed on August 2, 1776.

## II. Uses of Evidence

Evidence proves facts. Thus, **arguments pertaining to evidence** help the tribunal to find the facts.

Witnesses *A* testifies that the plaintiff habitually referred to her supervisor as "that scum bag," "that low life," or "that s.o.b." This testimony supports the employer's claim that he fired the plaintiff because of her insubordination, not because of her age.

# § 9

# POLICY ARGUMENTS

Policy arguments are based on social welfare and the public good. A policy argument is a consequential argument. It is forward looking. It asserts that the consequences of the tribunal's decision will be good if our side wins or bad if the other side wins. Policy arguments are grounded on legislative facts and are used to influence courts, legislatures, and administrative agencies.

> It is necessary to secure our borders. Otherwise, we will be overrun by illegal immigrants, who commit crimes and take away jobs from citizens.
>
> America was built by the energy and ambition of immigrants. The crime rate of undocumented immigrants is lower than the overall crime rate, and they take jobs that citizens are unwilling to perform.

Public policy may be found in a specific source, such as a constitution or a statute, or in a general source, such as notions of public welfare.

Public policy is neither clear nor bounded, and the same is true of policy arguments.

## I. The Nature of Policy Arguments

A policy argument contains at least one normative claim. The normative claim is often implicit, but unstated.

### A. Normative Claims

#### 1. *Values*

A **normative claim** is an assertion of value; it is about what is good and bad. A normative claim usually contains a word like "should," "ought," "right," "wrong," "good," "value," or "purpose."

Not every sentence containing words like "should" or "good" is a normative claim, however. The following sentences are not normative claims.

> At this time of the year, the high temperature should be about 65 degrees.
> Tom is a good deal taller than Jerry.

Also, a normative claim is a *reason* for action; accordingly, the *action* for which an advocate calls is not a normative claim, though "should" is often used in such a sentence. For example—

> The Board should find that the union committed an unfair labor practice and order the union to cease and desist from picketing the employer's premises.

is an exhortation to action, not a normative claim.

Explicit disagreements about what is valuable are uncommon in cases and briefs (although such disagreements are becoming more common). Reasons for this (apparent) agreement on values may include—

   (1)  Most persons in our society share many values. For example, we generally agree that an employer should not exploit or oppress a worker (though we might disagree on what constitutes exploitation and oppression).

(2) One who genuinely disagrees with a widely held value is often reluctant to publicize the disagreement. For example, employers who operate sweatshops (paying less than the minimum wage and demanding long hours, sometimes in dangerous working conditions) admit their belief, when they speak candidly, that the workers who take such jobs are not fully human. These employers believe of the workers that "they don't feel things the way we do," "they don't deserve any better," "they're not forced to take these jobs," and "they are better off than they used to be." Knowing, however, that such values are unpopular or against public policy, sweat-shop employers rarely express their values publicly; confessing to such values in an argument might scuttle a case that otherwise could be won.

(3) Statutes reflect values, and a tribunal is obliged to render decisions that further those values. Therefore, expressing a value that is inconsistent with a statute would provide a reason to ignore any argument based on that value. For example, many employers believe that unions are not legitimate institutions. The Labor Act, however, incorporates the opposite value. An employer would encounter little success by arguing for a given result explicitly on the ground that it would weaken unions.

(4) We lack a way to settle disagreements about values. A theocracy does not have this problem; sacred texts or prophets reveal the divine will. Nor does a society—typically small, homogenous, and old—in which a single system of values prevails. If we were all utilitarians (or deontologists or egoists) we would know how to resolve disputes about values. But in a large, heterogeneous, and dynamic society like modern America, conflicts of values are not easily resolved. An environmentalist asserts that old growth forests deserve protection; a logger claims that people need jobs and houses. Who is right? Congress may decide conflicts of values, but, in the absence of a statute, courts and administrative tribunals historically prefer not to.[1]

---

1. In recent years, courts and administrative agencies may have decided proportionally more cases involving conflicts of values than in the past.

## 2. Varieties of Arguments about Values

Although one party rarely denies the values in the other party's normative claims, parties commonly advance competing values and argue that one is more important than the other, at least in the context of the case at bar. Consider the safety of automobiles. Advocates of requiring safer cars assert that life and protection from injury are important, and argue that the government should require safer cars in order to protect people. Critics assert that freedom and efficiency are important, and argue that consumers who are satisfied with today's cars should not be forced to pay for heightened safety, and that consumers who want safer cars will pay for them. Thus, the debate is over which values are more important.

When parties disagree about competing values in a case, the arguments come in two varieties. One variety is **the lesser of evils**: what the other side fears may be bad; but if it gets its way, something even worse will also happen. For example, consider the issue of gun control. Liberals argue:

> Gun control will limit the right to bear arms, but what is the value of the Second Amendment to a dead man or his family?

Translation: gun control is the lesser evil; slaughter of Americans is the greater evil. Conservatives reply:

> Guns don't kill people; people kill people. Until we amend the Constitution, we must honor it.

Translation: loss of life is the lesser evil; disregard of Constitutional rights is the greater evil.

The other variety of argument when parties disagree about legitimate values is **the greater of goods**: what the other side wants may be good, but what we want is even better. Consider, for example, the issue of whether to raise or lower taxes. Fiscal conservatives argue:

> We must raise taxes in order to pay down the national debt and insure the solvency of Social Security and Medicare.

Translation: reducing taxes is good, but paying down the national debt and insuring the solvency of Social Security are a greater good. Neoliberals reply:

> We must cut taxes because Americans know how to spend their money better than the government does.

Translation: some government spending may be good, but cutting taxes so Americans can decide how to spend their money is better.

When the parties agree about values in a case (or even if they disagree), they typically argue about the best means to promote those values. Suppose the parties agree that the value of individual liberty is at stake in the case at bar. A party might argue:

> The result I advocate will effectively and efficiently promote liberty because . . . whereas the result advocated by my adversary will undermine liberty and increase costs because . . .

Reading briefs and cases, one finds arguments that one value outweighs another or that one policy serves a value whereas another policy undermines the value. But one does not find a formula for deciding which competing value is more important or which policy will promote a value more effectively.

### 3. Sources of Values

How does a tribunal know that a public policy exists, or that a given rule will promote or undermine a policy? In some cases, a policy can be drawn from a strong source, such as the federal constitution, a state constitution, a statute, or a precedent. In other cases, evidence, especially from experts, might seem appropriate, but such evidence is uncommon. Instead, a tribunal often relies on its intuition and takes judicial notice (after some coaching from a party) that a policy exists or that a rule will serve or disserve a policy.

### B. ASSERTIONS OF FACT

In addition to normative claims, policy arguments contain assertions of fact. Factual assertions may be divided into two categories, retrospective facts and prospective facts.

*1. Retrospective and Prospective Facts*

**Retrospective facts** have already occurred. Parties may disagree about what happened in the past. For example, the union says:

> The employer raised pay in order to win the election.

The employer says:

> I raised pay in order to match my competitor's raises.

Disagreements about retrospective facts are resolved by evidence, such as testimony and documents. Retrospective facts figure in policy arguments chiefly as the basis for predicting the future: if something happened in the past (especially if it happened often), it may happen again.

**Prospective facts** have not yet occurred, but a party predicts that they will occur if a rule is adopted or not adopted. Parties frequently disagree about what will happen in the future. For example, suppose a union is trying to organize a shop and is soliciting workers to sign membership cards. Some workers say they are interested, but do not want to pay a hefty initiation fee to join the union. In response, the union says it will waive the fee, but only for workers who sign cards before the election. An election is held, which the union wins. The employer asks the Board to set the result aside on the ground that the waiver of initiation fees interfered with the workers' freedom of choice because the waiver was tantamount to a bribe. The employer predicts:

> Some of the workers who sign cards to save the fee are likely to feel obligated to follow through on their commitment and to vote for the union.

The union predicts:

> When a worker steps into the voting booth, the worker knows that one is completely free to vote for or against the union, regardless of whether one has signed a card.

The tense of verbs can be misleading. The facts immediately above are stated in the present tense. In truth, they describe events in the past. But they are really predictions about the future. The union and the employer are arguing that the pattern of the past will continue in the future.[2]

Disagreements about prospective facts are occasionally resolved by predictions from experts. More often, a member of a tribunal simply uses one's own intuitions about the future.

Assertions of fact, whether retrospective or prospective, can be explicit or implicit (in other words, expressed or implied). **Explicit assertions of fact** are stated openly, such as:

> Some workers sign authorization cards, not because they support the union, but only because they want to get the union organizer off their backs.

Explicit assertions of fact can easily be identified, after which they can be evaluated.

More difficult to identify and evaluate are **implicit assertions of fact** (which are often called "assumptions"). An implicit assertion is a necessary part of an argument, but is not articulated. For example:

> Workers commonly change their minds after signing authorization cards, which therefore should not be used in support of a bargaining order.

This argument contains a significant implicit assertion of fact, namely:

> The workers did not change their minds because of the employer's serious unfair labor practices.

This assertion, while perhaps true in cases in which employers do not commit serious unfair labor practices, may well be false in cases in which

---

2. In *National Labor Relations Board v. Savair*, 414 U.S. 270 (1973), the Supreme Court agreed with the employer. A fee waiver that expires before an election interferes with the workers' freedom of choice because the waiver is analogous to an employer's raising pay before an election in order to sway the workers' votes against the union. Also, workers might fear retaliation from the union if they do not sign cards, but it wins the election. In subsequent cases, the Board has held that a waiver is permissible if it does not expire before election but remains open after the election.

employers have wantonly broken the law. When implicit assertions are identified and exposed, they can be refuted; but if they are not exposed, they can give a poor argument influence that it does not deserve. Therefore, it is important to examine arguments carefully to identify any implicit factual assertions and then to evaluate them.

### 2. Sources of Assertions of Fact

One would think that retrospective facts used in a policy argument would be proved in the same ways that other facts are proved, that is, with witnesses, documents, and the like. In fact, however, tribunals often take judicial notice of retrospective facts in policy arguments. The Labor Board simply "knows" that workers often change their minds after signing union authorization cards.

Prospective facts cannot be proved in the same way that retrospective facts can be proved. Predictions are always problematic. In other contexts, expert testimony is used for predictions. For example, a physician might testify that a plaintiff will probably never regain the use of her legs. One might think that experts would also be the source of prospective facts in a policy argument, but they rarely are. Once again, we find that tribunals simply take judicial notice of prospective facts.

## II. Uses of Policy Arguments

Policy arguments may be used to identify or interpret the governing rule of law. For example:

#### Lockouts

The National Labor Relations Act is intended to promote the public policy of labor peace, which is crucial to the national economy. The issue at hand is whether employers should be allowed to lock out workers during a labor dispute. A lockout is the opposite of labor peace. The typical lockout occurs when collective bargaining has stalemated, but the union has not called a strike. Thus, a lockout provokes industrial strife that would not occur otherwise. As long as workers are willing to stay on the job for the wages and under the working conditions that the employer specifies, the employer should be prohibited from locking out the workers and instigating industrial warfare.

This argument uses the public policy in favor of labor peace in order to argue that lockouts should be illegal.[3]

Policy arguments may also be used in applying law to fact.

### Employees or Independent Contractors?

The Labor Act gives employees the right to join unions and bargain collectively with their employers. The Act does not give any rights to independent contractors. In the *National Labor Relations Board v. Hearst Publications,* newsboys who sold several publishers' papers authorized a union to bargain for them. The newsboys had the right to bargain through a union if they were employees; but if they were independent contractors, the publishers had the right to refuse to bargain with the union. The threshold question was, how should the terms "employee" and "independent contractor" be defined under the Labor Act? The employer argued for the common law definition, under which the newsboys were independent contractors. The union responded that new definitions of these terms were necessary in order to serve the purposes of the Labor Act:

> The common law definitions of "employee" and "independent contractor" were created to serve the purposes of the day, such as deciding when a company is responsible for damage to third parties caused by workers, but these are not the purposes of the Labor Act. The purpose of this Act is to promote collective bargaining because it leads to industrial peace and protects workers from exploitation by large and powerful corporations. The definitions of "employee" and "independent contractor" under this Act should be fashioned to serve its purpose. Accordingly, any worker who is subject to the evils that the Act was passed to eradicate—that is, any worker who is subject to exploitation by powerful corporations—should be included as an employee under the Act.

This argument uses the public policy in favor of collective bargaining to argue that newsboys should be classified as employees, not independent contractors.[4]

---

3. The Supreme Court rejected this argument and approved lockouts in *American Ship Building v. National Labor Relations Board.*

4. This argument convinced the Supreme Court, but shortly thereafter Congress amended the Labor Act to require that tribunals use the common law definitions of "employee" and "independent contractor."

## III. Evaluating Policy Arguments

Like any other argument, a policy argument must be evaluated for validity and soundness. Unfortunately for the student, policy arguments (also
like other arguments) often omit or imply elements which must be made
explicit before they can be evaluated. Here follows an example of implied
normative claims in policy arguments that must be made explicit.

### The Case of the Bargaining Order

Local 347 of the Food Store Employees attempted to organize the workers
of the Gissel Packing Company. Members of the local solicited the workers to sign cards that authorized the local to represent the workers in collective bargaining with Gissel. When the local had collected authorization
cards from a majority of the workers, it demanded that Gissel begin collective bargaining. Gissel refused, as was its right, and the local took the cards
to the Labor Board and petitioned it to conduct a representation election.

The Board scheduled an election in which the workers would vote on
whether or not to be represented by the union. During the weeks preceding the election, Gissel intimidated the workers by committing numerous
unfair labor practices, such as discharging union activists; the workers got
the message and voted against unionization. After an investigation and a
trial, the Board determined that the unfair labor practices had tainted the
election and its result had to be disregarded. The Board also determined
that the unfair labor practices were so serious, and the workers so intimidated, that a rerun election would also have been tainted.

The issue then became, what is the appropriate remedy? The law is
clear that a union may represent a unit of workers only if the majority of
them desire union representation. Therefore, the Board could issue a bargaining order (i.e., compel the employer to bargain with the union) only
if the union presented evidence that it once had majority support which
the employer's unfair labor practices had vitiated. Such evidence often
consists of authorization cards signed by workers. But Gissel argued that
authorization cards are unreliable evidence of majority support:

> The only proof that the majority of workers ever wanted Local 347 to rep-
> resent them is a pile of authorization cards, each stating that the worker
> who signed the card authorized the union to bargain on his behalf. But

union agents put heavy social pressure on workers to sign cards. Also, workers do not always understand the significance of signing cards. And workers who sign cards might change their minds after hearing their employer's arguments against unionization. Consequently, the Board should not order Gissel to bargain with the union. Instead, the Board should order Gissel to refrain from further unfair labor practices and to post a notice in the shop, stating that the Board has found Gissel guilty of unfair labor practices and promising to refrain from any further unfair labor practices; and the Board should postpone the rerun election until sufficient time has elapsed that the workers no longer feel intimidated.

The lawyer for the union replied that Gissel's argument must be rejected:

Authorization cards are a valid measure of workers' support for a union. Workers are adults who can stand up to social pressure from their peers. Workers know the consequences of signing a document. Nevertheless, they are human beings, and they can be intimidated by their employer, who has considerable power over them. The effect of intimidation lasts a long time. If the Board accepts Gissel's proposal and postpones the election until the employer's intimidation wears off, the election would often be postponed for months. A lengthy postponement would be tantamount to a victory for the employer because it is next to impossible for a union to maintain workers' support when, not having the right to bargain, it cannot do anything for them. But even if the effect of intimidation were short lived, and even if the employer committed no further unfair labor practices, postponing the election would allow the employer to benefit from its own wrongdoing: for during the postponement the employer would not have to bargain with the union and could continue campaigning against the union.

Let us focus on one of the arguments stated by Gissel's lawyer: "workers do not always understand the significance of signing a card." This single sentence contains a policy argument, most of which is implied. On its face, it may seem plausible, but we cannot judge whether it is valid and sound until we coax out its implied elements.

Before we analyze this argument, an admonition and a suggestion are in order. The admonition is that, as an advocate identifies implied elements in an adversary's argument, the advocate should state those elements as forcibly as possible. An advocate might be tempted to state the elements of an adversary's argument so as to contain errors of logic or fact, but such a tactic makes the advocate vulnerable to embarrassment. One's adversary need only reply, "That's not what I had in mind at all. Here is what I meant." An advocate should never underestimate one's adversary. An advocate should construct an implied argument in its strongest possible form.

The suggestion is that one should begin the analysis by stating the issue to which the argument applies. We have two reasons for making this suggestion. The first reason is that, although it is not technically an element of a syllogism, the issue should be stated because even the best of minds wander on occasion. The second reason is that the *resolution* of the issue will be the *conclusion* of the syllogism that the advocate needs to construct. (Recall issue-and-resolution pairs discussed in §1.) As a result, stating the issue, and the resolution associated with the issue, does part of the work of analyzing the argument.

With the foregoing advice in mind, we are prepared to state the issue which the argument of Gissel's lawyer addresses: Do authorization cards prove workers' will regarding unionization? Of course, Gissel's lawyer wants the resolution of this issue to be no. Accordingly, the conclusion of the syllogism that we are constructing will be, authorization cards do not prove workers' will regarding unionization.

With the issue (and, therefore, the conclusion of the syllogism) stated, the next step in evaluating this policy argument is to articulate the normative claim. In the argument of Gissel's lawyer, a normative claim is implied, but fairly obvious: the true will of the workers must be the basis for deciding whether or not they will be represented by a union.

Now the question becomes, what premises lead to the conclusion that authorization cards do not prove workers' will? Gissel's lawyer stated one of them: workers do not always understand the significance of signing authorization cards.

At this point, we have a premise and a conclusion, but the conclusion does not follow from the premise. They must be connected by an additional premise. Gissel's lawyer did not state it, and so we say that it is implied. What is implied? At this point, the advocate must think creatively. Workers do not understand authorization cards . . . cards do not prove workers' will regarding unionization . . . the implied premise is, if a person signs a document which the person does not understand, the document is not proof of the person's will.

Now we have analyzed the argument of Gissel's lawyer into the following syllogism:

MAJOR PREMISE

If a person signs a document which the person does not understand, the document is not proof of the person's will.

MINOR PREMISE

Workers do not understand authorization cards.

CONCLUSION

∴ Authorization cards do not prove workers' will regarding unionization.[5]

Once an argument is expressed as a syllogism, it can be checked for validity and soundness. The major premise of the lawyer's argument makes common sense, but common sense and the law sometimes diverge—and they do in the present example. Common sense may allow an adult to offer evidence that one did not understand the document and, therefore, that the document does not express the one's will. The law, however, presumes that an adult always understands the documents one signs, and therefore (with some exceptions) presumes that a signed

---

5. Above we admonished the student to state the elements of an adversary's argument as forcibly as possible. One who is careless about the logic of arguments might state the implied premise thus: if a person understands a document, it represents the will of the person. The resulting syllogism would state—

MAJOR PREMISE

If a person understands a document, it represents the will of the person.

MINOR PREMISE

Workers do not understand authorization cards.

CONCLUSION

∴ Authorization cards do not prove workers' will regarding unionization.

This syllogism commits the fallacy of denying the antecedent. (See § 4.) An advocate who analyzed the argument of Gissel's lawyer into this syllogism might gleefully argue that the lawyer's argument is invalid. But the glee would vanish when Gissel's lawyer replied that the correct statement of the major premise (as in the text) is part of a logically valid argument.

And so we repeat the admonition: Never underestimate one's adversary. Always construct an adversary's implied argument in its strongest possible form.

document expresses the will of the signer. Therefore, the major premise of the syllogism is at least doubtful. But the law might recognize an exception regarding union authorization cards, and so research is in order.

Suppose arguendo that our research reveals that the major premise is correct regarding authorization cards. Now attention shifts to the minor premise. It is an assertion of fact. Three questions pertain to assertions of fact. The first is whether the assertion is relevant to the issue at hand. If the law is that a signed authorization does not express the will of the signer if the signer did not understand the card, it is relevant that workers do not always understand authorization cards. Thus, the assertion in the minor premise is substantively relevant.

The second question is whether the assertion is true. It is not common knowledge or true beyond dispute that workers do not understand authorization cards, so judicial notice is not appropriate. Rather, evidence is in order. The advocate must search for evidence pro and con and weigh it carefully.

If the assertion is relevant and true, the third question is whether the assertion operates at the appropriate level of abstraction. The answer depends on the level of abstraction of the issue. In this example, the issue operates at a fairly high level because the resolution of the issue will apply to all employers and unions in similar circumstances. It follows that the assertion must also operate at a high level. The minor premise in the syllogism applies to workers across the country, so the assertion is at the appropriate level.

## IV. Review

1. Which of the following statements is true? More than one answer may be correct.
   - ☐ (a) Public policy is too amorphous to serve as a source of legal arguments.
   - ☐ (b) Policy arguments pertain to the good of the community.
   - ☐ (c) Policy arguments are consequential in nature.
   - ☐ (d) Policy arguments involve predictions.

2. In the Case of the Bargaining Order—
   a. State two normative claims (either explicit or implicit) (i) in the argument of Gissel's lawyer (other than the claim discussed in the text above) and (ii) in the argument of the union's lawyer.

b. State two implicit facts (i) in the argument of Gissel's lawyer and (ii) in the argument of the union's lawyer.

c. In the argument of the union's lawyer concerning social pressure, (i) identify the normative claim, (ii) analyze the argument into one or more syllogisms, and (iii) evaluate the argument for validity and soundness.

## V. References

*American Ship Building Company v. National Labor Relations Board,* 380 U.S. 300 (1965).

*National Labor Relations Board v. Gissel Packing Co.,* 395 U.S. 575 (1969).

*National Labor Relations Board v. Hearst Publications et al.,* 322 U.S. 111 (1944).

*National Labor Relations Board v. Savair Manufacturing Company,* 414 U.S. 270 (1973).

# § 10

# DOCTRINAL ARGUMENTS

Arguments may be based on legal doctrine. Doctrine is expressed in authorities, which include, for example, constitutions, precedents, and treatises. Authorities may be binding or advisory.

## I. Varieties of Authority

### A. BINDING AUTHORITIES

Some authorities are binding on a tribunal. A binding authority literally makes the law, and tribunals must follow it. For example, a statute states, "A tax of 8 percent shall be collected by a merchant on each sale in the state, and the merchant shall transmit such taxes to the state treasury quarterly."

Some binding authorities make public law; they state the rules that govern everyone. Three such authorities are—

*constitutions*
*statutes*
*precedents*

CONSTITUTION

Article I, section 9, clause 8 of the Constitution of the United States of America provides: "No Title of Nobility shall be granted by the United States: And no Person holding any Office of Profit or Trust under them, shall, without the Consent of the Congress, accept of any present, Emolument, Office, or Title, of any kind whatever, from any King, Prince, or foreign State."

STATUTE

Section 7 of the National Labor Relations Act provides, "Employees shall have the right to self-organization, to form, join, or assist labor organizations, to bargain collectively through representatives of their own choosing, and to engage in other concerted activities for the purpose of collective bargaining or other mutual aid or protection, and shall also have the right to refrain from any or all of such activities."

PRECEDENT

Precedents are prior decisions of the tribunal that is hearing the case at bar or of a higher tribunal in the same jurisdiction. As we mentioned in § 1 ISSUES, the word "precedent" has two meanings. In a broad sense, "precedent" can mean any decision made prior to the case at bar. In a narrow sense, "precedent" can mean a prior decision that governs the outcome of the case at bar. The narrow sense is applicable here. For example, in 1896 the Supreme Court held in *Plessy v. Ferguson* that segregated railway cars—and, by extension, segregated public schools—did not violate the Constitution. The Court followed that precedent until 1954.

Other binding authorities make private law; they state the rules that govern only specific persons. Two such authorities are—

*contracts*
*wills*

CONTRACT

Paragraph 18 of the agreement between the employer and the union provides, "The base wage of retail clerks will be $19 per hour."

WILL

In his will, miser Madison "left River City the library building / But he left all the books to" Marian (from the musical *The Music Man*).

## B. ADVISORY AUTHORITIES

Advisory authorities do not make the law. Instead, they help a tribunal to interpret the law. Advisory authorities may enjoy the respect of tribunals, but are not binding on them. If a law review articles says, "The Emoluments Clause of the Constitution prohibits the president from doing private business with a foreign government," a tribunal may accept or reject this interpretation. Two advisory authorities are—

*legislative history*
*scholarly commentary*

LEGISLATIVE HISTORY

The record of reports and debates in the legislature or constitutional convention on proposals that were adopted or rejected, e.g., the *Congressional Record.*

SCHOLARLY COMMENTARY

Treatises, e.g., *Williston on Contracts*
Law review articles, e.g., Cooper and Sobel, *Seniority and Testing under Fair Employment Laws: A General Approach to Objective Criteria of Hiring and Promotion,* 82 HARVARD LAW REVIEW 1598 (1969).

## II. Uses of Authority

Doctrinal arguments, whether grounded on binding or advisory authority, may be used in any of the functions in the resolution of a dispute. Here follow a few examples.

A DOCTRINAL ARGUMENT USED IN AN ARGUMENT AS TO THE ISSUE IN A CASE

The plaintiff urges that the issue in the case at bar is whether the statute outlawing automatic firearms is unconstitutional because it infringes on her Second Amendment rights. The State urges that the issue is whether the Constitution allows the State to protect citizens from murder by firearm. The case at bar is analogous to the decision of the Supreme Court of this state in *Lions v. Martyrs*, in which the court framed the issue as the plaintiff in the case at bar frames it, and this court will address that issue.

### A DOCTRINAL ARGUMENT USED IN AN ARGUMENT AS TO THE FACTS

The collective bargaining agreement between the employer and the union contains a grievance/arbitration procedure; it provides that if a grievance cannot be settled by negotiation between the parties, the grievance may be referred to a neutral arbitrator for decision. The parties agree that the union's grievance over a worker's promotion is covered by this procedure. The agreement also contains a no-strike/no-lockout clause regarding several issues that are listed in the agreement; the union agrees not to strike, and the employer agrees not to lock out workers, over issues on the list. The list does not include disputes over promotions.

The union filed a grievance over a promotion. When the grievance could not be settled by negotiation, the union could have demanded arbitration but, instead, went on strike. The issue in this case is whether the strike was barred by the no-strike clause in the labor agreement. The Supreme Court held in *Teamsters Local 174 v. Lucas Flour Company* that parties normally intend that, if a dispute is subject to arbitration, the union waives the right to strike over the dispute. Accordingly, this court finds that the union waived the right to strike over grievances pertaining to promotions. The union's remedy is arbitrations.

### DOCTRINAL ARGUMENTS USED IN AN ARGUMENT AS TO THE LAW

#### Choosing the Governing Authority

The Fair Labor Standards Act allows a labor contract to supersede certain provisions of the Act that protect workers in the absence of a union. The contract in the case at bar specifically addresses compensation for workers' time spent donning and doffing protective gear, and therefore the contract, not the Act, governs the present dispute.

Interpreting the Governing Authority

The parties agree that this case is governed by § 99 of the Statute of Spirits, but they disagree about whether the section applies to zombies. During the debate in the Senate on the bill that was later enacted, Senator Blowhard asked Senator Bilgewater, who was the sponsor of the bill, to define the term "spirits." The latter replied, "'Sprits' include angels, banshees, cherubim, demons, dybbuks, ghosts, phantoms, poltergeists, seraphim, spooks, sprites, and wraiths, but not elves, doppelgangers, fairies, goblins, gremlins, leprechauns, nymphs, Santa Claus, or zombies." 666 CONGRESSIONAL RECORD 2577–2578 (1964). § 99 does not apply to zombies.

### DOCTRINAL ARGUMENTS USED IN APPLYING LAW TO FACT

Ann had two daughters, Laura and Phyllis. Laura was married to Glenn and they had four children. Phyllis was unmarried without issue.

The first issue is whether Ann's will is valid. As she lay dying in a hospital on January 4, 2016, Ann summoned two nurses to her bedside at 6:00 p.m. and said, "I want you to witness my will." She then wrote the following on a blank piece of paper: "I leave all of my property to my children." She dated and signed her name at the bottom, and each nurse attested to have seen Ann sign the paper. This document meets the requirements of § 88 of the Statute of Wills and, therefore, is a valid will in the State of Confusion.

The next issue is, how should Ann's estate be divided? Ann died two hours after signing her will. Phyllis survived Ann. However, unbeknownst to Ann, Laura had predeceased Ann; Laura had been driving to the hospital to visit her mother on January 4 when a bridge collapsed on Laura's car at 5:30 p.m., killing her instantly. Accordingly, the issue arises, should Ann's estate be distributed half to Phyllis and half to Laura's estate, or should all of Ann's estate pass to Phyllis? In *Age v. Beauty,* 18 Conf. 77 (1911), our supreme court held that the estate of a decedent who is named as a beneficiary of a will may inherit from the will only if the testator expressly acknowledges that the decedent is or may be dead; in other words, it is presumed in this state that a testator does not intend to leave an inheritance to a dead person. Accordingly, all of Laura's estate passes to Phyllis.

### *People v. Ledfoot*

Ledfoot was cited for speeding as she cut through the parking lot of Central School at 6:00 p.m. on January 15. She argued that the relevant authority was § 1 of the Motor Vehicle Code, which states, "A driver shall not exceed the reasonable and safe speed under the circumstances" and that it was reasonable and safe to drive 25 miles per hour through the school parking lot at the date and time in question. The prosecutor argued that the relevant authority was § 2 of the Motor Vehicle Code, which states, "The speed limit near a school is 15 miles per hour." Judge Janus wrote:

> Section 2 of the Motor Vehicle Code is the applicable rule if a school parking lot is "near a school." The lot was certainly "near a school" in terms of geography, but was 6:00 p.m. "near a school" in terms of *time* on January 15? In *People v. Speedy Gonzales*, the defendant was cited for driving past a school at 30 miles per hour at 5:00 a.m. The court held that § 2 did not apply because "near a school" refers both to both geography and to time, and no children were likely to be in the vicinity of a school at 5:00 a.m. The same is true of 6:00 p.m. of a winter's night. (The fact might be different of a summer's eve.) Because § 2 applies only to the period of time before, during, and after school when children are likely to be present, it does not apply to the case at bar.
>
> Section 1 of the Code applies at all times in all places. The issue is, therefore, what was the reasonable and safe speed in the school parking lot at 6:00 p.m. on January 15? *Left v. Right* teaches that the reasonable and safe speed is affected by various factors, including time, place, and weather conditions. Time matters because it is harder to see during the night than during the day, so the reasonable and safe speed may be lower at night. The sun set at 4:58 p.m. on January 15, *see* http://aa.usno.navy.mil/cgi-bin/aa_rstablew.pl (website of the U.S. Naval Observatory), and so by 6:00 p.m. it was full dark. Place matters because in general one may safely go faster on a divided highway than on an arterial boulevard, faster on a boulevard than on a side street, and so forth. Ledfoot was driving in a parking lot. The report of the Governor's Special Committee on Motor Vehicle Safety, which was the basis for the most recent revision of the Motor Vehicle Code, stated on p. 18, "Per mile of vehicle operation, many more collisions and injuries occur in parking lots than on streets." Thus, a slower speed is generally appropriate in a parking lot than on a street. Weather conditions

matter because they affect visibility and traction. The *Star Gazette* for January 16 reported on page 2 that two inches of snow fell the preceding day and that the high temperature was 28 degrees F. These conditions suggest that the surface of the parking lot was at least partially covered with snow and, therefore, probably slippery, at least in spots. Taking all of these facts into account, this court concludes that Ledfoot exceeded the reasonable and safe speed under the circumstances.

This case illustrates a tribunal's use of doctrinal arguments to perform three of the functions necessary to resolving an issue.

1. FUNCTION: CHOOSING THE GOVERNING RULE OF LAW

   (a) The issue

   What is the governing rule of law? The court had to choose § 1 or § 2 as the governing rule of law.

   (b) The court's argument

   The court used a doctrinal argument based on a precedent, *People v. Speedy Gonzales*, to choose § 1.

2. FUNCTION: APPLICATION OF LAW TO FACT

   (a) The issue

   Determining the reasonable and safe speed under the circumstances called for application of law to fact.

   (b) The court's argument

   The court used a doctrinal argument based on a precedent, *Left v. Right*, to identify the factors that were relevant to this determination, namely, time, place, and weather conditions.

3. FUNCTION: FINDING FACTS

   Fact 1

   (a) The issue

   Was it light or dark at 6:00 p.m.?

   (b) The court's argument

   The court used an authoritative text, namely, the website of the U.S. Naval Observatory, to find the fact that the sun set at 4:58 p.m., from which it followed that it was dark at 6:00 p.m.

Fact 2

(a) The issue

Is driving in a parking lot more dangerous than driving on a street?

(b) The court's argument

The court found as fact that driving in a parking lot is more dangerous than driving on a street; this finding was the result of a doctrinal argument based on an authoritative text, namely, the Report of the Governor's Special Committee on Motor Vehicle Safety.

Fact 3

(a) The issue

Was the surface of the parking lot slippery or dry?

(b) The court's argument

The court found that the surface of the parking lot was slippery by relying on another authoritative text, the weather report in the local newspaper.

## III. Varieties of Doctrinal Argument

Doctrinal arguments come in several varieties, for example, syllogisms, analogies, and purpose of a statute. Several varieties of doctrinal argument are discussed in subsequent sections of this book.

## IV. Review

### Questions

1. One source of legal argument is authority. Authorities include (more than one answer may be correct)—
   - ☐ (a) statutes and treatises.
   - ☐ (b) precedents.
   - ☐ (c) papal bulls.
   - ☐ (d) expert witnesses
   - ☐ (e) treatises

### *Sure-Tan v. National Labor Relations Board*

A leather-processing firm in Chicago employed eleven workers, several of whom were Mexican nationals who were illegally present in the United States. Eight of the workers signed cards authorizing a union to represent them. The Labor Board scheduled an election, and the majority of workers voted for the union. Immediately after the election, the employer objected to the election on the ground that the undocumented workers were not employees as defined in the Labor Act and should not have voted in the election.[1] The Board disagreed and certified the union as the workers' bargaining agent. In retaliation, the employer wrote a letter to the Immigration and Naturalization Service, asking it to check on the status of several of the workers. The INS investigated, and the undocumented workers returned to Mexico. The Board accused the employer of discriminating against these workers.

The employer argued that undocumented workers take jobs illegally, and Congress could not have intended to afford them the rights that lawful workers enjoy. Also, giving rights to undocumented workers would create a conflict between the Immigration and Nationality Act and the National Labor Relations Act. The Immigration Act is intended to guard America against an influx of foreign workers, and treating undocumented workers as employees under the Labor Act would encourage them to sneak into America.

---

1. Like all statutes that apply to workers, the coverage of Labor Act is limited. The Act does not apply to every worker; e.g., it does not apply to agricultural workers. Congress expressed this limitation by giving the word "employee" a special definition for the purpose of the Labor Act alone. Thus, although the undocumented workers in *Sure-Tan* were employees under the common law because they worked for money and under the direction of the employer, the issue could arise whether they were employees as defined by the Labor Act.

The significance of being, or not being, an employee under the Labor Act is that the Act gives legal rights to employees but not to other workers. For example, the Act gives employees the right to join a union, and forbids an employer to discriminate against employees for exercising this right. If a worker is not an employee (as the Act defines "employee"), the worker does not have this right and the employer is not forbidden to discriminate against the worker for joining a union. Thus, agricultural workers are not employees under the Act, and the Act does not forbid an employer to discriminate against them for joining a union. (The laws of some states protect agricultural workers, but the federal law does not.)

The Labor Board replied that the Labor Act defines "employee" broadly: "The term 'employee' shall include any employee" except for those whom the Act specifically excludes (such as agricultural and domestic workers). Undocumented workers are not specifically excluded. Also, the Act is intended to promote collective bargaining in order to improve workers' wages and working conditions. If undocumented workers are barred from collective bargaining, they will take jobs on substandard wages and working conditions, thereby depressing the wages and working conditions of legal workers. As for a conflict with the Immigration Act, that statute has little concern with employment of illegal entrants; it does not make it a crime either for an employer to hire an undocumented worker or for an undocumented worker to accept employment.[2]

Section 8(a)(3) of the Act makes it illegal for an employer to discriminate against workers. To discriminate under the Labor Act is deliberately to disadvantage a worker because of the worker's concerted activity. The employer conceded that its letter to the INS was motivated by the workers' voting to unionize, but argued that it had not caused them harm because the proximate or real cause of the workers' deportation was their status as illegal aliens, not the letter. The Board replied that the proximate cause was the employer's letter because, but for the letter, the INS would not have investigated the workers.

2. (a) State one of the issues in the case.
   (b) State the employer's argument(s) on the issue and classify the argument by function and by basis.
   (c) Ditto for the Labor Board's argument(s).

---

2. Immigration law was later amended. The Immigration and Control Act of 1986 makes it a crime for an employer knowingly to hire an undocumented worker, but does not make it a crime for an undocumented worker to hold a job in America unless the worker presented forged documents.

3. (a) State the other issue in the case.
   (b) State the employer's argument(s) on the issue and classify the argument by function and by basis.
   (c) Ditto for the Labor Board's argument(s).

## V. References

*Plessy v. Ferguson*, 163 U.S. 537 (1896).
*Sure-Tan v. National Labor Relations Board*, 467 U.S. 883 (1984).
*Teamsters Local 174 v. Lucas Flour Co.*, 369 U.S. 945 (1962).

# Analogies and Precedents: The Structure and Criteria for Evaluation of Legal Analogies

## I. Analogies, Similes, and Metaphors

### A. The Nature of Analogies

An **analogy** has two elements, which are called the **antecedent** and the **consequent**. As these names imply, the antecedent occurs first and the consequent, thereafter.[1] Similes

> O, my luve's like a red red rose
> That's newly sprung in June
> O, my luve's like the melodie
> That's sweetly play'd in tune.
>         —Robert Burns (1794)

---

1. In some analogies, the antecedent and the consequent are contemporaneous. Such analogies are otherwise like any other analogy.

and metaphors

> All the world's a stage,
> And all the men and women merely players:
> They have their exits and their entrances;
> And one man in his time plays many parts,
> His acts being seven ages.
> —Shakespeare, *As You Like It* (Act V,
>                                      Scene VII)

> To-morrow, and to-morrow, and to-morrow,
> Creeps in this petty pace from day to day,
> To the last syllable of recorded time;
> And all our yesterdays have lighted fools
> The way to dusty death. Out, out, brief candle!
> Life's but a walking shadow, a poor player,
> That struts and frets his hour upon the stage,
> And then is heard no more. It is a tale
> Told by an idiot, full of sound and fury,
> Signifying nothing.
> —Shakespeare, *Macbeth* (Act V, Scene V)

are analogies.

### Exercise

1. What are the antecedents and the consequents of the foregoing analogies?

Not all analogies are arguments. But when an analogy is an argument, it points out that at least one aspect of the antecedent has a counterpart in the consequent, and maintains that because we observe that the antecedent and the consequent are similar in this way, they are probably similar in some other way as well. The form of an analogy is—

The antecedent has aspects 1 and 2.
The consequent has aspect 1.
Therefore, the consequent has aspect 2.

In ordinary English, an analogy points out that the antecedent and the consequent have something in common and, therefore, they have something else in common. "My luve's like a red red rose" and so she is beautiful and sweet (and can prick you as well as please you). "All the world's a stage" and so our lives fall into acts or phases. "Life's but a walking shadow" and so it is fleeting and insubstantial.

Aspect 1 of an analogy can be a single fact or several facts. Aspect 2 of an analogy is usually a single fact, but can be more. Thus, it may be argued that, in addition to the points of similarity identified in aspect 1, the antecedent and the consequent have one additional fact in common, or that they have many additional facts in common.

As a rule, the more facts in aspect 1 (that is, the more ways in which the antecedent and the consequent resemble one another) and the fewer facts in aspect 2, the stronger the analogy.[2]

Although the antecedent and the consequent are usually explicit in an analogy, the aspects of similarity between them may be either explicit or implicit. Here is a simile in which the antecedent, the consequent, and both aspects of similarity are explicit:

> Goats are like cows: they nurse their young. Humans can drink cows' milk, and so we can drink goats' milk as well.

Cows are the antecedent; goats are the consequent. Aspect 1 is that cows and goats nurse their young, and aspect 2 is that humans can drink cows' milk. The argument of this analogy is—

[Aspect 1] Cows nurse their young, and [Aspect 2] humans can drink their milk.
[Aspect 1] Goats nurse their young.
Therefore, [Aspect 2] humans can drink goats' milk.

---

2. This rule is consistent with the point in § 5 INDUCTION that the more particulars that support a generalization, the greater our confidence in the generalization. For this purpose, aspect 1 of an analogy is like the particulars of an inductive generalization, and aspect 2 of an analogy is like the conclusion of an inductive generalization. Indeed, analogies are a form of inductive reasoning.

The argument would still be an analogy if it were written so that aspect 1 is implied and aspect 2 is explicit:

We can drink goats' milk because we can drink cows' milk.

Here is a metaphor in which aspect 1 is explicit and aspect 2 is implicit:

You might as well use a boa constrictor to measure your neck as go to a lawyer for advice.—An old saying

The antecedent is a boa constrictor; the consequent is a lawyer. Aspect 1 is that it is possible to do something, namely, use a boa constrictor to measure your neck. Aspect 2, which is implicit, is that if you do this, the boa will squeeze the life out of you. The argument of the analogy is—

[Aspect 1: explicit] You can use a boa constrictor to measure you neck;
     [Aspect 2: implicit] but if you do, it will squeeze the life out of you.
[Aspect 1: explicit] You can go to a lawyer for advice.
[Aspect 2] But if you do, the lawyer will squeeze the life out of you.

## B. The Danger of Analogies

Analogies are slippery. Simply that the antecedent and the consequent have one, two, or even twenty things in common does not guarantee that they have anything else in common. For example:

Monkeys and dogs have a lot in common. The range of sizes of monkeys and dogs is roughly the same. Both are mammals. Both have tails. Both have four limbs of equal length and use them to walk on the ground. Monkeys can walk on the canopy of the forest, and so dogs should be able to do it as well.

Analogies are more suggestive than probative. They are fine for poetry and political rhetoric, but must be used with care in reasoned argument.

### Aspasia

Aspasia was one of the most famous and accomplished women of ancient Athens, indeed, of the ancient world. Greek women at that time were strictly cloistered and played no role in public life; but being a foreigner (she was from Miletus, a Greek city in what is now southwestern

Turkey) Aspasia was free of this repression. Her house was an intellectual center of Athens, attracting the leading figures of the city, including Socrates and Pericles. Cicero reports an argument that she made to Xenophon's wife:

| | |
|---|---|
| ASPASIA: | If your neighbor had finer jewelry than you have, would you prefer hers or yours? |
| XENOPHON'S WIFE: | Hers. |
| ASPASIA: | If she had finer clothing than you have, would you prefer hers or yours? |
| XENOPHON'S WIFE: | Hers. |
| ASPASIA: | And if she had a better husband? |

Xenophon's wife blushed. Then Aspasia said to Xenophon:

| | |
|---|---|
| ASPASIA: | If your neighbor had a better horse than yours, would you prefer his or yours? |
| XENOPHON: | His. |
| ASPASIA: | If he had a better farm than yours, which would you prefer? |
| XENOPHON: | His. |
| ASPASIA: | And if he had a better wife? |

Xenophon did not reply.

### Exercise

2. Were Aspasia's analogies sound?

## II. The Legal Analogy

### A. DIFFERENCES BETWEEN AN ORDINARY ANALOGY AND A LEGAL ANALOGY

In the daily life of a judge, a precedent is a blessing. It means that the judge need not rethink the issue, and someone else is to blame if the precedent is undesirable. Precedents are even better for a lawyer. If a precedent is on point, a lawyer can give a client a definite answer. Clients like that. If no precedent is on point, a lawyer can run up a large bill analyzing cases. Ex-spouses like that.

Most people know how important precedents are in the law. *Argument based on precedent is argument based on analogy.* Indeed, often an analogy is one of the premises of a legal syllogism:

MAJOR PREMISE

Analogous cases should be decided similarly.

MINOR PREMISE

The case at bar is analogous to case X.

CONCLUSION

∴ The case at bar should be decided as case X was decided.

An issue is to a case as a gene is to a species. An issue can be isolated in a case and serve as a precedent, regardless of any other issues in a case. Accordingly, the word "issue" may be substituted for the word "case" in the foregoing syllogism.

MAJOR PREMISE

Analogous issues should be decided similarly.

MINOR PREMISE

The issue in the case at bar is analogous to issue X in a precedent.

CONCLUSION

∴ The issue in the case at bar should be decided as issue X was decided in the precedent.

Nonetheless, some important differences exist between analogies in ordinary discourse and legal analogies. One difference is that the antecedent and the consequent in a legal analogy go by different names. The antecedent is an earlier decision, which is known as the **precedent**. The consequent is the case presently before the tribunal for decision, which may be called the **case at bar**.[3]

---

3. Numerous synonyms exist for "case at bar," such as "case (or situation or matter) at hand (or under consideration)," "present (or instant) case (or situation or matter)," and "case (or matter or issue) sub judice."

A second difference between ordinary and legal analogies is that aspects 1 and 2 of an ordinary analogy may be facts, feelings, intuitions, or anything else. In a legal analogy, aspect 1 is the facts of the precedent and aspect 2 is the outcome of the precedent. If the issue or case at bar shares aspect 1 (has similar facts), the issue or case should also share aspect 2 (have a similar result).

A point bears repetition and emphasis: in a legal analogy, aspect 1 is the *facts* of the precedent and the case at bar. *Facts are as important to a lawyer as to an empirical scientist.*

A third difference between ordinary and legal analogies is that the precedent in a legal analogy is an authority. Therefore, as pointed out in § 10 DOCTRINAL ARGUMENTS, the legal analogy is a type of argument from authority. The precedent must be followed except in extraordinary circumstances. Your roommate's fury may be like a hurricane, but you may ignore her. A tribunal may not ignore a precedent on point.

A fourth difference is that a legal analogy contains an element that ordinary analogies omit, namely, a rationale. The ordinary analogy merely observes that the antecedent has aspects 1 and 2, that the consequent also has aspect 1, and concludes that the consequent has aspect 2 as well. No attempt is made to argue why this conclusion should be so. A good legal analogy makes such an argument. It is called the rationale. The **rationale** gives the reasons why the facts of the precedent led to the outcome of that case, and then argues that the same reasons demonstrate that analogous facts of the case at bar should lead to the same outcome.

## B. THE STRUCTURE OF A LEGAL ANALOGY

Whereas the ordinary analogy is flexible in form (witness, for example, the similes and metaphors at the beginning of this section), the legal analogy has a formal structure. Here is the structure of a legal analogy—

**Issue**
**Precedent**
　**Facts of the precedent**
　**Rationale of the precedent**
　**Result of the precedent**
**Case at bar**
　**Facts of the case at bar and their similarity to the facts of the precedent**

**Argument that the rationale of the precedent applies to the facts of the case at bar**

**Claim**

We frequently use analogies in daily life that have a legal flavor to them, and it may be helpful to analyze one of them at this point. Consider—

### Exercise

#### The Captain's Analogy

The captain of a ship is responsible for everything that happens on and to the ship. Because one who may be held responsible for events should have the power to control them, the captain has absolute authority over all persons and objects on the ship. The general of an army is also responsible for everything that is done by and happens to the army and, like the captain of a ship, must have absolute authority over all persons and objects in or that might affect the army.

3. It is easy to see in this analogy that the antecedent (precedent) is the captain of a ship and the consequent (case at bar) is the general of an army. It may be more difficult to identify the three parts of each element. Try your hand at it: complete the following sentences.

ISSUE

*The issue is*

PRECEDENT *The captain of a ship*

Facts of the precedent

*The facts of the precedent were*

Rationale of the precedent

*The rationale of the precedent was*

Result of the precedent

*The result of the precedent was*

CASE AT BAR *The general of an army*

Facts of the case at bar and their similarity to the facts of the precedent

*The facts of the case at bar are similar to the facts of the precedent because*

Argument that the rationale of the precedent applies to the facts of case at bar

*The rationale of the precedent applies to the case at bar because*

CLAIM

*The result of the case at bar should be*

## C. TRUNCATED ANALOGIES

As indicated above regarding the analogy of the milk of cows and goats, an analogy can be truncated, and one often encounters analogies in truncated form. Here is the *Captain's Analogy* as one might hear it from a friend:

> Like the captain of a ship, a general of an army should have absolute authority over all soldiers under one's command.

Two truncations are particularly nettlesome: (1) failure to demonstrate that the facts of the precedent are similar to the facts of the case at bar, and (2) failure to demonstrate that the rationale of the precedent applies to the case at bar. Both must be avoided. Let us now consider each.

### 1. Failure to Demonstrate That the Facts of the Precedent Are Similar to the Facts of the Case at Bar

Sometimes one who draws an analogy fails to demonstrate the similarity of the facts of the precedent and of the case at bar. Perhaps the facts are so obviously similar or analogous that one feels it would be superfluous, even condescending to the audient, to argue for their similarity. However, subtle differences in the facts often engender a distinction between a precedent and a case at bar, and a distinction can destroy an analogy. (Distinctions are discussed in § 12 DISTINCTIONS.) For example—

#### *The Case of Illegal Questions*

In *Case 1* a union was organizing the workers of a factory. A manager held a conversation with a worker in the manager's office in the factory. During the conversation, the manager asked the worker how she felt about the union. The union filed an unfair labor practice charge, and the Labor Board held that the question was illegal because a reasonable worker would fear that if the manager knew that she supported the union, the employer might retaliate against her.

In *Case 2* a manager holds a conversation with a worker as they eat at the same table during the lunch hour in the cafeteria of the factory. During the conversation, which addresses a variety of topics, the manager asks the worker how he feels about the union. The union files an unfair labor practice charge, and the union's advocate seeks to draw an analogy between *Cases 1* and *2* (i.e., use *Case 1* as a precedent for *Case 2*). The advocate argues:

> In *Case 1* the Board held it illegal for a manager to hold a conversation with a worker in the factory and ask whether the worker supported

the union. The facts of the case at bar are the same, and the outcome should be the same as well.

This argument is unsatisfactory because the advocate merely *asserts,* but fails to *argue*—fails to *demonstrate*—that the facts of the precedent and the case at bar are similar.

Two practical reasons should motivate every advocate to demonstrate the similarity of facts of the precedent and the case at bar. First, a demonstration of similarity impresses the strength of the analogy on the mind of the tribunal, thereby making it more difficult for one's opponent to undermine the analogy by distinguishing the cases. Second, given the procedures of trials and hearings, an advocate may not have an opportunity to respond to a distinction suggested by one's opponent, in which event the advocate's initial statement of the analogy must be strong enough to deflect any distinction. For example, in the *Case of the Illegal Questions,* the employer's advocate might argue:

> The manager's office is the locus of power in the factory, so a question about union allegiance in the office would be coercive. By contrast, workers feel that the cafeteria during the lunch hour is their space. The atmosphere is informal, and other workers are likely to overhear a conversation there. If a manager threatened a worker in this space, other workers would bear witness. It is therefore unlikely that a manager would intentionally threaten a worker in the cafeteria. It is equally unlikely that a worker would interpret a question about the union as a threat when the question was asked in the course of a conversation that touched a variety of topics.

The union's advocate having forfeited the opportunity to demonstrate that the facts of the precedent and the case at bar are similar, in other words, to argue that any factual differences between the cases are unimportant, the employer's advocate is able to present an unanswered argument. The union's advocate should have written something like this:

> In *Case 1* the Board held it illegal for a manager to hold a conversation with a worker in the manager's office and ask whether the worker supported the union. In the case at bar the manager held a conversation with the worker in the cafeteria during the lunch

hour and asked whether the worker supported the union. The facts of the two cases are analogous. The only difference between them is the location of the conversation, and this difference is not significant. Like the manager's office, the cafeteria is in the factory. The employer owns both, and the workers know it. A manager is a manager wherever one is, and workers know this fact as well. A manager's inquiry into a worker's union allegiance is fully as coercive in a cafeteria as in an office, even if the question is slyly embedded in a more general conversation.

This argument might not have succeeded, but at least it would have had a chance.

- **An analogy must demonstrate explicitly that the facts of the precedent are similar to the facts of the case at bar.**

### The "Phantom Analogy"

What we will call the "phantom analogy" is a variety of the failure to demonstrate that the facts of the precedent are similar to the facts of the case at bar, yet this variety is important enough to warrant separate treatment. A phantom analogy occurs when an advocate extracts from a prior case a few words, a sentence, or a passage, and applies it to the case at bar without drawing an analogy between the facts of the cases (hence, the analogy is a phantom). The phantom analogy is an instance of a broader error of argument with which the student is surely familiar, namely, taking something out of context. Here follows an example of a phantom analogy.

#### *The Seat Belt Cases*

##### Getgo's Case

The legislature of the State of Confusion has enacted § 789 of the Motor Vehicle Code, which reads: "Every person riding in a motor vehicle shall wear a seat belt at all times." Getgo gets going in her car, fastens her seat belt, and drives on a toll road. When she reaches her exit, she hands the toll card to the clerk in the booth; the clerk says that she owes $1.35. Her money is in her purse, which is on the back seat. She needs to unfasten her seat belt in order to reach her purse; she opens it and pays the toll. Before she can drive away, State trooper Persnickety, who has been hiding under a rock near the toll booth, cites her for not wearing a seat belt while riding in a motor vehicle. Her case comes before Justice Janus, a reasonable judge, who says:

> "Getgo has violated the letter of the § 789. I do not believe, however, that the legislature intended the law to apply to this situation. The law was meant to protect persons involved in automobile crashes. Few if any crashes occur while a passenger is reaching for money to pay a toll while the vehicle is standing at a toll booth at an exit from the road. Also, the legislature intended that tolls be paid, and it is lawful to keep one's money in a purse on the back seat. The citation is dismissed."

Justice Janus interpreted the law in light of its purpose ("The law was meant to protect persons involved in automobile crashes").

### Francisco's Case

Francisco lives on Penny Lane. It is a short, dead end street with only two houses on each side. The other houses are occupied by elderly retirees who rarely rise before 10:00 a.m.

Francisco is somewhat rotund and, when his seat belt is fastened, he finds it difficult to turn around to look through the rear window as he backs up his car. He therefore does not fasten his seatbelt as he backs out of his driveway. On this particular morning, he is absorbed in a story on the radio about the #MeToo Movement, and he forgets to fasten the seatbelt when he shifts into forward gear and drives down the street. When he stops at the corner, Officer Persnickety steps out from behind a tree and cites Francisco for driving without a seatbelt. In a hearing before Judge Devorah, Francisco argues:

> "I left for work, as I always do, at 7:00 in the morning. My neighbors on Penny Lane were still sleeping. What Judge Janus said in *Getgo's Case* applies to my case: "The law was meant to protect persons involved in automobile crashes." There was no chance that I would crash into my neighbors or their cars, and so my case should be dismissed."

Francisco has made a phantom analogy. He quoted from a prior case a sentence that seems to apply to his case, but he has failed to draw an analogy between the facts of the cases. Accordingly, Judge Devorah says to him:

> "Your case is nothing like *Getgo's Case*. Her car was fully stopped at a toll booth, and she was reaching for her purse on the back seat. Her

chance of being involved in a crash was negligible. You, however, were driving your car on a public street, and a crash was entirely possible. Your neighbors might have awakened early. A vehicle might have turned into Penny Lane, or you might have crashed with another vehicle as you turned out of the street. I find you guilty as charged."

One would not be mistaken to think that Judge Devorah merely distinguished *Getgo's Case*, but we classify Francisco's argument as a phantom analogy because he did not as much as attempt to drawn an analogy between *Getgo's Case* and his. Even an experienced advocate should draw a complete analogy in one's mind before truncating it. A beginning student should always draw an analogy fully.

### 2. Failure to Demonstrate That the Rationale of the Precedent Applies to the Case at Bar

The other nettlesome truncation of an analogy is the omission of an argument that the rationale of the precedent applies to the case at bar. Such an argument is necessary because sometimes the facts of a precedent seem similar to the facts of a case at bar, but the rationale of the precedent—the reason for the tribunal's decision—does not apply to the case at bar. In this event, the precedent is not an appropriate precedent and should not be used. Perhaps the classic example involves a statute, not a precedent (but, as the student learned in § 1 ISSUES, using a statute as authority is like using a precedent as authority in that both uses rest on an analogy between the facts of the authority (the facts contemplated by the statute or the facts of the precedent) and the facts of the case at bar).

#### Church of the Holy Trinity v. United States

At the end of the nineteenth century, a church in New York contracted with a pastor in England to come to America for employment in the church. A federal statute prohibited an employer from contracting with foreign laborers to come to America for employment. The prosecutor argued that the statute applied to the church because he believed that the facts contemplated by the statute, as indicated by its text, were analogous to the facts of the case at hand. The prosecutor was right insofar as a pastor is a kind of laborer. But the prosecutor failed to take into account the rationale of the statute or, to say the same thing, the purpose of the statute. It was aimed at a particular evil:

> It had become the practice for large capitalists in this country to contract with their agents abroad for the shipment of great numbers of an ignorant and servile class of foreign laborers, under contracts, by which the employer agreed, upon the one hand, to prepay their passage, while, upon the other hand, the laborers agreed to work after their arrival for a certain time at a low rate of wages. The effect of this was to break down the labor market, and to reduce other laborers engaged in like occupations to the level of the assisted immigrant. (pp. 463–464)

In light of the rationale of the statute, it did not apply to the church and the pastor. As Justice Brewer wrote, "It is a familiar rule, that a thing may be within the letter of the statute, yet not within the statute, because not within its spirit" (p. 459).

Here is a more recent case in which the facts of two cases were analogous, and the rationale of the precedent made all the difference.

### The Case of Gay Marriage

In 2013 the U.S. Supreme Court decided *Hollingsworth v. Perry*. The voters of California approved an amendment to the state constitution that prohibited gay marriage. Advocates of gay rights sued, claiming the amendment violated the federal Constitution. The State of California chose not to defend the case, and the federal Court of Appeals held that the amendment was unconstitutional. The Supreme Court affirmed that judgment.

Two years later, the Supreme Court entertained another gay marriage case, *Obergefell v. Hodges*. The laws of four states prohibited gay marriage. Was *Hollingsworth* a precedent for *Obergefell*? In other words, did *Hollingsworth* dictate that the state laws in *Obergefell* were unconstitutional? If one looked only at the facts of the cases, the answer was yes: they were analogous because, in both cases, state laws prohibited gay marriage. But if one looked at the rationale of *Hollingsworth*, the answer was no.

To understand why *Hollingsworth* was not a precedent for *Obergefell*, one must know the rationale of the earlier case. In *Hollingsworth*, the advocates proposed three rationales on which the Court could affirm the judgment of the lower court. The first rationale was that marriage is a fundamental right of all persons. If the Supreme Court had relied on this rationale, the decision would have applied to the whole nation and same-sex marriage would become legal in all states. In this event, *Hollingsworth* would have been the controlling precedent in *Obergefell*. The second rationale was that because California allows same-sex couples all of the other rights and privileges that opposite-sex couples enjoy, denying same-sex couples the right to marry is irrational and discriminatory. If the Court had chosen the second rationale, the decision would have applied only to California and the seven other states that gave same-sex couples the same rights as opposite-sex couples except marriage; the decision would have no effect on the other forty-two states. In this event, *Hollingsworth* would have controlled *Obergefell* only if the plaintiffs in *Obergefell* lived in one of those eight states. The third rationale was that no one had the legal right to challenge the decision of the Court of Appeals because California declined to defend the amendment. Had the Court chosen the third rationale, the decision would have applied to this particular constitutional amendment in California, but not to any law that a state chose to defend. In this event, *Hollingsworth* would not have been a precedent for *Obergefell* because the states defended their laws.

The Court in *Hollingsworth* upheld the judgment that the amendment was unconstitutional based on the third rationale. As a result, although the facts of *Obergefell* were analogous to the facts of *Hollingsworth*, the latter was not a precedent for the former.[4]

Thus, an advocate should always identify the rationale of a precedent and consider whether it applies to the case at bar. If the rationale does apply, the advocate should demonstrate how it applies in the analogy. If the rationale does not apply, the advocate should abandon the analogy and look for another argument.

- **An analogy must demonstrate explicitly that the rationale of the precedent applies to the case at bar.**

### 3. Legal Citations as Truncated Analogies
The most truncated of analogies is simply a citation to an authority. For example, a tribunal often draws a rule of law from a statute. A tribunal

---

4. Nonetheless, the Court in *Obergefell* held that same-sex marriage is a constitutional right—but not on the basis of *Hollingsworth*.

might write, "The weight limit of any vehicle on the roads of the State of Confusion is 10,000 pounds per axle. Section 123, Conf. Mot. Veh. C. (1999)." A student expects that § 123 of the Motor Vehicle Code of the State of Confusion would specify this weight limit.

Similarly, a tribunal frequently draws a rule of law from a case. For example, a tribunal might write, "State laws restricting marriage to persons of opposite sexes are unconstitutional. *Obergefell v. Hodges*, 576 U.S. ___, 135 S.Ct. 2584 (2015)." A student expects that *Obergefell* held that gay marriage is a constitutional right.

Truncated analogies like these must not be taken at face value. The advocate must examine the antecedent (statute or precedent) and the consequent (case at bar) to verify that the implied analogy is sound and that the rationale of the antecedent applies to the consequent.

Analogies arise in two contexts: other persons' arguments that are made to us, and our own arguments that we make to other persons. Truncated analogies can occur in both contexts. In the first context—

- **the advocate must analyze another person's truncated analogy into its components.**

The advocate must make explicit the precedent, the case at bar, and each of their parts. Only then can the advocate evaluate the argument. In the second context—

- **the beginning advocate should never present an argument in the form of a truncated analogy.**

An experienced advocate knows when an analogy may be truncated, but the beginner does not.

### Exercise

4. Analyze the following analogy into its elements.

#### The Case of the Second Bite

Janus, J.

Δ was walking her dog, Brutal, on a leash. Brutal broke free and bit π, who was playing hopscotch on the sidewalk. Brutal had bitten a stranger a month before. Is Δ liable for π's injuries?

The law of this state is that if a dog bites a person and on a subsequent occasion bites another person, the dog's owner is liable for the second bite. This rule was established in *Fershing v. Norlander*, 123 Conf. 456 (1978). In that case, Norlander owned a dog named Terror. In 1975 while Norlander was walking Terror on a leash, the dog broke free and bit Turayhi, who had done nothing to provoke the animal. Six weeks later, again while Norlander was walking Terror, the dog broke free and bit Fershing, who was napping on a bench in the park. The court held that Terror's first bite put Norlander on notice of the beast's tendency to bite and, therefore, Norlander had a duty to control it. Norlander breached this duty and was liable to Fershing for damages. Based on *Fershing*, which is analogous to the case at bar, we hold that Δ is liable in damages to π.

ISSUE

*The issue is*

PRECEDENT

Facts of the precedent

*The facts of the precedent were*

Rationale of the precedent

*The rationale of the precedent was*

Result of the precedent

*The result of the precedent was*

CASE AT BAR

Facts of the case at bar and their similarity to the facts of the precedent

*The facts of the case at bar are similar to the facts of the precedent because*

Argument that the rationale of the precedent applies to the facts of case at bar

*The rationale of the precedent applies to the case at bar because*

CLAIM

*The result of the case at bar should be*

\* \* \*

Because tribunals write their opinions for professionals, the foregoing reasoning is commonly truncated. Thus, Judge Janus might write:

> The defendant is liable to the plaintiff. If a dog bites a person and on a subsequent occasion bites another person, the dog's owner is liable for the second bite because the owner is presumed to know of the dog's propensity to bite. *Fershing v. Norlander*, 123 Conf. 456 (1978).

### Exercise

5. Which elements of a complete legal analogy has the tribunal omitted?

The student is not a judge. Therefore—

- **The beginning student should never truncate an analogy in this way.**

## D. The Uses of Analogies

In daily life, an analogy is often the support for a proposition. For example:

PROPOSITION

I should not eat those Macadamia nuts.

SUPPORT: AN ANALOGY

The last time I ate Macadamia nuts, I broke out in hives.

The same is true of legal argument. An analogy can be used in any of the functions necessary to resolve a dispute.

### 1. Using an Analogy to Identify the Issue

As discussed in § 1 Issues, one identifies an issue by drawing an analogy between the facts of the case at hand and the facts of a precedent. If the facts of the precedent generated a certain issue, the facts of the case at hand generate the same issue. For example—

#### Ford Motor Company v. National Labor Relations Board

For many years, the Ford Motor Company provided food for its workers in cafeterias and vending machines. When the company announced a substantial increase in the prices of food and beverages, the Auto Workers Union asked to bargain over the prices. The company refused, and the union charged the company with violating the duty to bargain in good faith required by § 8(a)(5) of the Labor Act. All parties concerned with this charge—Ford, the Auto Workers, the Labor Board, and the federal courts—knew what the issue in the case was. How did they know?

They knew the issue because they were familiar with the Supreme Court's decision in *National Labor Relations Board v. Wooster Division of Borg-Warner*. In *Borg-Warner*, the employer proposed a clause in the contract providing that the union would not strike unless a majority of workers voted by secret ballot to reject the employer's latest offer. The union objected to the clause, but conceded when the employer insisted that it would not agree to a contract without the clause. Then the union filed an unfair labor practice charge with the Labor Board, accusing the employer of refusing to bargain in good faith because of the employer's insistence on the ballot clause. The Labor Board ruled that a party need not bargain over every topic raised by the other party. Rather, topics are divided into three classes: (1) mandatory subjects, over which a party must bargain if the other party raises them (e.g., wages and hours); (2) permissible subjects, over which a party may either bargain or decline to bargain if the other party raises them (e.g., the company's investment policy); and (3) illegal subjects, which no party may raise in bargaining. Accordingly, the issue in *Borg-Warner* was whether the ballot clause was a mandatory subject of bargaining. If so, the employer lawfully insisted on incorporating it in the contract. If not, the employer violated § 8(a)(5).[5]

In *Ford*, the parties perceived that their case was analogous to *Borg-Warner*. In both, one party asked to bargain over a proposal, and the other party declined. On these facts, *Borg-Warner* held that the controlling issue was whether the proposal in question was a mandatory subject of bargaining. Therefore, the issue was the same in *Ford:* were the prices of food and beverages in Ford's cafeterias and vending machines a mandatory subject?

As the *Ford* case demonstrates, we use analogies to identify the issue in a case.

## 2. Using an Analogy to Find the Facts

Analogies can be used to find facts. Fact finding is beyond the scope of this book, but an illustration from daily life may be useful. Your old dog, Harlequin, has regular habits. She is used to being walked at 7:15 a.m. before you leave for work, and at 5:30 p.m. as soon as you return home. One day an emergency keeps you at work late, and you reach home at 7:00 p.m. As you insert your key in the lock, you look through the glass in the door and see Harlequin urinating on the floor of the entry hall. A few weeks later, you are again detained at work and reach home at 7:30 p.m. When you open the front door, you espy a yellow puddle on the floor of the entry hall. You know exactly what has happened.

---

5. The Board held, and the Supreme Court agreed, that the employer violated the duty to bargain because the ballot clause was a permissible, not a mandatory subject of bargaining.

## 3. Using an Analogy to Identify and Interpret the Governing Rule of Law

Analogies may be used to choose the governing authority and to interpret that authority. For example—

### The Taggers' Cases

A rooky police officer noticed Anderson spray-painting a picture on the wall of city hall. The officer cited Anderson for violating § 98.76 of the municipal code, which prohibits damaging public property. Anderson insisted on a hearing. The officer testified to what she had observed. Anderson admitted it, but argued to the judge, "I didn't damage public property. The building is as sturdy as ever."

Judge Devorah replied, "You are correct. In *Long v. Gone* the court of appeals dismissed a complaint against a tagger for violating § 98.76 because 'damage' in that section means harm to the physical integrity of the building. But you did violate § 54.32 of the code, which prohibits defacing public property—"

Anderson, whose only knowledge of courtroom procedure came from watching *Judge Judy*, interrupted the judge: "I didn't deface that building. I made it more beautiful."

Being in a good mood, the judge ignored Anderson's breach of decorum. "I am inclined to agree with you," said the judge, "but a recent tagging case, *City v. Basquiat,* holds that painting on a public building without permission constitutes defacing. However, you were not cited for violating § 54.32. Case dismissed."

The officer subsequently apprehended Banks in the act of spray-painting a design on the wall of a fire house, and cited Banks for violating § 54.32. The judge found Banks guilty.

Three analogies were used in the *Taggers' Cases*. (1) One issue for the judge was, did § 98.76 govern Anderson's case? The analogy was between *Long v. Gone* and Anderson's case. In both of those cases, a tagger was accused of violating § 98.76. The court of appeals had held in *Long v. Gone* that tagging did not violate this section. Because *Long v. Gone* and Anderson's cases were analogous, the judge knew that § 98.76 did not govern Anderson's case.

(2) Another issue for the judge was, how should § 54.32 be interpreted, specifically, does defacement include tagging? The analogy was between Anderson's case and *City v. Basquiat*. In both cases, a tagger had painted on a public building without permission. *City v. Basquiat* held that painting without permission is defacing. Because Anderson's case and *City v. Basquiat* were analogous, the judge knew that defacement in § 54.32 includes tagging.

(3) An issue for the officer was, did § 54.32 govern Banks's case? The analogy was between Anderson's and Banks's cases. The judge in Anderson's case said that Anderson had violated § 54.32. Because Anderson's and Bank's cases were analogous, the officer identified § 54.32 as the governing rule in Banks's case and cited Banks for violating it.

*4. Using an Analogy to Apply Law to Fact*
Analogies are used to apply law to fact—

### Ford Motor Company v. National Labor Relations Board (continued)

The Board held that the prices of food and beverages in Ford's cafeterias and vending machines were a mandatory subject of bargaining. The Board based its holding in part on analogies to prior cases. For example, *Preston Products Company* had held that improvements in lunchroom equipment and supplies were a mandatory subject, and *Fleming Manufacturing Company* held that provision of free coffee and scheduling of coffee breaks were mandatory subjects. The facts of these cases were analogous to the facts of the *Ford* case in that all affected the material conditions of employment and (as the Supreme Court pointed out when it affirmed the Board's decision) the availability of food during working hours and the conditions under which it is to be consumed are matters of deep concern to workers.

To apply law to fact is to ask, what are the legal consequences of the facts? The Board in *Ford Motor Company* (continued) had found the facts: the company refused to bargain over the prices of food and beverages in its cafeterias and vending machines. The Board had identified the issue as whether these prices were a mandatory subject of bargaining. Then the Board turned to applying law to fact and used an analogy: the prices of food and beverages were analogous to lunchroom equipment and supplies and to free coffee and coffee breaks. Therefore, the prices of food and beverages were a mandatory subject.

## E. Four Criteria for Evaluating Legal Analogies

A sound analogy must satisfy at least four criteria. In other words, an analogy can be rebutted in at least four ways:

> **The precedent must be authoritative.**
> **The precedent and the case at bar must be analogous.**
> **The analogy must be relevant to the issue at hand.**
> **No other analogy may be more convincing.**

### 1. The Precedent Must Be Authoritative; If the Precedent Can Be Vitiated, the Analogy Fails

The precedent must be authoritative, a criterion that divides into three parts. First, the facts and result of the precedent must be stated correctly. Sometimes a party misstates the facts or result of a precedent; more commonly, a party shades the statement so as to give the impression that the precedent is more favorable to oneself than an objective statement would warrant.

Second, the precedent must be interpreted correctly. A precedent can often be interpreted in various ways, and the advocate's task is to convince the tribunal that one's interpretation, and not the interpretation of one's adversary, is correct.

Third, the precedent must have been decided correctly. When a precedent damages one's case and cannot be interpreted away, one may have no choice but to argue that the precedent was mistaken and should not be followed. Given the strength of stare decisis, however, such an argument rarely succeeds.

### 2. The Legally Significant Facts of the Precedent and the Case at Bar Must Be Analogous in the Important Ways; If the Case at Bar Can Be Distinguished from the Precedent (that is, if the legally significant facts of the case at bar and the precedent differ), the Analogy Fails

The second criterion or test of an analogy is that the legally significant facts of the precedent and of the case at bar must be similar. To say the same thing, the second way to rebut an analogy is to demonstrate that the legally significant facts of the precedent differ from the facts of the case at bar. In legal parlance, the precedent is shown to be *distinguishable* from the case at bar. Because some differences of fact are important and some are not, an advocate must state why a difference of fact is important.

Distinctions are a major topic. They are discussed in some detail in § 12 DISTINCTIONS.

### 3. The Analogy Must Be Relevant to the Issue at Hand

An analogy may be convincing for one purpose and irrelevant and misleading for another purpose. For example, a professor once said, "Enrolling in college is like joining a health club. It doesn't mean anything unless you do the work." This analogy is convincing if the issue is whether the college or the student is responsible for the student's education. The argument is that the student will not benefit from enrolling in college unless one attends classes and does the assignments, just as a member of a health club will not benefit from joining it unless one goes to it regularly and works out vigorously.

But suppose the issue is, should the faculty or the students determine the curriculum? The analogy to a health club may seem appealing: as a customer of a health club chooses which equipment to use and which exercises to perform, so a student should choose which courses count toward a degree. But the appeal of this analogy is only superficial, for the issues are different. The issue in the second example is whether students are qualified to determine the body of knowledge necessary to earn a particular degree. The analogy establishes that a student cannot learn without working, but says nothing about whether a student, who by definition lacks knowledge, is qualified to decide what must be learned.

### 4. No Other Analogy May Be More Convincing

Two or more prior cases may resemble the case at bar in some ways and differ from it in other ways. Thus, one's adversary may propose an analogy between the case at bar and case *A*, which leads to a judgment in favor of one's adversary; but an analogy between the case at bar and case *B* may lead to a judgment in one's own favor. In this event, the tribunal must choose as a precedent the prior case that more closely resembles the case at bar. Accordingly, the third criterion or test of an analogy is that no other analogy is a closer fit, and the third way to parry an analogy is to identify a competing prior case, the facts of which are more similar to the facts of the case at bar than are the facts of the precedent suggested by one's adversary.

Competing analogies are common in legal argument. For instance, in § 9 POLICY ARGUMENTS, the student learned that employees are protected by the Labor Act, but independent contractors are not. Thus, employees have the right to form or join a union and bargain collectively with their employer, whereas independent contractors have no right to bargain collectively. Also (though a consequence of the common law, not of the Labor Act), employers are responsible for the job-related conduct of their employees that results in harm to others, such as damage caused by an employee's negligent operation of a motor vehicle, but employers are not responsible for the harm caused by independent contractors.

A number of criteria are used to determine whether a worker is an employee or an independent contractor. In effect, two models exist—one of the ideal employee, the other of the ideal independent contractor. Rarely do the characteristics of any individual worker match all and only the elements of either of these models; typically, a worker has some of the characteristics of each model. Therefore, in each case the issue is whether the worker is more like one model or the other. In effect, the models are competing analogies.

In the case of *Thomas the Mover*, which follows in the text, Thomas is like an employee in some respects (precedent *A*) and like an independent contractor in other respects (precedent *B*). Thus, the question for the tribunal becomes, is Thomas more like an employee or more like an independent contractor?

### *Thomas the Mover*

Thomas owns and maintains his own moving van and purchases its fuel. He works exclusively for Plymouth Movers, which advertises and secures customers for him. He does not have a regular work schedule; when Plymouth has a job, it calls Thomas (or another driver), who is free to decline the assignment. If Thomas accepts an assignment, Plymouth contacts the customer and arranges the dates on which Thomas will pick up and deliver the load.

Thomas hires day laborers to help him load and unload his van. Plymouth does not supervise Thomas as he picks up and delivers the load, nor does Plymouth specify the route Thomas must follow as he drives between cities. Plymouth insures the load; Thomas insures his van. Plymouth inspects Thomas's van monthly and specifies what Thomas may and may not carry in the van. Thomas wears a uniform supplied by Plymouth, and "Plymouth Movers" is painted on the van. Plymouth pays Thomas by the job, does not remit payroll taxes on his work, and does not withhold income taxes from his check.

Unfortunately, as Thomas is delivering a load, his van negligently collides with a wayward dirigible, and a lawsuit results. An issue is whether Thomas is an employee of Plymouth Movers, in which event Plymouth would be liable, or whether he is an independent contractor, in which event he, but not Plymouth, would be liable.

In some regards, Thomas is like an employee: Employees usually work for one company. Employees wear uniforms supplied by their companies. Companies put their names on their motor vehicles. Companies advertise for and secure customers and arrange when employees will perform services for customers. Companies inspect their employees' equipment, specify how that equipment may be used, and insure products that employees handle.

In other regards, Thomas is like an independent contractor: He owns, maintains, and insures his own van and purchases its fuel. He does not have a regular work schedule, and he is free to decline an assignment. The company does not supervise him as he picks up and delivers a load. He chooses the route he will follow between cities, and he employs workers to help him load and unload his van. The company pays him by the job, not by wages or salary, does not remit payroll taxes, and does not withhold income taxes.

Is Thomas an employee or an independent contractor? The answer depends on which is the better analogy to his case.

An advocate who uses an analogy as part of an argument would not explicitly evaluate the analogy in one's argument. Presumably, the advocate has evaluated the analogy before using it. The advocate's adversary, however, must always evaluate an advocate's analogy and criticize it using one or more of the criteria above.

## III. Review

### *The Fine Print Cases*

The case of *Daniel v. Drop-Your-Call* arose in the State of Grace. The facts were that Daniel had a telephone that he used for both business and personal calls. He decided for tax reasons to use that telephone only for business and to obtain another telephone that he would use only for personal matters. For his personal calls, he signed a two-year contract with Drop-Your-Call Cell Phone, Ltd. The contract contained several pages of legalese in fine print. Clause *Z* of the contract provided that any disputes between the parties would be governed by the law of the State of Decay. Drop-Your-Call dropped so many of Daniel's calls in the first month that he felt its service was worthless, and he wrote to the company cancelling his contract. When the company did not reply to this (and several subsequent) letters, Daniel sued in the State of Grace. But the company invoked clause *Z* and argued that the law of the State of Decay law governed the case. The case was assigned to Judge Devorah.

The law of the State of Grace provides that a party to a contract of at least one year's duration may cancel the contract if the other party provides unreasonably poor service. The law of the State of Decay provides that a party may not cancel a contract for poor service, but instead may sue the other party for damages for any economic loss caused by the poor service. Consequently, if Judge Devorah applied the law of the State of Grace (and if Drop-Your-Call's service was unreasonably poor), Daniel would not owe the company any further monthly fees; if the judge applied the law of the State of Decay, Daniel could not cancel the contract, would owe all monthly fees, and could not collect damages for economic loss because he used the telephone only for personal matters.

It is generally lawful for parties to a contract in one state to specify that the laws of another state or nation will govern their contract. Under this principle, Daniel's contract with Drop-Your-Call would be governed by the law of the State of Decay, and Daniel would lose his case. He had one hope, however. He believed that clause *Z* was unintelligible to an ordinary person and, therefore, it should be void. The State of Grace had neither statute nor precedent on whether a clause in a contract could be voided because an ordinary person could not understand the clause, and

Judge Devorah asked the parties to present arguments on the issue. Daniel's attorney cited the case of *David v. Goliath* in the State of Elah. In that case, the lease between Goliath Rentals and David, a tenant, consisted of twenty-three pages of lawyer speak. In particular, a clause on page 5 defined "to live" to mean "to sleep in the apartment." A clause on page 12 prohibited anyone other than the tenant from living in the apartment. A clause on page 22 provided that the monthly rent would double for the remainder of the lease if a person in addition the tenant lived in the apartment. David had a party one night in February; several friends attended. A blizzard struck, and the police closed the roads and advised people to stay indoors. David's guests spent the night in his apartment and departed the next day. When David went to pay his rent the next month, Goliath rejected his check, demanding double the normal rent. David refused to pay, and he and Goliath sued each other. The court held in favor of David on the principle that a consumer is not bound by fine print that no person of ordinary intelligence and education could understand.

Drop-Your-Call's attorney replied that the courts of the State of Grace should not adopt a new principle like Elah's, but should leave it to the legislature to change the law; also that it would be a bad law because an adult should be held responsible for the contracts one signs and, if one does not understand the contract, one should either not sign it or get legal advice.

Judge Devorah decided to follow the rule of *David v. Goliath*. The issue then became, could an ordinary person understand clause $Z$? This was an issue of application of law to fact, and both parties invoked precedents. Daniel cited *Far v. Away*, in which Doris had obtained a credit card from Usurious Bank of the South Seas. A dispute arose between Doris and the bank. Clause $Y$ of the application that Doris had signed for the credit card was similar to clause $Z$ of Daniel's contract, and on that basis the bank asserted that the dispute was governed by the laws of the State of Decay. The court ruled that Doris was not bound by clause $Y$ because a person of ordinary education and intelligence could not understand the clause. Given that clause $Y$ of Doris's contract and clause $Z$ of Daniel's contract were similar, Daniel urged Judge Devorah to follow the precedent of *Far v. Away* and hold that clause $Z$ was invalid because it could not be understood by an ordinary person.

In response, Drop-Your-Call cited *Over v. Out*, in which clause $X$ of the contract between the Cable Television Company and the Nightly News

Network was similar to clause Z of Daniel's contract. The court ruled that the clause was not beyond the ken of the parties to the transaction, and so the case was governed by the laws of the State of Decay. Drop-Your-Call urged the court to follow the precedent of *Over v. Out* and hold that Daniel could understand clause Z and, therefore, that the dispute between Drop-Your-Call and Daniel was governed by the laws of the State of Decay.

Judge Devorah discounted the holding of *Over v. Out* because the contract was between large businesses that were advised by legal counsel. The court followed the holding of *Far v. Away* because the contract was between a large business and an individual consumer, as was the contract in the case at bar. Accordingly, the court held that clause Z could not be understood by an ordinary person and released Daniel from his contract with Drop-Your-Call.

## Questions

6  (a) Analyze each analogy in the *Fine Print Cases* into its elements; if an element is omitted, so indicate and supply it.
   (b) Categorize the issue by function.
   (c) State the use to which each analogy is put.
   (d) Evaluate each analogy.

## IV. References

*Church of the Holy Trinity v. United States*, 143 U.S. 457 (1892).

*Fleming Manufacturing Company*, 119 NLRB 452 (1957).

*Ford Motor Company*, 230 NLRB 716 (1977), affirmed *Ford Motor Company v. National Labor Relations Board*, 441 U.S. 488 (1979).

*Hollingsworth v. Perry*, 570 U.S. ___, 133 S.Ct. 2652 (2013).

Marcus Tullius Cicero, *De Inventione* 1.51–52, cited in *How to Win an Argument* (James M. May trans. (Princeton University Press, 2016).

*National Labor Relations Board v. Wooster Division of Borg-Warner Corp.*, 356 U.S. 342 (1958).

*Obergefell v. Hodges*, 576 U.S. ___, 135 S.Ct. 2584 (2015).

*Preston Products Company*, 158 NLRB 322 (1966).

## § 12

# DISTINCTIONS: DISTINGUISHING
# PRECEDENTS, DISANALOGIES,
# AND PRECEDENTS AND LEVELS
# OF ABSTRACTION

One of the three criteria for evaluating analogies is whether the facts of the antecedent and the consequent are analogous or distinguishable. This section discusses distinctions in some detail and relates them to the level of abstraction at which an issue is resolved, and also discusses disanalogies.

*B* distinguishes a precedent in order to undermine *A*'s analogy. Thus, *A* has argued (or is likely to argue) that the case at bar and a precedent are analogous and, therefore, should be decided similarly. *B* can refute this argument by identifying a significant difference between the case at bar and the precedent, in other words, by distinguishing them.

We often distinguish precedents in daily life. Here is an example from a film:

### The Musician's Case

A young musician needed money to make a demonstration record-ing for his band. His friend offered to give him the money, but the musician refused it because his friend had acquired it dishonestly. The friend said:

"When Jesus healed the blind man, did the blind man ask where the mercy came from?"

The musician replied:

"You're not Jesus, and I'm not blind."

Here is our analysis of the *Musician's Case*.

### The Fiend Draws an Analogy

In the friend's analogy, he was like Jesus and the musician was like the blind man. The analogy implied this argument: "You need money, and I can give it to you. The blind man needed vision, and Jesus gave it to him. The blind man didn't question Jesus's gift, and you shouldn't question mine. So take the money."

The friend's analogy had two parts. One part operated on the level of abstraction at which all needs are the same: the musician needed money, and the blind man needed vision. The other part operated on the level of abstraction at which all gifts are the same: the friend had the power to give money, and Jesus had the power to give vision.

### The Musician Distinguishes the Precedent

The musician distinguished both parts of the analogy. One part was that all gifts were the same. When the musician said, "You're not Jesus . . . ," the musician made the point that his friend's gift would be tainted because the friend had acquired the money dishonestly, whereas Jesus's gift was pure because the power of healing is an attribute of divinity. Thus, the musician took the analogy to a lower level of abstraction. Instead of the level on which all gifts are the same, the musician thought about the issue on the lower level on which an additional fact was significant, namely, the legitimacy of the gift. On this level, a gift of tainted money is not the same as a gift of divine grace.

The other part of the analogy was that all needs were the same. When the musician said, ". . . and I'm not blind," he made the point that his need for money was less compelling than the blind man's need for vision. Once again, he took the analogy to a lower level of abstraction. Instead of the level on which all needs are the same, the musician preferred to decide the issue on the lower level of abstraction on which an additional fact was significant, namely, the degree of need. On this level, the blind man's need for vision was more compelling than the musician's need for money to make a record.

## I. The Elements of a Distinction

The elements of a distinction are—

### The Other Party's Analogy

Issue
Precedent
    Facts of the precedent
    Rationale of the precedent
    Result of the precedent
Case at bar
    Facts of the case at bar and their similarity to the facts of the precedent
    Argument that the rationale of the precedent applies to the facts of the case at bar
Claim

### The Distinction

**Difference(s) of fact between the precedent and the case at bar**
**Importance of the difference(s) of fact**
**Conclusion**

The student may be wondering why the analogy is included as a part of the distinction. After all, they are offered by different parties and for different purposes in a case. We include the analogy for two reasons, one theoretical and one practical. The theoretical reason is that a distinction is meaningful only in light of the analogy, which the distinction attacks. It follows that the analogy is, by implication, a part of the distinction. The practical reason is that a distinction will fail unless it is aimed precisely at the analogy. Accordingly, it is wise for the beginning student to analyze the analogy into its elements before distinguishing the precedent. Including the analogy as a part of the distinction will help the student to keep this advice in mind.

In practice, an advocate who includes a distinction in a *brief,* which is meant to persuade a tribunal, would not state the analogy in detail. Rather than reinforcing the analogy in the tribunal's mind, the advocate would mention only enough about the analogy—indeed, might mention nothing more than the name of the precedent being distinguished—in order to refresh the tribunal's recollection so that the distinction could take effect. By contrast to the advocate, one who is writing a *memorandum,* which is meant to identify the issues in a dispute and evaluate the arguments in an evenhanded way before reaching a conclusion, would state the analogy fully before drawing any distinctions (or would refer to another place in the memorandum where the analogy is stated fully).

The elements of the analogy were discussed in § 11 Analogies. Here follows a discussion of distinctions.

## A. Difference(s) of Fact between the Precedent and the Case at Bar

*A distinction rests on facts.* A distinction must state a difference (or several differences) of fact between the antecedent (precedent) and the consequent (case at bar). This point is clear if one considers a situation in which two cases have analogous facts, but different outcomes. These cases cannot be distinguished; they are simply inconsistent.

## B. The Importance of the Difference(s) of Fact

### 1. Some Differences Do Not Matter

Some differences of fact are not important and may not serve to distinguish an antecedent from a consequent. This assertion is obviously true in a trivial way. All cases differ from one another in regard to time (they happened at different times) and most differ in regard to place and person (they happened in different places and involved different persons), yet such differences must be ignored—else analogies would not exist.

The assertion is true in a significant way as well. An analogy is a simplified comparison of situations. It must be simplified because, if an advocate had to state and compare every knowable fact of two situations, analogies would be impractical if not impossible. An analogy invariably assumes that a few facts (and sometimes only one fact) of the antecedent and the consequent are similar, and the rest may be disregarded. If the captain in the *Captain's Analogy* wore a navy blue uniform, does it matter that the general wore an olive green uniform? If the employer in a precedent had red hair, does it matter that the employer in the case at bar has blond hair? A distinction that rests on unimportant facts like these is, as lawyers like to say, a distinction without a difference.

Another way to express this idea is that an analogy is an abstracted comparison of events. To say that some facts are important, and some are not, is to say that an analogy operates at a certain level of abstraction (usually a fairly high level when one takes into account all of the ways in which situations can differ). A distinction drawn at a lower level of abstraction would rest on facts that are considered unimportant.

For example, suppose the General Counsel of the Labor Board accuses Seth of an unfair labor practice. The General Counsel draws an analogy (relies on a precedent), and Seth seeks to distinguish it—

### Seth's Case:
### An Unsuccessful Distinction

Roger, an employee of Ariana & Co., became dissatisfied with his wages and began talking to his coworkers about unionizing. Ariana got wind of Roger's conversations and wanted to know which of her workers supported unionizing. She paid another worker, Kristen, to spy on Roger and report what he said, to whom he said it, and what the other workers said. The Labor Board held in *Ariana's Case* that she had engaged in surveillance of Roger and other workers in violation of § 8(a)(1) of the Labor Act, which prohibits an employer from interfering with or coercing workers as they engage in concerted activity. The Board reasoned that spying on workers makes them fearful of retaliation and, therefore, reluctant to exercise their rights under the Act.

Jamila, an employee of Seth & Sons, became dissatisfied with her work schedule and began talking to her coworkers about unionizing. Seth wanted to know which of his workers supported unionizing and promised another employee, Victor, to hire his sister if he would "keep an eye" on

Jamila and report what she and the other workers said. The General Counsel filed a complaint against Seth and relied on the precedent of *Ariana's Case*. Seth sought to distinguish his case from *Ariana's Case* on the grounds that Roger was concerned about his wages whereas Jamila was concerned about her work schedule, and that Kirsten received money to spy whereas Victor himself received nothing.

Here is an analysis of *Seth's Case*.

## The General Counsel's Analogy

PRECEDENT (*Ariana's Case*)

Facts

> Roger was an employee of Ariana & Co. He became dissatisfied with his wages and began talking to his coworkers about affiliating with a labor union. Ariana wanted to know which of her employees supported unionizing, and so she paid another employee, Kristen, to spy on Roger and report what he and the other workers said.

Rationale of the precedent

> Spying on workers makes them fearful of retaliation and, therefore, discourages them from exercising their rights under § 7 of the Labor Act to form, join, and assist labor unions.

Result of the precedent

> Ariana engaged in surveillance of Roger and other workers, which was an unfair labor practice under § 8(a)(1) of the Labor Act.

CASE AT BAR (*Seth's Case*)

Facts of the case at bar and their similarity to the facts of the precedent

> Jamila was an employee of Seth & Sons. She began talking to her coworkers about affiliating with a labor union. Seth wanted to know which of his employees supported unionizing, and so

he promised to Victor to hire his sister if Victor would report what Jamila and the other workers said. *Seth's Case* is like *Ariana's Case* because in both cases the employers used workers to spy on other workers in order to learn which of them supported unionization.

Argument that the rationale of the precedent applies to the facts of the case at bar

Seth's spying on his workers would reasonably make them fearful of retaliation and, therefore, discourage them from exercising their rights.

Conclusion

Seth violated § 8(a)(1).


### Seth's Unsuccessful Distinction

DISTINCTION

Difference(s) of fact between the precedent and the case at bar

*Seth's Case* differs from *Ariana's Case* because Roger was concerned about wages whereas Jamila was concerned about the work schedule, and Kristen received money whereas Victor himself received nothing.

Importance of the difference(s) of fact

Not stated.

Conclusion

Therefore, *Ariana's Case* does not establish that Seth violated the Labor Act.


Seth's attempt to distinguish the cases fails. Although we cannot deny that the facts of the precedent and of the case at bar differ, the differences are plainly unimportant. Seth has not given (and probably cannot give) a good reason why the issues that motivated the workers, or the nature of the compensation given to the spies, should justify ignoring the precedent in *Ariana's Case*.

### 2. Merely Identifying Difference(s) of Fact Does Not Distinguish a Precedent from a Case at Bar: The Importance of the Difference(s) of Fact Must Be Explained

A successful distinction includes *both* a difference of fact *and* an explanation of why the difference matters. Often the importance of a difference of fact seems so obvious that the advocate omits the explanation; however,

- **one must always include an explanation of why a difference of fact matters.**

Here is a simple example:

#### A Brick and a Rose Petal

π sues Δ for damages, claiming that Δ dropped an object from the second story of a building and the object struck π on the head. As a precedent, π cites the case of *Down v. Out*, in which the defendant dropped a stone on the plaintiff's head and the court ruled that the defendant was liable to the plaintiff for damages. Δ attempts to distinguish π's precedent: "*Down v. Out* is distinguishable from the case at bar because I did not drop a stone on π's head."

This argument gets Δ exactly nowhere. He has not even identified difference(s) of fact between the precedent and the case at bar. Suppose he adds:

I dropped a brick, not a stone.

It is obvious that this distinction will not help his case because the difference is not important. If he had attempted to explain the "distinction," he would have known at once that a brick can cause as much injury as a stone.

Now suppose Δ dropped a rose petal instead of a brick. He might say:

I dropped a rose petal, not a brick.

In this event, he has drawn a distinction, but he has relied on the audient to supply the explanation of why the difference(s) of fact should matter. Far better for Δ to say:

> As we all know, some falling objects are not harmful. A significant part of π's case depends on precisely what was dropped. If someone drops a marshmallow on your head, you are not hurt and you have no case. π cites *Down v. Out*, in which the defendant dropped a stone. If I had dropped a stone, *Down v. Out* would establish my liability. But I did not drop a stone. I dropped a rose petal. The difference between a stone and a rose petal is important because a stone can do serious damage to a person's head; a rose petal, like a marshmallow, cannot do any damage at all.

Now consider this more complicated example:

### Daniela's Case:
### A Successful Distinction

Joshua filed a charge of unfair labor practice against Daniela for unlawfully spying on her workers. The facts were that Joshua was an employee of Daniela & Daughters. He became dissatisfied with his wages and began talking to his coworkers about affiliating with a labor union. After a few weeks, he scheduled a meeting with Daniela. He was accompanied to the meeting by Andrew, the business agent of Local No. 39 of the Chattelers, Tattlers, and Dawdlers of the World. Andrew presented Daniela with a list of fifteen of her employees and said, "All the workers on this list want to be represented by Local 1. Fifteen is a majority of your employees, and I hereby demand that you recognize and bargain with Local 1 on their behalf." Daniela looked at the list and returned it to Andrew, saying, "I will not recognize Local 1. You could have put any names you like on this list. I demand an NLRB election."

The General Counsel investigated and, relying on the precedent of *Ariana's Case*, filed a complaint against Daniela. Daniela sought to distinguish the case at bar from *Ariana's Case* by pointing out that Ariana had learned which of her workers supported unionizing by spying on them, whereas Daniela learned who supported the union when the union's business agent gave her a list of union supporters and demanded recognition.

Daniela argued that her workers wanted her to know that they supported the union because their support was the basis of the union's demand for recognition; thus, the workers had no reason to fear retaliation from her. Also, spying is an illegal way to gather information about workers, but receiving information from a union's business agent is not illegal.

Here is an analysis of *Daniela's Case*:

## The General Counsel's Analogy

PRECEDENT (*Ariana's Case*)

CASE AT BAR

### Facts

Roger was an employee of Ariana & Co. He became dissatisfied with his wages and began talking to his coworkers about affiliating with a labor union. Ariana wanted to know which of her employees supported unionizing, and so she paid another employee, Kristen, to spy on Roger and report what he and the other workers said.

### Rationale of the precedent

Spying on workers makes them fearful of retaliation and, therefore, discourages them from exercising their rights under § 7 of the Labor Act to form, join, and assist labor unions.

### Result of the precedent

Ariana engaged in surveillance of Roger and other workers, which was an unfair labor practice under § 8(a)(1) of the Labor Act.

CASE AT BAR (*Daniela's Case*)

### Facts of the case at bar and their similarity to the facts of the precedent

Andrew, the business agent of a union, gave Daniela, an employer, a list containing the names of the majority of her employees, and demanded that she recognize and bargain with the union. Daniela looked at the list, rejected Andrew's demand, and insisted on an NLRB election. *Daniela's Case* is like *Ariana's Case* because in both cases the employers learned which workers supported unionization.

Argument that the rationale of the precedent applies to the case at bar

When an employer learns which workers support unionization, the workers reasonably fear retaliation for concerted activity.

Conclusion

Daniela violated § 8(a)(1).

Then Daniela distinguished her case from *Ariana's Case*:

### *Daniela's Successful Distinction*

DISTINCTION

Difference(s) of fact between the precedent and the case at bar

Daniela conceded that, in both cases, the employers learned which workers were supporting unionization. But she argued that her case differed from *Ariana's Case* because Ariana learned who supported unionization by spying on her workers, whereas Daniela learned who supported unionization when the union's business agent gave her a list of supporters and demanded recognition.

Importance of the difference(s) of fact

Learning who supports a union by spying differs from learning who supports a union from its business agent because, in the latter case, the workers will not fear retaliation. Instead, they want the employer to know of their support so the employer will recognize the union. Also, spying on workers is an illegal way to gather information, whereas receiving information from the union's business agent is not illegal.

Conclusion

*Ariana's Case* does not establish that Daniela violated the Labor Act.

Daniela falsified the analogy; she distinguished her case from *Ariana's Case*. She did this by (1) pointing out a factual difference between the precedent and the case at bar *and* (2) presenting a good argument that the difference of fact was significant.

The need to state the importance of the difference of fact between the precedent and the case at bar cannot be overemphasized. The importance may seem so obvious that one is tempted not to mention it, and advocates often do fail to give reasons why the difference is important. Nevertheless, *the best practice is always to indicate why a distinction matters.*

Two of the elements of a distinction have now been considered: a difference of fact that matters, and an explanation of why the difference is important. The following case illustrates both of these elements and leads us to a definition of "distinction."

### Seymour's Case

Esme, aged twelve years, was a girl of normal intelligence and average experience for her age. She was bequeathed $1,000,000 by the old man who had lived across the street, and the next day she signed a contract to purchase a 1960 Volvo from Shady Sam's Pre-Owned Cars for $8,000. Her parents learned of the contract that afternoon and at once sent Sam a registered letter, which was delivered the next day. It said that the contract was void and Esme would not honor it. Shady Sam sued, and in *Shady Sam v. Esme* Judge Janus held that the contract was not enforceable against Esme.

Subsequently, in the same jurisdiction, Seymour, aged eleven years, signed a contract to purchase a 1963 Corvette from Hard Luck Hank's Good-as-New Vehicles for $25,000. Seymour was a boy of high intelligence. He had been trading stocks profitably via the internet for three years, and he had just earned $2,000,000 by anticipating that Microsoft would declare a huge dividend. Seymour rode his scooter home and told his mother about the car. A little later Hank was offered $100,000 for the same car by a person who knew (what neither Hank nor Seymour knew) that this car had been owned by Elvis. Hank immediately telephoned Seymour's home. Seymour's mother answered. Hank said he had just realized that "little Seymour" was too young to sign a contract and, therefore, it was void. Seymour's mother, a sports car buff, immediately drove to Hank's car lot and inspected the

Corvette. She did not know it had belonged to Elvis, but she decided that it was worth $25,000. Thinking to herself that Seymour could use the car only if she drove it, which she would enjoy, she told Hank that she expected him to honor the contract. When he refused, she sued him on behalf of Seymour. The case is now before Judge Devorah of the State of Confusion, who has to decide whether *Esme's Case* is a precedent for Seymour's.

Regrettably for judges and scrupulous attorneys, precedents and cases at hand are never exactly identical. As we noted above, different parties are involved and the events occurred at different times and places. Therefore, an advocate can always argue that the case at hand is distinguishable from an earlier case in some regard.

Judge Devorah notices that the facts of *Seymour's Case* differ from the facts of *Esme's Case* in several regards:

- Esme was twelve years old, whereas Seymour was eleven years old.
- Esme inherited her money, whereas Seymour earned his.
- Esme had $1,000,000, whereas Seymour had $2,000,000.
- Esme bought a Volvo, whereas Seymour bought a Corvette.
- Esme agreed to pay $8,000 for her car, whereas Seymour agreed to pay $25,000.
- Esme's parents notified Shady Sam by registered letter, whereas Seymour's mother spoke to Hard Luck Hank in person.
- Shady Sam learned that Esme would not honor the contract the day after it was signed, whereas Hank learned that Seymour's mother intended to enforce the contract on the same day it was signed.
- Esme had normal intelligence, whereas Seymour had superior intelligence.
- Esme had no business experience, whereas Seymour had substantial business experience.

Should any of these differences matter to the judge? Some obviously do not; they are not legally significant. It is not significant that Esme was a girl and Seymour was a boy. It is also not significant that Esme had $1,000,000 whereas Seymour had $2,000,000, that Esme's parents notified Shady Sam by registered letter whereas Seymour's mother spoke to Hard Luck Hank in person, or that Esme's dream was a Volvo whereas

Seymour's was a Corvette.[1] But other distinctions between the cases might well be legally significant. For example, Esme had normal intelligence, whereas Seymour was exceptionally bright. Esme had no business experience whereas Seymour had ample business experience.

Hard Luck Hank wants to escape the contract with Seymour, and his lawyer argues to the judge that *Esme's Case* is the controlling precedent:

> In *Esme's Case*, a contract between a twelve-year-old and an adult was void. In the case at bar, the contract was between an eleven-year-old and an adult. A fortiori, Seymour's contract with Hank is void.[2]

Seymour's lawyer now seeks to distinguish *Esme's Case*. Notice how the lawyer explains the significance of the difference(s) of fact between the cases:

> *Esme's Case* must be distinguished from *Seymour's Case* because in *Esme's Case* the adult sought to enforce the contract against the minor, whereas in *Seymour's Case* the minor is trying to enforce the contract against the adult. This difference matters a great deal. In general, minors are not required to keep their promises to adults because minors do not have sufficient maturity and experience to realize what they are doing; an adult who tries to enforce a contract against a minor is taking advantage of the minor's youth. But adults should be required to keep their promises to minors. An adult has no more excuse for backing out of a contract with a minor than for backing out of a contract with another adult.

The definition of the term "distinction" can now be stated.

- **A distinction is a difference in facts between an earlier case and the case at bar *plus* an explanation of why those facts are legally significant.**

---

1. These facts might be legally significant in other contexts. The children's sexes might matter, for example, when they are assigned roommates in college.

2. "A fortiori" means "by even greater force" or "all the more so." An argument a fortiori takes the form, "If proposition $p$ is true of Case 1, $p$ is even more certainly true of Case 2." For example: If two inches of rain in a day will cause a flood in this valley, a fortiori three inches in a day will cause a flood.

## C. The Conclusion

Distinguishing a precedent leads to the conclusion that the precedent is irrelevant to the case at bar. *No other conclusion is appropriate.*

Nevertheless, one sometimes encounters the conclusion of a distinction in which the advocate argues that, because the precedent is distinguishable, the result of the case at bar should be the opposite of the result of the precedent. Let us analyze this argument.

MAJOR PREMISE

> If a prior case t is analogous to the case at bar, the outcome of the case at bar must be the same as the outcome of the prior case.

MINOR PREMISE

> Prior case $X$ is not analogous to (is distinguishable from) case at bar.

CONCLUSION

> The outcome of the case at bar must not be the same as the outcome of prior case $X$.

Expressed in symbols, the argument takes this form:

If $p$, then $q$.
Not $p$.
∴ Not $q$.

As the student will recall from § 4 DEDUCTION, this argument commits the logical fallacy of denying the antecedent.

Two lines of commonsense reasoning lead to the same conclusion. First, consider the extreme case: the prior case and the case at bar have absolutely nothing in common. Thus, the prior case is easily distinguished from the case at bar. Is there any reason that the outcome of the case at bar should be influenced in any way by the outcome of the prior case? Second, distinguishing a case simply takes it out of the picture. The case is irrelevant. We must ignore it. But ignoring something is not the same thing as doing the opposite of it. Your mother may advise you not to hang out with Bianca because she will lead you astray. You may reject your mother's argument because you are not afraid that Bianca will lead you astray. Nonetheless, you may decide not to hang out with her for some other reason, for example, that you dislike her tattoos.

To express the idea in more legal terms, a distinction merely demonstrates that a prior case does not control the case at bar. Yet it remains possible that a legitimate precedent for the case at bar does exist and that the outcomes of this precedent and of the distinguished case—and therefore the outcome of the case at bar as well—happen to be the same. Accordingly, the student must bear in mind the principle that

- **distinguishing a precedent demonstrates that it does not control the case at bar—and nothing more.**

## II. The Uses of Distinctions

What the student has just learned about distinctions—that distinguishing a precedent merely negates its effect on the case at bar—is a matter of *substantive* law. A prior case that has been distinguished has no force. The parable of Jesus and the blind man did not control the outcome for the musician who needed money. *Seth's Case* did not dictate how *Daniela's Case* should be decided. *Esme's Case* did not resolve *Seymour's Case*.

But for *procedural* reasons, distinguishing a precedent can have a significant effect on the case at bar. Consider the most common form of litigation: the plaintiff accuses the defendant of having broken the law. Within this context, in lawsuits arising in the common law countries (England and its former colonies) and in Western Europe, the initial presumption is liberty: an individual may do whatever one wants unless a law prohibits it. Therefore, when a plaintiff sues a defendant for having performed a certain act, the initial presumption is that the defendant was free to perform that act; and the burden is on the plaintiff to convince the tribunal that the law prohibited the defendant's act.[3] If the plaintiff does not carry this burden—if the plaintiff does not convince the tribunal that a law prohibited the defendant's act—the defendant wins the case.

---

3. Liberty also implies that an individual may do nothing at all unless the law requires a certain act. Sometimes a plaintiff sues a defendant for having failed to perform a certain act. The discussion in the following text applies to this situation mutatis mutandis.

In trying to carry this burden, a plaintiff may cite a precedent. The idea is that the act of the defendant in the case at bar is analogous to the act of the defendant in the precedent; the precedent held that act was illegal and, therefore, the same result should obtain in the case at bar. If the plaintiff's analogy is plausible, the defendant may attempt to distinguish the precedent, that is, identify a difference of fact and argue that the difference is legally significant. If the distinction is successful, the precedent effectively disappears from the case. Without the precedent, no law says that the defendant's act was illegal. Thus, because of the initial presumption of liberty, when the defendant successfully distinguishes a precedent on which the plaintiff relies, the defendant has implicitly given the tribunal a reason why the defendant should win the case.[4]

For example, recall *Daniela's Case*, in which the business agent of Local 1 demanded that Daniela recognize and bargain with the union. In support of the demand, the business agent presented Daniela with a list of workers who supported the union. She looked at the list, then refused to accede to the union's demand. The General Counsel filed an unfair labor practice complaint against Daniela. The complaint alleged that Daniela's looking at the list of union supporters was tantamount to surveillance because she learned who supported the union and could retaliate against them. The General Counsel relied on the precedent of *Ariana's Case*, in which Ariana committed an unfair labor practice by paying a worker to spy on another worker who was organizing support for a union. Daniela distinguished *Ariana's Case* by pointing out that, whereas Ariana was actively spying on the workers, Daniela merely read a list which the union's business agent handed to her; and that, whereas in *Ariana's Case* the workers who supported unionization had reason to fear retaliation if their employer learned their names, the workers in *Daniela's Case*, via the union's business agent, deliberately informed their employer of their names in support of their demand for recognition of the union. This distinction was successful, and the precedent on which the General Counsel relied disappeared from the case. There being no other legal support for the complaint, Daniela won the case.

---

4. This reasoning does not mean that the defendant automatically wins the case, but rather that the burden is back on the plaintiff to demonstrate that the defendant's act was illegal. The plaintiff might advance another argument to convince the tribunal that the defendant broke the law; for example, the plaintiff might rely on another precedent, or argue that a new precedent should be set.

Now let us reverse the roles of the parties regarding the precedent: the defendant relies on the precedent, and the plaintiff seeks to distinguish it. Commonly, the plaintiff presents a plausible argument that the defendant has broken the law.[5] As we have just seen, it is now the defendant's task to offer evidence and argument that the act was lawful. Toward this end, suppose the defendant invokes a precedent which held that act $\alpha$ is an exception to the law on which the plaintiff relies. The idea is that the act of the defendant in the case at bar is analogous to act $\alpha$ of the defendant in the precedent; the precedent held that act $\alpha$ was lawful and, therefore, the act of the defendant in the case at bar was also lawful. If the defendant's analogy is plausible, the plaintiff would have to distinguish the precedent or lose the case.[6]

Suppose now that the plaintiff successfully distinguishes the defendant's precedent, in other words, points out a difference of fact and convincingly argues that the difference is important. In this event, the precedent disappears from the case. Because the precedent created an exception for the defendant's act, the exception also disappears from the case. Due to the structure of a lawsuit, the result is that the plaintiff has implicitly given the tribunal a reason why the plaintiff should win the case.[7]

For example, in *Seymour's Case* the defendant, Hard Luck Hank, relied on the precedent in *Esme's Case*, which held that the contract to purchase a 1960 Volvo for $8,000 was unenforceable because Esme was a minor. Hank argued his contract with Seymour was also unenforceable because Seymour was a minor. Seymour sought to distinguish *Esme's Case* on the grounds that, whereas in *Esme's Case* an adult had sought to enforce a contract against a minor, in his case the minor sought to enforce the contract against an adult; that whereas Esme was inexperienced in business, Seymour had substantial business experience; and so forth. The distinction was successful, and the precedent disappeared from the case. The

---

5. For example, the plaintiff might argue that a statute outlaws the defendant's act. The precise nature of the plaintiff's argument is unimportant for the present purpose.

6. This example assumes that the plaintiff presents only one line of argument. Often a plaintiff presents two or more lines of argument showing the defendant's act was illegal. If the defendant vitiates one of these lines of argument with a successful precedent, the plaintiff could still win the case on the basis of another line of argument.

7. This reasoning does not mean that the plaintiff automatically wins the case. The defendant might use some other type of argument to convince the tribunal that the law was not broken. For example, the defendant might rely on another precedent or argue that a new exception should be recognized.

general rule is that contracts are enforceable. Hank tried to escape the rule via the exception for minors in *Esme's Case*. When Seymour distinguished *Esme's Case*, Hank could no longer rely on the exception. Unless he had another arrow in his quiver, he would lose the case.

## III. Disanalogies

An advocate typically draws a distinction in response to a precedent invoked by one's adversary. Sometimes, however, an advocate distinguishes a precedent that one's adversary has *not* invoked; this sort of distinction, which may be called a **disanalogy**, is a preemptive strike. Why would an advocate essay a disanalogy? Does it not call attention to an argument that one's adversary might never advance—and that might backfire if the tribunal finds the disanalogy unconvincing? A few reasons for using a disanalogy may be suggested. First, if the precedent is obvious, a disanalogy may defuse its force; rebutting an argument before the other side states it may weaken its effect. Second, if the disanalogy is presented forcibly, the other side may decide not to mention the precedent at all. Third, a disanalogy may have an emotional effect separate from its logical force. Suppose a defendant is accused of act *A*, which (if she did it) is undoubtedly illegal. Her advocate may attempt to cast her in a good light by arguing that she did not perform acts *B* or *C* or *D*, which happen to be more reprehensible than *A*, and thereby cast her in a good light. Finally, although tribunals in their opinions often use arguments advanced by the parties, tribunals also create their own arguments. When a tribunal creates its own argument, the party against whom it is directed usually has no chance to reply to the argument. Arguments created by tribunals are generally sound, but occasionally a tribunal's argument may be fallacious, or a convincing counterargument may exist that did not occur to the tribunal. Thus an argument created by a tribunal can tip the balance in a case that would have gone the other way if the tribunal had been aware of the counterargument. A disanalogy is a way of reducing this hazard.

It is usually a mistake to attempt to evaluate or rebut an adversary's disanalogy (unless it is misleading). To do so is to allow the adversary to fight the battle on favorable terrain, that is, to focus the argument on an issue on which the adversary has a strong position. Normally, the best response to a disanalogy is simply, "No one said you did that" or "That's irrelevant to the case at bar."

## IV. Distinctions and Levels of Abstraction

If the decision on an issue in one case is precedent for an issue in a subsequent case, the issues must exist on the same level of abstraction and within the same universe of significant facts with respect to the issue.[8] The reason is that one case is precedent for another only if their legally significant facts are analogous. If either case contains an additional significant fact, the earlier case is not a precedent for the later one. This statement is true by definition: a fact is legally significant because it affects the outcome of a case.

These ideas are perhaps clearer in schematic form.

> *Case A*. The legally significant facts are 1, 2, and 3. We also know that proposition $p$ is true of *Case A* where $p$ indicates which party prevailed.
>
> *Case B*. The facts are 4, 5, and 6. Fact 4 is like fact 1, fact 5 is like fact 2, and fact 6 is like fact 3. Accordingly, *Case B* is analogous to *Case A* and, therefore, proposition $p$ is also true of *Case B* (the

---

8. An exception to this rule occurs when the precedent sets a general standard that operates at a high level of abstraction. That precedent will control subsequent cases in which the issue operates at a lower level of abstraction. For example, suppose $X$ uses an automatic weapon to kill a large number of persons. The magazine of the weapon holds 100 bullets. $X$ would kill more persons, but he is tackled when he has to stop firing in order to load another magazine. The state legislature hurriedly passes a law that the magazine for an automatic weapon may contain no more than ten rounds. The constitutionality of the law is challenged in *A v. B*. The challengers raise three issues. First, does the Second Amendment prohibit a state from placing any limit on the capacity of a magazine? Second, assuming that a limit is constitutional, may it be as low as the state chooses, or is there a limit to the limit? Third, assuming there is a limit to the limit, is ten rounds too low a limit? The court holds, first, a state may limit the capacity of a magazine for an automatic weapon; second, any limit must be reasonable; and third, ten is not a reasonable limit because it is irrational in that it was not supported by evidence before the legislature. The first two issues and their resolutions operate at a high level of abstraction because they apply to many situations and persons; the third issue and resolution operate at a lower level because they apply only to a limit of ten rounds (and, a fortiori, to any limit of fewer than ten). The appellate court affirms this judgment.

The state responds by holding hearings, taking expert testimony, and increasing the limit to twenty rounds, and this limit is now challenged in *C v. D*. The issue is, is a limit of twenty rounds reasonable? This issue operates at a low level of abstraction because it applies only to a limit of twenty rounds, yet it is controlled by the ruling at a high level of abstraction in *A v. B* that a limit must be reasonable. Thus, although it is generally true that a precedent and an issue that the precedent controls must operate on the same level of abstraction, a case that sets a general standard, which operates at a higher level of abstraction, may be a precedent on an issue in a case that operates at a lower level of abstraction.

party in *Case B* who is in the same position as the winner of Case A should prevail.).

   *Case C.* The facts are 7, 8, 9, and 10. Fact 7 is like fact 1, fact 8 is like fact 2, and fact 9 is like fact 3; but fact 10 is not like facts 1, 2, or 3. Is *Case C* analogous to *Case A*? The answer depends on whether fact 10 is legally significant. If fact 10 matters to us, *Case C*, which contains fact 10, is not analogous to *Case A*; and therefore we do not know whether or not proposition *p* is true of *Case C*. That is, *Case A* does not dictate which party should win *Case C*. The outcome of *Case C* could be the same as, or different from, the outcome of *Case A*. All we know is that *Case A* is not a precedent for *Case C*. But if fact 10 does *not* matter to us, we can ignore it; in this event, *Case C* is analogous to *Case A*, and proposition *p* is true of *Case C* (the party in *Case C* who is in the same position as the winner of Case A should prevail.)

   *Case D.* The facts are 11 and 12. Fact 11 is like fact 1, and fact 12 is like fact 2; but nothing corresponds to fact 3. Is *Case D* analogous to *Case A*? The answer is no because fact 3 is legally significant, and therefore we do not know whether or not proposition *p* is true of *Case D*. *Case A*, therefore, does not dictate which party should win *Case D*. The outcome of *Case D* could be the same as, or different from, the outcome of *Case A*. All we know is that *Case A* is not a precedent for *Case D*.

| Case A | | Case B | | Case C | | Case D | |
|---|---|---|---|---|---|---|---|
| Leg. Sig. Facts | | Leg. Sig. Facts | | Leg. Sig. Facts | | Leg. Sig. Facts | |
| 1 | = | 4 | = | 7 | = | 11 | |
| 2 | = | 5 | = | 8 | = | 12 | |
| 3 | = | 6 | = | 9 | | | |
| | | | | 10 | | | |
| ∴ Proposition *p* | | ∴ Proposition *p* | | ∴ Proposition *p*? | | ∴ Proposition *p*? | |

**Figure 12.1** To distinguish a case is to move to a different level of abstraction

It is obvious that analogous cases like *A* and *B* exist on the same level of abstraction within the same universe of facts; they contain the same significant facts. It is equally obvious that distinguishable cases exist on different levels of abstraction or in different universes of significant facts. Assume that, in the preceding example, fact 10 in *Case C* is legally significant. Accordingly, *Case A* is not analogous to (a precedent for) *Case C*. Also, because *Case C* has more legally significant facts than *Case A*, *Case C* exists on a lower level of abstraction. Similarly, as long as fact 3 is significant, *Case A* is not analogous to (a precedent for) *Case D*. And because *Case D* has fewer legally significant facts than *Case A*, *Case D* exists on a higher level of abstraction.

The upshot of this analysis is that the process of

- **distinguishing cases involves moving to a different level of abstraction.**


## V. *Seymour's Case* Expanded

A busy judge has little time for research and necessarily relies on the attorneys to identify and interpret precedents. Judges often say that a bad decision is the result of bad lawyering. Nevertheless, a judge sometimes undertakes independent analysis of prior cases, in which event the judge must read and reflect on the leading precedents.

Let us suppose, then, that Judge Janus is satisfied with the arguments of neither Seymour's lawyer nor Hard Luck Hank's lawyer. The judge is certain that Hank's analysis (the only legally significant facts are a contract between an adult and a minor) is simplistic. The judge believes that Seymour has a good point (it is also significant whether the minor is seeking to enforce or avoid the contract), but thinks the issue is even more complex than this. Accordingly, the judge studies the decision in *Esme's Case*. It read:


### Shady Sam v. Esme

123 Confused Reports 456 (1982)

Janus, J.

This action was brought by Shady Sam, a used car dealer, against Esme, a 12-year-old girl, for breach of a contract for the purchase of a 1960 Volvo. The contract price was $8,000.

Esme contracted to buy the car the day after learning that she was the beneficiary of a $1,000,000 bequest in the will of a neighbor. She has average intelligence. Her only business experience has been babysitting. She showed the contract to her parents when she returned from Sam's car lot. They immediately sent a registered letter to Sam, declaring that the contract was void and they would not allow Esme to honor it. Sam received the letter the following day, and two days later sold the car at its market value of $1,000.

If the contract were valid, Sam would be entitled to damages of the difference between the contract price and the market value of the car ($8,000–$1,000 =) $7,000. However, based on the foregoing facts, this court concludes that the contract is not enforceable. The case is dismissed.

If Judge Janus had stated his reasoning or rationale, it would have identified the legally significant facts and explained why they are significant. In this event, subsequent judges would have been required to work within the limits of *Esme's Case* (or make new law and say why). Instead, the judge did not state a rationale. As a result, judges in subsequent cases have considerable discretion in how they interpret *Esme's Case*. Judge Devorah could interpret the case at the high level of abstraction that Hank's lawyer wishes (the significant facts are that an adult and a minor enter into a contract), or adopt the argument of Seymour's lawyer and move to a lower level of abstraction (the significant facts are that an adult and a minor enter into a contract, and the minor seeks to enforce it against the adult), or deem even more facts to be legally significant and decide the case at a still lower level of abstraction. After some reflection, the judge chooses the last of these alternatives.

### Seymour v. Hard Luck Hank

234 Confused Reports 567 (2008)

Devorah, J.

Seymour is a remarkable eleven-year-old boy. He is exceptionally intelligent. (The court has been apprised of Seymour's IQ. It is not reported herein out of consideration for his youth and his privacy.) Without his mother's knowledge, he began trading stocks and futures on the internet at the age of eight. When his mother learned of this activity, she also learned that he was well ahead of the game; and she allowed him to continue. Recently, he foresaw that Microsoft would declare a dividend exceeding $30 billion, and he leveraged this foresight into a profit of $2 million.

Like his mother, Seymour is an aficionado of vintage sports cars. He had noticed a 1963 Corvette for sale on the lot of Hard Luck Hank's Good-as-New Vehicles for $34,999. The day after making the killing in Microsoft, Seymour rode his scooter to Hank's and, after an hour's dickering, signed a contract to buy the automobile for $25,000.

No sooner had Seymour left Hank's lot than Harland Sanders expressed interest in the Corvette. Hank said he was sorry, it had just been sold, but he had a nice MG available. Sanders knew that the Corvette had belonged to Elvis. Licking his fingers but not disclosing the automobile's provenance, Sanders offered Hank $100,000 for it. Hank said he would see what he could do.

Hank immediately telephoned Seymour's home. The latter had not arrived yet, and his mother took the call. Hank said he had just realized that "little Seymour" was too young to sign a contract and, therefore, it was void. Seymour's mother immediately drove to Hank's car lot, inspected the Corvette, and decided that it was worth $25,000 or more. Accordingly, she informed Hank that she expected him to honor the contract. He offered her a sum of money (he said $1,000, she said $100; the actual sum is irrelevant) to rescind the contract. When she refused, he said he would not honor the contract.

Suspecting from Hank's behavior that the automobile had some special value, Seymour's mother called an attorney, who appeared before this court the same day and asked for a temporary restraining order, enjoining Hank from selling the automobile until the dispute could be resolved. This court granted the restraining order and calendared a hearing for the fifth succeeding day. That hearing was held as scheduled. Represented by counsel, the parties appeared, submitted affidavits, and gave testimony. The parties have agreed that this court may dispose of the case on this record.

The parties have brought to the court's attention one precedent in this state (and the court's research has revealed no others), to wit: *Sam v. Esme*, 123 Confused Reports 456 (1982). In this case . . . [the court's recitation of the facts of *Esme's Case* is omitted]. Our analysis of this case indicates

that a contract involving a person under the age of sixteen is legally binding depending on—

- the age, intelligence, and experience of the minor
- the nature of the transaction (e.g., whether for necessities or non-necessities)
- the complexity of the transaction
- the relevant information of which the adult and the minor were aware, and
- a comparison of the hardship that would result from enforcing the contract versus the hardship that would result from voiding the contract.

Thus, in *Sam v. Esme*, the contract was voided because the minor had only average intelligence and no business experience, purchasing a used auto-mobile is a complex transaction, and the minor had no idea of the market value of the automobile whereas Sam of course did. The hardship on the minor of enforcing the contract would have been paying $8,000 for an old automobile worth $1,000. The hardship on Sam of voiding the contract would have been losing a windfall of $7,000. Losing a windfall is a lesser hardship than overpaying $7,000 for a used automobile; thus, the hard-ship on the minor was greater. All the factors pointed toward voiding the contract, as the court did.

In the case at bar, some facts suggest the contract should be voided. In *Sam v. Esme* a contract with a minor twelve years old was not enforced. At eleven years, Seymour is even younger. This fact tends toward the conclu-sion that the contract between Seymour and Hank should be voided. Sey-mour agreed to pay $25,000 for an automobile actually worth $100,000. If the contract is voided, he will lose a windfall of $75,000. If the contract is enforced, Hank will be forced to sell an automobile for $75,000 less than its value. Normally, the court would weigh Hank's hardship heavily. However, given that Hank was a specialist in the sale of used automobiles, and therefore presumably an expert who should have known the value of his merchandise, the court discounts the hardship. Nevertheless, it is still a hardship, and this fact, like Seymour's age, suggests that the contract should be voided.

But other facts militate toward enforcing the contract. Esme had nor-mal intelligence; Seymour has superior intelligence. This fact cuts in favor

of honoring Seymour's contract. Likewise, Esme had no business experience, whereas Seymour has considerable experience in the stock market;
he may not have previously purchased a car, but he knows about bargaining over price. This fact also favors enforcing the contract. Neither party
knew the true value of the automobile. In the context of this case, this fact
favors enforcing the contract, not only because Hank is an adult, but also
because he is a dealer in used automobiles.

Weighing all of these facts, the court concludes that Seymour's contract
with Hank was valid and should be enforced. Given that an automobile
once owned by Elvis is a rare item, the court grants specific performance
of the contract and orders Hank to sell the car to Seymour for $25,000.

Judge Devorah's opinion reveals two points. The first is that precedents
can be interpreted, and the second is that level of abstraction is a major
element of interpretation. Each of the relevant factors identified by the
judge was a legally significant fact. The judge chose to decide the case at
a lower level of abstraction than the attorneys for the parties had urged.

## VI. Review

### The War between the Unions

The Labor Act allows a union to represent a unit of workers if the majority of them desire union representation. Majority rule is a coin with two
sides. If a union has the support of the majority of workers in a unit, the
employer *must* recognize the union and bargain with it regarding all of
the workers in the unit. If the union lacks the support of the majority, the
employer *must not* recognize the union or bargain with it regarding all of
the workers in the unit. This second rule is important in various contexts,
one of which arises when workers who are represented by a union change
their mind about it. In this event, the employer may no longer bargain with
the union concerning all the workers in the unit.[9]

In the *War between the Unions* union A had represented a unit of workers
for a few years. Some individual workers became dissatisfied with union A

---

9. Significant exceptions, not relevant here, exist to this rule.

and approached union *B*, asking the latter to represent them. Union *B* then commenced to recruit members in the unit. After a few weeks, union *B* believed that the majority of workers now supported it, and it sent this letter to the employer: "The majority of workers in the unit wish to be represented by union *B*. Hence we demand that you cease relations with union *A* and begin bargaining with us." The employer showed this letter to union *A*, which insisted that it continued to enjoy majority support. These conflicting claims put the employer in an awkward position. If union *B* were right about its support, the employer would violate the law by continuing to deal with union *A*. But if union *A* were right about its continued support, the employer would break the law by bargaining with union *B*. Thus, in order to obey the law the employer had to know which union the majority supported.

After receiving the letter from union *B*, the employer instructed its supervisors to ask the workers which union they supported. Union *A* filed an unfair labor practice charge, alleging that the questions were coercive because the employer would know which union the worker favored, and the worker might fear that the employer would use that knowledge to retaliate against the worker. The Board held the questions were permissible because the employer had a legitimate reason for asking, namely, to learn which union with which to bargain.

### The Case of the Supervisor's Questions

Along comes the *Case of the Supervisor's Questions*, in which a union is attempting to organize a unit of workers. Upon learning of the organizing campaign, a supervisor begins asking workers whether they support the union. The union files a charge with the Board, asserting that the supervisor's questions are coercive. The advocate for the employer likes the result of the *War between the Unions* and wants to draw an analogy between it and the case at bar. The advocate argues:

> In the *War between the Unions,* supervisors asked workers about their allegiance to a union, and the Board held that the questions were lawful. In the case at bar supervisors asked workers about their support for a union. These questions were lawful on the authority of the *War between the Unions.*

## Question

1. How can the advocate for the union distinguish the *War between the Unions*? HINT: Think about the rationale of that case.

### *Young Tom's Case*

Young Tom wants to buy the latest version of his favorite video game, but he does not have enough money. He asks his mother, who promises him that she will give him half the money for the game when he has saved the other half from his allowance. The next day he remembers that his mother keeps money at the back of a dresser drawer; she has told him she keeps that money for emergencies. When his mother leaves the house, Tom takes some of the money, buys the game, and plays it on the computer in his bedroom. A few days later, his sister Ashley is looking for him.

"Tom."

No answer.

"Tom!"

No answer.

"TOM!! It's time for your violin lesson."

No answer. She opens the door to his bedroom.

"What are you doing?" she asks.

"Not'in'," he replies.

"Isn't that the newest update of 'Space Commandos'?"

"No."

"Yes, it is, and I'm gonna tell Mom."

Ashley does just that, and Mother confronts Tom. "Where did you get the money?" she asks.

"Found it."

"Where?"

"I don't remember."

"Tom, I'm going to look in my drawer, and if any money is missing and you lied to me, you're going to be in double trouble."

"I didn't steal it. I was gonna pay you back."

"What you did was just like stealing."

"I saw Dad take some money from your drawer last week."

"That was different. Your father took five dollars because he didn't have enough money to pay for the pizza he ordered for you guys when I was late coming home. He told me about it that night, and he paid it back the next day."

"At least I didn't say Ashley took it."

"Yes, but you didn't ask first, and that's what matters."

## Question

2. *Young Tom's Case* is more complicated than it may seem. Mom drew an analogy and Tom attempted to distinguish it; Tom proposed a competing analogy and Mom distinguished it; and Tom stated a disanalogy and Mom refuted it. Analyze these arguments into the elements of analogies and distinctions. If an element is missing, so indicate and supply it.

### The Fine Print Cases

### Question

3. Review the Fine Print Cases in § 11. How did Judge Devorah distinguish *Over v. Out* from *Daniel v. Drop-Your-Call*? State both the analogy drawn by Drop-Your-Call and the distinction drawn by the judge.

# § 13

# Holding and Dictum

## I. Definitions

In order to understand how precedents are used in law, the student must understand the difference between holding and dictum. **Holding** is the judgment of a tribunal on an issue that must be resolved in order to decide the case; holding also can include the reasoning that supports the tribunal's judgment. **Dictum** (plural: **dicta**) is a statement of a tribunal on an issue which the tribunal need not resolve in order to decide the case. Holding says who wins and why; dictum is anything else of which the tribunal cares to unburden itself.

## II. Effect of a Holding

Holding is precedent; dictum is not. Holding is binding; dictum is not.

The first tribunal to decide an issue does not create a precedent for all time and for all other tribunals; precedent has a territorial (lawyers would say "jurisdictional") dimension and a hierarchical dimension. Beginning with jurisdiction, a precedent is binding only within the tribunal's jurisdiction. The holding of the Court of Appeals of New York is binding in the State of New York, but not in any other state; the holding of the U.S. Court of Appeals for the Fifth Circuit is binding in the Fifth Circuit, but not in any other circuit. Of course, the holding of a tribunal in one jurisdiction may be influential in another jurisdiction. A court in Texas may cite a case decided in Illinois in support of a point. Nevertheless, the Texas court is not bound to honor the Illinois precedent.

As for hierarchy, a precedent of a tribunal is binding on all tribunals beneath it in a given structure. Thus, a decision of the U.S. Court of Appeals for the Ninth Circuit is binding on all the lower federal courts in the Ninth Circuit. A dictum of a higher court also has considerable influence on lower courts in the same structure, but is not binding.

Is a precedent binding on the very tribunal that issued it? The answer is usually yes but sometimes no: yes in that tribunals normally follow their own precedents; no in that tribunals can overrule themselves. The policy of the U.S. Supreme Court is to adhere to its own precedents on statutory issues, that is, issues growing out of statutes enacted by Congress. With respect to interpretations of the Constitution, the Supreme Court feels freer to reexamine its precedents.[1]

## III. The Scope or Meaning of a Holding

*The scope or meaning of a holding derives from the facts of the case.* Here follows an example.

### Union Access to Company Property

In *Republic Aviation*, a company promulgated a "no-solicitation rule," which prohibited workers from soliciting one another on company property at

---

1. The Court's rationale is that, if the Court misconstrues a statute, Congress can correct the Court by amending the statute (thereby effectively overruling the Court's decision for subsequent cases). By contrast, correcting the Court's interpretation of the Constitution requires a constitutional amendment, which is so difficult to accomplish that more flexibility on the part of the Court is appropriate.

any time and for any purpose, for example, to sign a political petition, to buy a product, or to support a union. At common law, the owner of real property has the right to restrict the behavior of guests on the property; therefore, the company's no-solicitation rule was legal under common law. Workers challenged the rule under § 8(a)(1) of the Labor Act, which prohibits an employer from interfering with workers' union activity. The workers argued that the no-solicitation rule interfered with their right to organize into a union because the workplace, although it is company property, is "the natural place for workers to talk to one another and persuade one another to join the union" (p. 1195). The Board accepted this argument, and the Supreme Court agreed with the Board. The Court held that (absent special circumstances) an employer may not prohibit a worker on company property from soliciting other workers to join a union.

Workers who think they would benefit from union representation usually know nothing about organizing, and they often consult a union for help. Most unions have at least one officer or employee, called an "organizer," who is responsible for organizing new shops. When workers ask for help, the organizer will provide advice and encouragement to these workers, and may also communicate directly with other workers as well. In *Babcock & Wilcox*, a company relied on its no-solicitation rule to ban a union organizer from distributing leaflets on company property. The union argued that this case was controlled by *Republic Aviation* because the workplace is the natural place for workers to learn about the union, and the organizer was helping the workers exercise their rights, doing only what the workers could not do themselves. The Supreme Court disagreed. *Republic Aviation* did not control *Babcock & Wilcox* because in the former case the no-solicitation rule applied to employees of the company, whereas in the latter case the ban applied to a nonemployee, a union organizer who was a stranger to the property. This difference in fact allowed the company to exercise its common law right of property against the organizer.

A point that we made at the beginning of the previous paragraph is a cardinal principle of the common law. If the student learns nothing else from this book, learn this:

- **The scope or meaning of a holding derives from the facts of the case.**

Thus, *Republic Aviation* held that the right to concerted activity includes the right of workers to solicit for a union on company property. Does this holding mean that workers may solicit during working hours? No. It was a fact of the case that the workers wished to solicit during nonworking hours. Therefore, the case held nothing about solicitation during working hours. Does the holding mean that nonemployees may solicit for a union on company property? No. Another fact of the case was that employees wished to solicit one another. Therefore, the case held nothing about solicitation by nonemployees.[2]

## IV. References

*National Labor Relations Board v. Babcock & Wilcox*, 351 U.S. 105 (1956).
*Republic Aviation*, 51 NLRB 1186 (1943).
*Republic Aviation v. National Labor Relations Board*, 324 U.S. 793 (1945).

---

2. The principle that the scope of a holding derives from the facts of the case is similar to the principle, discussed in § 16 INTERPRETING STATUTES, that the scope or meaning of a statute derives from the facts of the cases decided under the statute.

# § 14

# Reductios ad Absurdum

The type of argument known as **reductio ad absurdum** (proof by contradiction) disproves a proposition by showing that it leads to an absurd result such as a contradiction, a falsehood, an anomaly, or an otherwise unacceptable conclusion. The logical form of a reductio is modus tollens (if *P*, then *Q*; not *Q*; therefore, not *P*). Reductios are prominent in mathematics[1] and are used in various other kinds of argument, including legal argument.

## I. The Elements of a Reductio ad Absurdum

The elements of a reductio ad absurdum are—

### Proposition

An assertion that the advocate intends to falsify

---

1. Indirect proof in mathematics falsifies a proposition by showing that it leads to its own contradiction or to a conclusion that is demonstrably false.

### Contradiction or absurdity

The contradiction or absurd result to which the proposition, if true, leads

### Argument that the proposition leads to the contradiction or absurdity

The reasoning that demonstrates that the proposition leads to the absurdity

### Conclusion

The proposition is false.

The master of the technique of reductio ad absurdum was the ancient Greek philosopher Zeno of Elea (born c. 490 BCE). Zeno's teacher, Parmenides (born c. 512 BCE), advocated the doctrine that change was an illusion: our senses may perceive change, but our reason proves that the world is indivisible, unchangeable, and eternal. Zeno supported this doctrine with paradoxes—arguments that a belief in change led to absurdities, in other words, reductios ad absurdum. Here are two famous examples.

#### The Paradox of the Arrow

As reported by Aristotle, Zeno said, "If everything when it occupies an equal space is at rest, and if that which is in locomotion is always occupying such a space at any moment, the flying arrow is therefore motionless."

Zeno's argument was that, for motion to occur, an arrow (or any other object) must move from one place to another, that is, change the position that the arrow occupies. But in any one moment of time, the arrow is not moving to where it is, nor is it moving to where it is going: it cannot move to where it is because it is already there, and it cannot move to where it is going because, during that moment, no time elapses during which the arrow can move. In other words, at every moment of time no motion occurs.[2] If everything is motionless at every moment, and time is composed of a series of moments, motion is impossible.

-----

2. Compare the Heisenberg Uncertainty Principle: the position and velocity of an object cannot both be measured.

The *Paradox of the Arrow* can be analyzed into the elements of a reductio ad absurdum:

PROPOSITION

Motion is possible. Motion means going from one point to another point in a period of time.

CONTRADICTION OR ABSURDITY

Motion is impossible.

ARGUMENT THAT THE PROPOSITION LEADS TO THE CONTRADICTION OR AN ABSURDITY

Belief in motion leads to the contradictory result that motion is impossible. In order for motion to occur, an object must change the position that it occupies. Imagine an arrow in flight. In any given moment of time, which has no duration, the arrow is neither moving to where it is because it is already there, nor moving to where it is going because no time elapses during which the arrow can move. In other words, at every moment of time, no motion is occurring. If an object is motionless at every moment, and if time is composed of moments, motion is impossible.

CONCLUSION

The possibility of motion leads to the contradiction that a body cannot move from one point to another. Therefore, motion is impossible.

Of course, this conclusion—that motion is impossible—is also absurd, and the result is a paradox. One way to resolve a paradox is to identify an internal contradiction. Another way is to demonstrate that the paradox rests on a false assumption.

## Question

1. Can the *Paradox of the Arrow* be resolved?

### The Paradox of Achilles and the Tortoise

As reported by Aristotle, Zeno said, "In a race, the quickest runner can never overtake the slowest, since the pursuer must first reach the point whence the pursued started, so that the slower must always hold a lead."

This paradox is commonly presented as a race between Achilles and a tortoise. Zeno's argument is that, because Achilles is the swifter one, the tortoise is allowed to start some distance ahead on the course. Both begin at the same moment. Before Achilles can overtake the tortoise, he must first reach the point at which the tortoise began. When Achilles reaches this point, the tortoise will have moved forward to another point; therefore, in order for Achilles to overtake the tortoise, Achilles must first reach this new point. But when he gets there, the tortoise will have moved yet again, and Achilles must now reach that point; and so on. Achilles will constantly reach points that the tortoise no longer occupies and, therefore, never overtake it.

The *Paradox of Achilles and the Tortoise* can be analyzed into the elements of a reductio ad absurdum.

PROPOSITION

A moving body can overtake and pass another moving body.

CONTRADICTION OR ABSURDITY

Achilles cannot overtake a tortoise.

ARGUMENT THAT THE PROPOSITION LEADS TO THE CONTRADICTION OR ABSURDITY

Belief that Achilles can overtake and pass a tortoise leads to the contradictory result that he cannot overtake and pass the tortoise. In a race between Achilles and a tortoise, the tortoise begins at point T-1, which is some distance in front of Achilles. Before Achilles can overtake the tortoise, he must reach point T-1. When he reaches this point, the tortoise will have moved forward to point T-2. Therefore, before Achilles can overtake the tortoise, he must reach point T-2. But by the time that Achilles reaches point T-2, the tortoise will have moved forward to point T-3, which Achilles must reach before overtaking the tortoise. And when Achilles reaches T-3, the tortoise will have progressed to point T-4, and so on. Thus, Achilles will never overtake the tortoise.

CONCLUSION

The possibility that a moving body can overtake and pass another moving body leads to the contradiction that Achilles cannot overtake a tortoise.

## Question

2. Can the *Paradox of Achilles and the Tortoise* be resolved?

A reductio may lead to a practical contradiction instead of a logical one. For example—

### The Paradox of the Minimum Wage

The purpose of the minimum wage is to improve the lives of low-wage workers. Conservative economists argue that increasing the minimum wage will have the perverse effect of worsening the lives of these workers. Here is their argument.

Assume that the expenses, revenues, and profits of a business are in an equilibrium that is satisfactory to the owner. If the minimum wage is increased, the labor costs of the business will rise, but its revenue will not. The logical step for the business will be to restore the equilibrium by reducing its labor costs. Reduction can be achieved by some combination of extracting more output from workers (a "speedup"), reducing their hours (a form of speedup because the same work must be performed in fewer hours), and substituting capital (machines) for labor. The workers who are most likely to suffer these consequences are the ones whose wages have just risen due to the increase in the minimum wage. The result will be that the very workers whom the increase was meant to benefit will be worse off.

### Questions

3(a). Analyze the conservative economists' argument into the elements of a reductio.

3(b). Can consequences occur other than those predicted by the conservative economists? Why or why not?

## II. The Criteria of a Sound Reductio ad Absurdum

An argument in the form of reductio ad absurdum is convincing only if it meets two criteria:

- **The proposition would surely or probably lead to a particular result in another case, or the result already exists.**
- **The result would contradict the proposition or be absurd.**

Zeno's paradoxes satisfied both of these criteria: they "proved" that the proposition that motion is possible led by logic to the conclusion that motion is impossible. The *Paradox of the Minimum Wage* also satisfied these criteria: the proposition that increasing the minimum wage would benefit low-paid workers led to the conclusion that an increase would worsen their lives, a result that was contrary to the purpose of the increase.

## III. Reductios ad Absurdum in Law

### A. REDUCTIOS AND PRECEDENTS

An advocate often argues that an adversary's proposition would be inconsistent with a precedent. Such an argument is tantamount to a reductio—

PROPOSITION

An employer committed an unfair labor practice by permanently replacing workers who went on strike.

CONTRADICTION OR ABSURDITY

*Mackay Radio* held that an employer may permanently replace strikers.

ARGUMENT THAT THE PROPOSITION LEADS TO THE CONTRADICTION OR
ABSURDITY

The law would contradict itself if it said that an employer may and
may not permanently replace strikers.

CONCLUSION

The employer did not commit an unfair labor practice by permanently replacing workers who went on strike.

In legal discourse, an argument that a result would violate a precedent is
nearly as powerful as proving a logical contradiction.

## B. REDUCTIOS AND FACT FINDING

Reductios are often used to prove that a putative fact is not true. For
example—

### The Philosopher's Reductio

Some Roman emperors are said to have believed that they were gods.
Suppose Augustus is about to proclaim an annual feast throughout
the empire in celebration of his birthday. Kendallacus, a particularly
brave (or foolhardy) philosopher, tries to dissuade the emperor as
follows:

| | |
|---|---|
| KENDALLACUS: | Augustus, the people say you are a god. Are they correct? |
| AUGUSTUS: | They are and I am. |
| KENDALLACUS: | Is it true that the gods are eternal? |
| AUGUSTUS: | It is true. |
| KENDALLACUS: | And yet you are about to proclaim your birthday as a holiday. Is that correct? |
| AUGUSTUS: | It is. |
| KENDALLACUS: | Does having a birthday mean that you were born on that day? |
| AUGUSTUS: | Of course. |
| KENDALLACUS: | Can anything exist before its birthday? |

| AUGUSTUS: | No. |
|---|---|
| KENDALLACUS: | But does not being eternal mean that one has always ex-isted and will always exist? |
| AUGUSTUS: | That is the correct meaning. |
| KENDALLACUS: | And so if you are a god, you are eternal and you have al-ways existed. Ergo, you must not have been born and you could not have had a birthday. And so proclaiming your birthday as a holiday would announce to the world that you are not a god. |
| AUGUSTUS: | Philosopher, do you think? |
| KENDALLACUS: | I do. |
| AUGUSTUS: | And do you wish to live? |
| KENDALLACUS: | I do indeed. |
| AUGUSTUS: | In that case, I advise you to think a little less lest you live no more. |

## Questions

4(a). Analyze the *Philosopher's Reductio* into its elements.

4(b). This reductio contains an error that vitiates its argument. Identify the error.

Lawyers, perhaps most especially when cross-examining witness, are fond of using reductios to prove that a fact to which the witness has tes-tified is untrue. The argument takes this form: if fact *A* is true, fact *B*, which presently exists or existed in the past and which is inconsistent with fact *A*, cannot be true. For example, a witness testifies to fact *A*. Pointing out that the witness previously said that fact *B* is true, the lawyer asks, "Which time were you lying?"

## C. Reductios and Policy Arguments

Most policy arguments are not reductios. A policy argument that predicts that a certain step will lead to good consequences is not a reductio; the argument satisfies the first criterion but not the second. Likewise, a policy argument that predicts that a certain step will lead to bad consequences is not a reductio. In addition, in many cases reasonable persons will disagree over whether the putative bad consequences are actually bad. One man's meat is another man's poison. For example, suppose a bill in a legislature would raise the age to buy cigarettes from eighteen to twenty-one. An opponent of the bill might argue that the bill would reduce the profits of tobacco companies. A proponent of the bill might believe that is a good consequence.

One type of policy argument, however, is a reductio, namely, an argument that predicts that a certain step will undermine rather than further its goal. The *Paradox of the Minimum Wage* is an example.

Like other policy arguments, a policy argument in the form of a reductio depends on a prediction of the future. Of course, predicted events may not occur. For this reason, a reductio that is based on a fact that presently exists, or existed in the past, is more convincing than a reductio based on a prediction of events that have yet to occur.

## IV. Review

In *A Brief History of the Paradox*, Roy Sorensen relates a story about Protagoras, who was the greatest of the Sophists.[3] He made a good living by teaching for money. He agreed that he would teach a young man named Euanthlus, and that Euanthlus would not have to pay the fee until he won his first case. After some years, Euanthlus had not sued anyone, nor had anyone sued him; so he had not won his first case, and he refused to pay Protagoras: whereupon Protagoras threatened to sue. "If I win," argued Protagoras, "you will have to pay me by virtue of the court's order; and if I lose, you will have to pay me by virtue of having won your first case." But Euanthlus had learned the lessons of sophistry well, and he replied: "If I win, in accordance with the court's judgment I won't owe you anything; and if I lose, I won't have to pay because I won't have won my first case."

---

3. Sophists were itinerant teachers in Greece in the fifth century BCE. Socrates thought they were disreputable because of their poor reasoning, their indifference to justice, and their willingness to accept money.

**Question**

5. Who was right?

## V. References

Aristotle, *Physics*, Book VI, ch. 9, 239b5, 10, 15 (W. D. Ross, trans., 1908).
Roy Sorensen, *A Brief History of the Paradox* (2003).

# § 15

# SUBJECTIVE AND OBJECTIVE STANDARDS

## I. Standards

Understanding law cases requires the student to be aware of two concepts. Neither is difficult; both affect not only the law, but also our everyday lives. The first of these concepts is a **standard,** which is a criterion, maxim, or test used in making a judgment. We often use standards in our daily lives. Suppose you find a wallet containing a driver's license, several credit cards, a few photographs, and $500 in cash. You have several alternatives, which can be placed on a spectrum: at one end of the spectrum, you could dispose of the wallet, sell the credit cards to a fence, and keep the cash; at the other end of the spectrum, you could return the wallet and all of its contents to the owner. What you do will depend on or reflect the standard you apply. If your standard is, "Life's a jungle, and each of us has to take care of oneself," you might choose the alternative at one end of the spectrum. If your standard is, "Do unto others as you would have them do unto you," you might choose the alternative at the opposite end of the spectrum.

## Exercise

1. State a standard that would result in your choosing an alternative that lies toward the middle of the spectrum (for example, you keep the cash and return the wallet and the rest of its contents).

The law uses standards extensively. For example, suppose your neighbor complains that your yard is messy. You respond, "That's none of your business!" Then your neighbor calls the mayor's office and learns that the city council has decided that yards full of junk are a public concern and has outlawed them. When your neighbor informs you of this fact, you reply, "My yard does not violate the ordinance." So your neighbor files a formal complaint with the city against you.

How will this controversy be resolved? Your neighbor thinks your yard is a mess. You disagree. Perhaps two other neighbors also think your yard is messy, and three others think it could be improved but is not all that bad. One way to decide the issue would be to take a vote of landowners in the neighborhood. But voting could lead to different results in similar cases, depending on things like the popularity of the people involved, who turns out to vote, and so forth. Another way to decide the issue would be to designate a judge with unrestricted power to decide. But an omnipotent judge could be arbitrary, inconsistent, irrational, or venal. Our legal system typically decides issues by reference to a standard. If the city council decides that messy yards are a public nuisance, the council will enact an ordinance. A good ordinance will not say, "Property must be neat and orderly" or "Property must not become littered with junk." Instead, the ordinance should be carefully worded so that it prohibits a yard from containing discarded appliances, old cars, and refuse, while it permits a yard to contain barbecue pits, dog houses, and vegetable gardens. In other words, the ordinance will contain a standard, and, when your neighbor complains, a neutral person will be able to apply the standard to the case and reach a result with which most reasonable persons would agree.

Standards come in two varieties, subjective and objective, and the distinction between them is the second concept of which the student needs to be aware. A **subjective standard** depends on the state of mind of the actor; the same act may be permissible or impermissible, depending on what the actor was thinking. An **objective standard** focuses on the actor's behavior; a given act is permissible or not, regardless of what the actor had in mind.

## II. Subjective Standards

Let us discuss these two kinds of standards in greater detail, beginning with subjective standards. In everyday life, an act may be acceptable to us if it is performed in good faith, but unacceptable if performed in bad faith. Criticism is an example. If *A* criticizes *B* with the purpose of helping *B* to improve, the criticism is (or should be) welcome; if *C* says exactly the same thing, but with the purpose of humiliating *B*, the criticism is unwelcome. In other words, we often judge a critic according to a subjective standard. (The standard is subjective because it focuses on the actor's (in this case, the critic's) state of mind.) Another example is one of the standards suggested above in connection with the lost wallet. If you follow the Golden Rule, your act is right if you are willing to be the other person in the situation.[1]

### Exercise

2. Devise a hypothetical situation in which an act is judged according to a subjective standard—that is, the act is acceptable if performed in good

---

1. The student should regard the word "subjective" in legal discourse as a term of art. It has one meaning in ordinary English and another meaning in law.

In *ordinary English*, the core idea of the word "subjective" is a focus on the mind of an individual. James might say, "I think Bob Dylan is the greatest musician of our time." And Carol might say of James, "That's just your subjective opinion." Carol means that James's statement is based on his own criteria, but not on anyone else's criteria. Also in ordinary speech, the word "subjective" has a connotation as well as a focus. The connotation is whimsy or caprice. Thus, Carol implies not only that James's criteria are his own, but also that reasonable persons do not share those criteria. Similarly, Carol might say, "Judge Picayune dismissed my case, but his opinion was totally subjective." Carol means that a fair judge, applying generally accepted standards, would have ruled otherwise.

The word "subjective" as used *in the law* refers to the core idea only—a focus on the mind of an individual whose action is being judged. When a subjective standard is used, legal consequences hinge on the state of mind of that individual, not the state of mind of another party to the case, or of society, or of the judge or jury that is deciding the legality of the act. In the example in the text, *A* criticizes *B*, and the question is whether *B* will accept or reject the criticism. Thus, *A* is the actor (the act was uttering criticism) and *B* is the judge (who will decide whether or not to accept the criticism). *B* applies a subjective standard: the criticism is accepted if *A* intended to help *B* improve; the criticism is rejected if *A* intended to humiliate *B*. By using a subjective standard, *B* focuses on the mind of *A*.

The legal meaning of "subjective" does not carry a connotation of capriciousness. When a legal issue is decided by a subjective standard, we ask, was a certain element operating in the actor's mind? If so, the case goes one way; if not, it goes the other way: and nothing is implied about whether that element would have been operating in the mind of a another person in the same situation.

faith and unacceptable if performed in bad faith. The act need not have legal consequences.

We use subjective standards in the law as well as in everyday life; accordingly, the legal consequences of an act may vary according to the actor's state of mind. For example, suppose C pushed you so hard that you fell to the ground. If C pushed you deliberately and with the intention of harming you, C committed the intentional tort of battery. You could sue C for compensation for your medical expenses, pain and suffering, and, if you missed work, lost pay; you could also sue for punitive damages (as a kind of punishment). If C pushed you carelessly—perhaps C was gesturing to a friend and didn't realize you were standing nearby— C may have committed the tort of negligence, and you could sue for compensation, but not for punitive damages. If C pushed you deliberately in order to move you out of the way of a speeding truck, you would have no case at all.

## III. Objective Standards

Now let us discuss objective standards. As important as state of mind is to our daily judgments, some acts are right or wrong, acceptable or unacceptable, regardless of the actor's state of mind. In other words, we often judge an act according to an objective standard. Sometimes objective standards take the form of a graded scale. For example, a real estate broker who regularly sells ten million dollars' worth of property a year is considered a better broker than one who sells only five million dollars' worth of property. Other times, objective standards take the form of a binary rule. For example, a good dog bites a burglar; a bad dog bites its master.[2]

---

2. Because an objective standard focuses on behavior, application of the standard may depend on what reasonable persons observing the behavior would think of it. In this sense, the idea of an objective standard in the law is similar to the meaning of the word "objective" in ordinary English usage. In daily life, an objective opinion is an opinion that is not influenced by something improper like bias and, therefore, is an opinion that reasonable persons would share. An objective fact is not a fact that cannot be false, but a fact that reasonable persons would believe to be true.

### Exercise

3. Name two acts that are commonly judged according to an objective standard—in other words, that are right or wrong without regard to the actor's state of mind; one act should be judged on a graded scale and the other, on a binary scale. The acts need not have legal consequences.

Objective standards are used in the law as well as in daily life. Thus, in the eyes of the law, some acts are also right or wrong, regardless of the actor's state of mind. However, objective standards in law, unlike those in daily life, usually do not contemplate a graded scale. The reason is that, in the view of the common law, an event occurred or did not occur, and an act is legal or illegal. Therefore, objective standards in law normally contemplate a binary scale. An example of the use of a binary objective standard to determine whether or not an event occurred can be seen in the law of defamation. Suppose a kosher butcher sues *D* because *D* has told many people that the butcher sells nonkosher meat. In order to win the case, the butcher must prove that *D* made those statements, that they were false, and that the butcher's reputation has been damaged. Whether each of these facts is true (whether the events occurred) will be determined on an objective standard. Did *D* say the butcher sells nonkosher meat? Did the butcher sell nonkosher meat? Did the butcher lose business? *D*'s state of mind will be irrelevant. It will not help him to prove—indeed, he will not be allowed to prove—that he honestly believed the butcher sold nonkosher meat, or that he was trying to help the butcher to attract gentile customers.

Another example of the use of a binary objective standard to determine whether an act is legal or illegal is your right to vote in a presidential election. If you are properly qualified and registered, it is lawful for you to vote for the candidate of your choice; your state of mind is irrelevant. Even if you hate your country and you vote for the candidate who you believe will bring down the system, it is legal for you to vote for this person.

## IV. Mixed Standards and Evidence

It is possible for a standard to have subjective and objective elements. Consider the example of homicide in the first degree. It has an objective element: *X* killed *Y*. It also has a subjective element: *X* premeditated the killing of Y. Because legal consequences flow from application of law to fact regarding each element of a standard, it is unnecessary to classify the standard as a whole as subjective or objective.

A fact is subjective when it exists in a person's mind. Nevertheless, the *evidence* that proves a subjective fact may be subjective or objective. Suppose the issue is whether Garrison bore ill will toward fans of the Whippets. Garrison's state of mind is a subjective fact, but the evidence of it may be subjective or objective. SUBJECTIVE EVIDENCE: Garrison says, "The Whippets are bums, and their fans are worse." OBJECTIVE EVIDENCE: Jill testifies, "Every time Garrison saw someone wearing a Whippets jacket, he cussed."

A fact is objective when it exists outside of a person's mind. Nevertheless, the *evidence* that proves an objective fact may be subjective or objective. Suppose the issue is whether Molly won the lottery. Whether or not she won the lottery is an objective fact, but the evidence of it may be subjective or objective. SUBJECTIVE EVIDENCE: Manny says, "Molly was depressed after she lost her job because she couldn't pay her bills, but the day after the lottery she told me she was on top of the world." OBJECTIVE EVIDENCE: Mary testifies, "A month after the lottery, Molly, who was unemployed, bought my house for $300,000 in cash."

## V. Subjective versus Objective Standards

Subjective standards are not intrinsically better or worse than objective standards. We use both kinds of standard in various situations. Indeed, sometimes a rule of law has both objective and subjective elements in it. For example, § 8(a)(3) of the Labor Act prohibits an employer from discriminating against a worker because of the worker's concerted (union) activity. To prove a violation of the section, the General Counsel must prove (i) that the employer disadvantaged the worker and (ii) that the employer's reason was that the worker performed a concerted act. (i) The determination of whether a worker was disadvantaged is objective; the employer's state of mind is irrelevant. Thus, suppose the General Counsel proved that an employer got so angry at a shop steward who filed numerous grievances that the employer awarded the steward a $500 bonus (assume the collective bargaining agreement allowed bonuses). Section 8(a)(3) has not been violated because, regardless of the employer's state of mind, the employer's act did not disadvantage the worker. (ii) By contrast, the determination of the employer's reason is subjective; it depends entirely on the employer's state of mind. Thus, suppose the General Counsel proved that an employer fired a worker who had been soliciting coworkers to join the union, but the employer proved that she was unaware of the solicitation and fired the worker because of poor performance on the job. Even though the effect of the discharge may have been to scuttle the union's organizing campaign, the discharge was lawful because the employer's state of mind was lawful.

Although we cannot say that either type of standard is generally superior to the other, we can say that, in a particular situation, one or the other is more likely to serve our purposes. For example, in order for a contract to come into existence, the parties must agree on the important terms. Thus, if Buyer wants to make a contract to purchase Seller's car, the two of them must agree on a price, a date of payment, and a date of delivery. Suppose the following facts occurred—

### The One-Year Misunderstanding

Buyer was a senior in the class of 2015. She wanted to drive across the country immediately after graduation, but she didn't have a car. Her roommate was Seller, a junior scheduled to graduate with the class of 2016. Each of them knew all of the following facts.

On May 27, 2015 Buyer said to her roommate, "I would like to buy your car."

Seller replied, "It will cost you $4,000."

Buyer said, "That's fair," took $4,000 in cash from her backpack, and handed it to her roommate. Buyer added, "I'll need the car on May 31st."

Seller responded, "No problem."

On May 31, 2015 Buyer asked her roommate for the keys. Seller refused to deliver them, saying, "I thought you meant May 31, *2016*."

Was Buyer entitled to the keys, that is, did Buyer and Seller make a contract? We could use either an objective or a subjective standard to determine whether agreement on the necessary terms was reached. On a subjective standard, the question would be, "Did each party, in her own mind, accept the same price, date of payment, and date of delivery?"

According to this standard, if Buyer believed that delivery would occur on May 31, 2015, but her roommate truly believed that delivery would occur on May 31, 2016, no contract was reached. On an objective standard, the question would be, "Would a reasonable person who observed the events have concluded that the parties accepted the same terms?" Judged by an objective standard, a legally enforceable contract could have been created even though the parties did not have the same ideas about the terms. Applying an objective standard, a judge might reason that because Seller knew of Buyer's plan to drive across the country and because it is unusual to pay for a car a year in advance of delivery, a reasonable person would have believed that the parties had agreed to the delivery of the car on May 31, 2015, regardless of Seller's misunderstanding.

Should we use an objective or a subjective standard to determine agreement to a contract? The answer depends on our purposes. If we want to ensure that no one ever is forced to do something that the person has not agreed to do, we should choose a subjective standard. If we want to ensure that a person can rely on reasonable perceptions of another person's promise, we should choose an objective standard.

## VI. Review

Over time, two standards have been used for determining when a contract is formed. The subjective standard is that a contract is formed when each party, in one's own mind, agrees to the same terms as the other party does—when there is a "meeting of the minds." The objective standard is that a contract is formed when the behavior of the parties indicates to a reasonable person that the parties have reached an agreement, regardless of what the parties were actually thinking.

### The House of Tantalus

Tantalus, king of Mycenae, had two grandsons, Atreus and Thyestes. The young men got into a dispute over the throne, and they sued one another.

Thyestes sued Atreus for breach of contract. Thyestes testified that Atreus had agreed to exchange his kingdom for a golden lamb, which Thyestes had tendered. Atreus testified that although he had said that he would trade his kingdom for a golden lamb, in his heart he had not truly agreed; he was just trying to avoid a fight with Thyestes.

4(a) If *Thyestes v. Atreus* were decided on a subjective standard, what would the issue be? If the case were decided on an objective standard, what would the issue be?

Thyestes won his case and assumed the throne. Then Atreus sued Thyestes for breach of contract. Atreus testified that he and his brother had a subsequent conversation in which Thyestes said, "I will relinquish the kingdom when the sun moves backwards in the sky." Zeus then caused the sun to move backwards.

4(b) If *Atreus v. Thyestes* were decided on a subjective standard, what would the issue be? If the case were decided on an objective standard, what would the issue be?

# § 16

# INTERPRETING STATUTES

## I. Sources

This section focuses on the interpretation of statutes. The principles of interpreting statutes also apply in large part to the interpretation of the other varieties of public documents such as constitutions and regulations.

When a party asserts that a statute provides the governing rule of law for the case at bar, the tribunal must interpret the statute. As it interprets a statute, the tribunal relies on a number of sources of information. The reason for consulting these sources is to determine the will of legislature.

*Ceteris paribus*, some sources are more influential than others, but no consensus exists on a hierarchy of influence. Nor is a hierarchy needed because all other things are rarely equal. Even if a particular source is usually more influential than another, in a given case an argument drawn from the more influential source may be comparatively weak, with the result that the argument may be outweighed by a strong argument drawn from a usually less influential source.

## A. Text of the Statute

The best indication of the will of a legislature is the text of the statute. If the meaning of the text is clear, a tribunal often decides the case at bar with no further research. But if the ordinary meaning of the words of a statute is ambiguous (i.e., open to more than one reasonable interpretation), the tribunal may refer to additional sources as it searches for the will of the legislature.

Even the presence or absence of a punctuation mark can affect how a tribunal interprets a statute. Here is an example from daily life—

The following message was posted on the bulletin board of κμα:

PARTY SATURDAY NIGHT!!!

Don't miss this one!! We've invited strippers, President Rawlings and Dean Katz!!

The punctuation of the second sentence of the message indicates that the words "President Rawlings" and "Dean Katz" are appositives of the word "strippers," and so the second sentence says that these venerable gentlemen are strippers. Surely the author of the message meant that strippers plus President Rawlings plus Dean Katz were invited. This meaning would have been clear if a comma (sometimes called the "Oxford Comma," that is, a comma before the word "and" in a series) had been inserted after "President Rawlings."

Here is a legal example—

The Landrum-Griffin Act guarantees democratic rights to union members. One section of the law protects union members from being disciplined for their speech by their union. In one of the last drafts of the bill, § 101(a)(2) read:

FREEDOM OF SPEECH AND ASSEMBLY.—Every member of any labor organization shall have the right to meet and assemble freely with other members and to express any views, arguments, or opinions and to express at union meetings his views, upon candidates in a union election or upon any business properly before the union meeting, subject to the organization's established and reasonable rules pertaining to the conduct of meetings.

The *Congressional Record*, which is the official record of debates and proceedings in Congress, records that Senator McClellan realized that, as written, this draft could be interpreted to protect union members' freedom of speech only in union meetings, whereas he believed (and the authors of the draft intended) that members' freedom of speech should be protected outside as well as inside the union hall. Accordingly, he suggested that the draft be amended to insert a semicolon after the word "members" in order to make clear that union members could not be disciplined for their speech, whether inside or outside of the union hall. His suggestion was adopted and, for good measure, another semicolon was added after the word "opinions" in the bill that became law. These semicolons influenced the decision of a federal appellate court in *Fulton Lodge v. Nix*.

## B. PURPOSE OF THE STATUTE

A legislature can foresee, and specifically provide for, only a limited number of situations. Yet the text of a statute can often be applied to situations that the legislature did not foresee. The task of deciding whether the statute should be applied to situations not foreseen by the legislature is delegated to the courts and to administrative agencies like the Labor Board. Such tribunals, it is often said, "fill in the gaps" in the statute.

The purpose or goal the legislature was trying to achieve—the evil to be eradicated or the good to be promoted—can be helpful in filling in the gaps. A statute sometimes contains a statement of its purpose. If not, purpose can be inferred from the text of the statute, from the reports of committees of the legislature that held hearings on, and perhaps amended, the bill that became the statute, and from remarks of legislators during debate on the bill on the floor of the legislature.

Knowing the purpose of a statute is especially helpful when its words seem to apply to unexpected cases. The student encountered one example in *Church of the Holy Trinity v. United States*, discussed in § 11. A statute prohibited employers from contracting with foreign laborers to work in America, and a church that had hired a pastor from England was prosecuted for violating this statute. The Supreme Court exonerated the church because the purpose of the statute was to protect American workers from competition from "great numbers of an ignorant and servile class of foreign laborers [who] agreed to work after their arrival for a certain time at a low rate of wages" (p. 463). Prohibiting a church from hiring a pastor from abroad would not have served this purpose. Another example grows out of § 6 of the Sherman Antitrust Act, which says, "Every contract . . . in restraint of trade or commerce . . . is hereby declared to be illegal." Suppose a spouse becomes a shopaholic. In order to avert bankruptcy, the other spouse and the shopaholic enter into a written agreement in which the latter promises to cut spending in half and, on condition that this promise is fulfilled, the former promises to stop kvetching. Such a contract, though it restrains trade or commerce, is plainly not within the purpose of the Sherman Act.

## C. Legislative History of the Statute

The legislative history of a statute includes the original bill that was introduced into the legislature; amendments to the bill, whether accepted or rejected; reports on the bill prepared by committees of the legislature; and statements by legislators on the floor of the legislature as they debated the bill. Legislative history can sometimes reveal the intent of the legislature. For example, suppose the text of a bill could reasonably be applied to facts $a$, $b$, $c$, and $d$. During debate on the bill, Senator Sanctimonious says, "I oppose this bill because it would outlaw $d$, which is a traditional American practice." To which the sponsor of the bill replies, "The senator's judgment is unimpeachable: $d$ is indeed a traditional American practice that should be encouraged, not outlawed. My bill would outlaw only $a$, $b$, and $c$; it would have no effect on $d$." A tribunal could reply on this legislative history to hold that the statute that resulted from the bill does not outlaw $d$.

Legislators' comments made after a statute is enacted are not admissible as evidence of legislative intent. Nor is the testimony in court of legislators as to the reach of a statute that has been enacted.

## D. Scholarly Publications

Scholarly writing on issues sometimes influences tribunals. Law professors, judges, law students, and practicing lawyers publish their ideas in law journals, books, and multi-volume treatises. Such scholarship has no direct force as precedent; but, if based on extensive research and sound reasoning, the views of legal commentators can influence tribunals much as precedents do. Occasionally, a treatise earns so much respect that it becomes an authoritative source.

## E. Public Policy

Policy arguments are discussed in § 9 Policy Arguments. Policy arguments may be used to interpret a statute. A statute should be construed so as to promote good public policy. For example:

### Cannery Row

A cannery operates only during the summer of the year, and it is staffed primarily with migrant workers and students on vacation. The labor contract between the cannery and a union provides that the opportunity to work overtime shall be offered to workers in order of their seniority in the job and that, if the cannery gives a junior worker overtime that rightfully belongs to a senior worker, the cannery owes the senior worker the amount of overtime wages that were paid to the junior worker.

Derr has worked in the cannery for two previous summers and this summer is the most senior worker in her job. Avraham, an adult, is the next most senior worker.

Derr is seventeen years old. By state law, she may work no more than eight hours per day and forty hours per week. Being the most senior worker, she claims shifts totaling forty hours per week. When overtime becomes available, the cannery gives it to Avraham. The union files a grievance, which goes to arbitration. The arbitrator, who is limited to enforcing the labor contract, sustains the grievance and awards Derr the amount of overtime that was paid to Avraham.

If the party that lost an arbitration refuses to obey the arbitrator's award, the party that won may ask a court to enforce the award. Accordingly, when the cannery refuses to obey the arbitrator's award, the union petitions a court for an order enforcing the award. The general rule is that a court must enforce an arbitrator's award unless the arbitrator was biased or the hearing was procedurally unfair (e.g., witnesses were not allowed to testify). In this case, the arbitrator was not biased, and the hearing was not unfair. Nevertheless, Judge Devorah refuses to enforce the award. She writes:

> The public policy of this state is that a minor may not work more than eight hours per day or forty hours per week. If this court enforced the arbitrator's award, in subsequent cases the cannery would have a strong incentive to give overtime hours to minors in violation of public policy. Therefore, this court declines to enforce the arbitrator's award.

## F. Administrative Interpretations

With increasing frequency during the twentieth century, legislatures charged administrative agencies with responsibility to interpret and enforce statutes, and this process seems to be continuing during the twenty-first century. For example, the Labor Board is responsible for administering the Labor Act. Courts give considerable respect to interpretations of a statute by the agency that administers the statute, especially when the interpretations are issued shortly after the statute was enacted. Thus, courts tend to accept the Labor Board's interpretations of the Labor Act.[1]

## G. Precedent

### 1. Analogous Statutes

If two statutes are similar, the interpretation already given to one may affect the interpretation given to the other. For example, the wording of some of the sections of the Age Discrimination in Employment Act of 1967 tracks *mutatis mutandis* the wording of some of the sections of the Title VII of the Civil Rights Act of 1964. When tribunals were called upon to interpret one of those sections of the Age Act, they followed the interpretation already given to the corresponding section of Title VII.

---

1. Some statutes give administrative agencies the authority to make rules. Properly issued rules have the force and effect of a statute. In most cases, however, an agency interprets a statute as it is applied to specific cases. In such cases, courts may review the agencies' interpretations, but usually defer to them.

## 2. *Other Tribunals' Interpretations*

Other tribunals' interpretations of a statute may also help a tribunal fathom the will of the legislature. To some extent, use of a precedent recapitulates the other sources; after all, the tribunal that issued the precedent must have based its decision on the text, legislative history, and so on of the statute. But, for at least three reasons, a precedent has independent force of its own.

First, strong arguments may be advanced on both sides of the question. That a judge has previously considered those arguments, and decided which are more convincing, can influence another judge in a subsequent case.

Second, stability in the law is usually a virtue. When an issue is decided, people adjust their behavior accordingly. Thus, the existence of a precedent creates reasonable expectations that would be upset if a subsequent tribunal declined to follow the precedent.

Third, judges are busy, and new issues are constantly arising. By following a precedent, a judge saves time that can be spent on other cases.

## II. Principles

Above we discussed sources from which courts draw information as they interpret statutes. Here we consider two principles of statutory interpretation. These principles apply regardless of the sources on which the tribunal relies.

### A. The Principle of Meaningfulness

- **Each clause, each sentence, each phrase—indeed, each word—of a statute must be given its own meaning.**

A statute is like holy writ: we mortals assume that every word was put there for a purpose. This assumption is remarkably strong. We do our utmost to honor every jot and tittle of the text. On occasion, we are not equal to the task; sometimes we must admit that the text is redundant or incomprehensible or that one passage is inconsistent with another. But admissions like this are rare. Tribunals expend great effort to avoid such admissions, and may resort to convoluted reasoning rather than admit that a statute is repetitious, unintelligible, or contradictory.

The Principle of Meaningfulness is sensible. Legislators (or, perhaps more accurately, legislative assistants and lobbyists) generally write statutes with care. Bills are scrutinized by competing interest groups and political factions, and compromises are made which are reflected in the text of the statute. Of course, the process is far from perfect. Errors occur. Some passages are hastily written. Sometimes the Principle of Meaningfulness is deliberately ignored; for example, a point may be so important to a legislator (or to the interests to which a legislator is beholden) that the point is repeated in a statute. On the whole, however, the principle is justified. And even if it is not justified, it is firmly established. For a lawyer to convince a judge that part of a statute should be disregarded would be a modern Labor of Hercules.

### Duplex v. Deering

The majority in *Duplex v. Deering* relied on the Principle of Meaningfulness. A union had been trying to induce the Duplex Company, which was one of four manufacturers of printing presses in America, to engage in collective bargaining. The union's reason was that it had organized and achieved wage gains for the workers of the other three manufacturers. Wage gains, of course, meant higher labor costs for these manufacturers. As long as Duplex remained nonunion, its labor costs would be lower than its competitors' and it could undersell them. Unfortunately for the union, only a few of Duplex's workers joined the union, and so a strike would not have been effective. The union tried another tactic: a nation-wide boycott of Duplex's presses, asking every union member to refuse to transport, install, use, or repair them. Duplex sought an injunction against the boycott, but the union pointed out that § 20 of the Clayton Act stated that no "injunction shall be granted by any [federal] court in any case between an employer and employees . . . involving, or growing out of, a dispute concerning terms or conditions of employment." The lower court accepted the union's argument and interpreted § 20 to prohibit an injunction. The Supreme Court disagreed. In the following passage from the Court's opinion, the "exceptional privilege" to which the Court referred was the exemption from injunctions for strikes and boycotts:

> Full and fair effect will be given to every word [of the statute] if the exceptional privilege be confined . . . to those who are proximately

and substantially concerned as parties to an actual dispute respecting the terms or conditions of their own employment, past, present, and future. [That is, the privilege applies to a labor dispute between a company and a union of its employees, but not to a dispute between a company and another union. The opinion of the lower court, however] virtually ignores the effect of the qualifying words [viz., "a dispute concerning terms or conditions of employment"]. "Terms or conditions of employment" are the only grounds of dispute recognized as adequate to bring into play the exemption; and it would do violence to the guarded language employed were the exemption extended beyond the parties affected in a proximate and substantial, not merely a sentimental or sympathetic, sense by the cause of the dispute.

The first clause of the first sentence of the foregoing quotation states the Principle of Meaningfulness. The third sentence accuses the lower court of ignoring the principle.

The Principle of Meaningfulness has many applications in daily life. For example, when two words are close in meaning, we seek to distinguish them. For example, consider the differences in meaning of the following words:

inherent/intrinsic
comprise/include
effect/impact

## B. The Principle of Wholeness

### 1. Within One Statute

- **A statute must be read as a whole. Each part of a statute must be interpreted in light of the other parts of the statute.**

A section or a title of a statute (a title is like a chapter) commonly addresses a single aspect of a larger subject; for example, § 8 of the Labor Act deals only with unfair labor practices, but not with representation issues or the structure of the Labor Board. Also, not every idea can be packed into each sentence, paragraph, and section to which the idea applies. For these (and probably other) reasons, the **Principle of Wholeness** dictates that the meaning of one part of a statute is influenced by the meaning of other parts of the statute.[2]

For example, § 20 of the Clayton Act read in relevant part:

> That no . . . injunction shall be granted by any [federal court] . . . in any case between an employer and employees, or between employers and employees . . . involving, or growing out of, a dispute concerning terms or conditions of employment, unless necessary to prevent irreparable injury to property. . . .
>
> And no such restraining order or injunction shall prohibit any person . . . from terminating any relation of employment, or from ceasing to perform any work or labor or from recommending, advising, or persuading others by peaceful means so to do; or from attending at any place where any such person or persons may lawfully be, for the purpose of peacefully obtaining or communicating information, or from peacefully persuading any person to work or to abstain from working; or from ceasing to patronize or to employ any party to such dispute, or from recommending, advising, or persuading others by peaceful and lawful means so to do.

The majority in *Duplex* used the second paragraph of § 20 to interpret the first paragraph. The Court wrote:

> The qualifying effect of the words [in the first paragraph] that descri[be] the nature of the dispute and the parties [viz., "a dispute concerning the terms or conditions of employment"] is further borne out by the phrases [in the second paragraph] defining the conduct that is not to be subjected to injunction or treated as a violation of the [antitrust law]:
>
> > "(a) terminating any relation of employment . . . or persuading others by peaceful and lawful means so to do;" (b) "attending at any place where any such person may lawfully be, for the purpose of peacefully obtaining or communicating information, or

---

2. This principle might be reduced to a corollary of the Principle of Meaningfulness; we separate them for clarity.

from peacefully persuading any person to work or to abstain from working;" (c) "ceasing to patronize or to employ any party to such a dispute, or . . . recommending, advising, or persuading others by peaceful and lawful means so to do."

The emphasis placed on the words "lawful" and "lawfully," "peaceful" and "peacefully," and the references to the dispute and the parties to it, strongly rebut a legislative intent to confer a general immunity for conduct violative of the antitrust laws, or otherwise unlawful. The subject of the boycott is dealt with specifically in the "ceasing to patronize" provision, and by the clear force of the language employed the exemption is limited to pressure exerted upon a "party to such dispute" [i.e., the primary employer] by means of "peaceful and lawful" influence upon neutrals. There is nothing here to justify defendants . . . in using either threats or persuasion to bring about strikes . . . [or boycotts against] complainant's customers or prospective customers.

*2. Between Statutes*

- **Statutes must be consistent with one another. A statute must be interpreted in light of other statutes.**

Just as one part of a statute must be understood in light of other parts of the same statute, so a statute must be understood in light of other statutes. It is somewhat more likely that one statute will conflict with another statute than that one part of a statute will conflict with another part of the same statute. The legislature, for example, might enact statute *B* without realizing that statute *A*, which already exists, could be interpreted to apply to some of the same cases as statute B. Tribunals try to maintain consistency across statutes and, therefore, the preceding discussion of the Principle of Wholeness applies to two (or more) statutes as well as to one statute.

## III. The Effect of Precedents on the Meaning of Statutes

When a tribunal interprets a statute, that interpretation effectively becomes a part of the statute (at least within the jurisdiction of that tribunal). Sometimes a tribunal's interpretation of a statute is explicit. For example, in *Duplex v. Deering* above, the Court wrote, "Full and fair effect will be given to every word [of the statute] if the exceptional privilege be confined . . . to those who are proximately and substantially concerned as parties to an actual dispute respecting the terms or conditions of their own employment, past, present, and future." Translated into ordinary English, this sentence meant that the privilege (exception) in the statute applied to a labor dispute between a company and a union of its own employees, but not to a dispute between a company and a union of other employees. For practical purposes, this interpretation became an amendment to the statute.

Other times, a tribunal's interpretation of a statute is not explicit, but rather is implicit in the application of law to fact. The tribunal does not expressly state what the words in the statute mean, but the holding of the case implies an interpretation. In the *First Seat Belt Case* discussed in § 12, Judge Janus considered the purpose of the law requiring use of seat belts, but did not expressly interpret the words of the statute. Nonetheless, by dismissing the citation, he implied that he interpreted the statute to mean that it did not require a driver to wear a seat belt when stopping at a toll booth and reaching for money to pay the toll.

*Duplex v. Deering* and the *First Seat Belt Case* illustrate a principle that cannot be overemphasized—

- **The meaning of a statute derives from the facts of the cases that apply it.**

This principle is so important to remember, yet is so often forgotten by beginning students, that we provide an additional example that we hope will stick in mind. A requirement for graduation provides, "Every student shall take at least one course in the Western Intellectual Tradition." Goofy proposes to meet this requirement by taking Hacking 101. The registrar informs him that Hacking 101 is not on the list of courses approved to satisfy this requirement. Goofy argues that successful hacking occurs frequently in the West and takes a lot of intellect. Of course, he loses the argument. The reason he loses is that the meaning of the requirement cannot be deduced from its name. Rather, the meaning of the requirement is exactly and only the courses that are approved to satisfy it.

Similarly, the meaning of a statute is exactly and only the holdings of tribunals that have applied the statute. *For practical purposes, cases that apply a statute amend it.* Thus, Judge Janus's decision in the *First Seat Belt Case* effectively amended the seat belt law to read, "Every person riding in a motor vehicle shall wear a seat belt at all times: provided that a person in a motor vehicle that is stopped at a toll booth may remove one's seat belt in order to reach for money to pay the toll." Likewise, the decision in *Duplex v. Deering* effectively amended the statutory words "in any case between an employer and employees" to read "in any case between an employer and *its* employees."[3]

## IV. References

105 *Congressional Record* 1230 (86th Cong., 1st sess., April 25, 1959).
*Duplex v. Deering*, 254 U.S. 443, 473–474 (1921).
*Fulton Lodge v. Nix*, 415 F.2d 212 (5th Cir. 1969).

---

3. This principle naturally assumes that a statute has been in force long enough to have been interpreted and applied by tribunals. When a statute has recently been enacted, or is applied for the first time to a particular situation, the other principles discussed in this section apply.

# § 17

# Prima Facie Case, Affirmative Defense, Burden of Proof

Basic to understanding a law case is an understanding of the ideas of the prima facie case, the defense, and the burden of proof. In brief, the prima facie case consists of the elements—that is, the facts—which the plaintiff in a civil case or the prosecution in a criminal case must prove in order to win on a claim.[1] The defense comes in two varieties. The first variety is an attack on the prima facie case; the defendant can win on a claim by destroying an element of the plaintiff's case. The second variety of defense, known as an "affirmative defense," is essentially an excuse; it is a way the defendant can prevail even if the plaintiff proves a prima facie case. The burden of proof is the obligation of a party to convince the tribunal that a fact is true.

---

1. A claim is the basis for relief; that is, a tribunal will grant a relief to a party who proves a claim. A lawsuit may include one or more claims, and they are separate. A party can win on one claim and lose on another. In a criminal case, a claim is called a "count." The rest of this section will refer to civil cases, but the principles are substantially the same in criminal cases.

## I. Prima Facie Case

### A. THE BASIC IDEA

The **prima facie case** is the set of facts (often called "elements") that a plaintiff must prove in order to prevail. Such facts are also called "material facts" or "ultimate facts." A more descriptive term would be "legally significant facts," as it emphasizes that these are the facts that the law deems important.

Many ideas in the law have a counterpart in everyday life. The trial of a lawsuit is analogous, in one respect, to the preparation of a dish in a kitchen. The cook decides which dish to prepare and then follows a recipe that specifies the ingredients of the dish and how they should be mixed and, if necessary, cooked. If the cook omits an ingredient, the dish will fail (or become something not intended).

The plaintiff in a lawsuit is like a cook, and the prima facie case is like a recipe. When a plaintiff files a lawsuit, the complaint invokes a particular substantive law, which is like the dish the cook has decided to prepare. As the cook must include each ingredient of the recipe or the dish will fail, so the plaintiff must prove that each element of the prima facie case is true. If the plaintiff fails to prove even one of the elements of the prima facie case (either because the plaintiff neglects to offer proof of the element or because the plaintiff's proof is not credible), the lawsuit fails.

For example, the tort[2] known as battery has the following elements:

1. The defendant (and not someone else)
2. intentionally (not accidentally)
3. caused a physical contact (e.g., landed a punch)
4. that was harmful or offensive (as opposed to pleasant or welcome)
5. to the plaintiff.

If π sues Δ for battery, π must prove elements 1–5, which are the prima facie case of battery. Like the cook who must mix in each ingredient

---

2. The word "tort" (from the French for "twist" or "distort") is an injury (other than a trespass to property or a breach of contract) that one person inflicts on another. A tort is considered an injury to a private person, not an injury to the public; thus, the legal remedy for a tort is a civil lawsuit, not a criminal proceeding. Negligence is the tort with which the student is most likely familiar.

of the recipe or it will fail, π must prove each of these facts or lose the case.

Another analogy to the prima facie case is a doctor's diagnosis of a disease. If conditions 1, 2, 3, and 4 are present, the patient has one disease. If conditions 1, 3, 4, and 5 are present, the patient does not have that disease, but instead has another disease or no disease at all.

Of these two analogies, the analogy to a disease is more helpful when we are thinking about how to govern our behavior. We do not wish to become ill, and therefore we attempt to avoid the conditions that constitute or cause a disease. For example, one who wishes not to contract atherosclerosis may reduce one's consumption of trans fats. Similarly, we do not wish to commit the tort of battery, and we attempt to avoid performing at least one of the elements of battery listed above. The analogy to a recipe is more helpful when we are thinking about what must be proved in a trial. If we want a perfect cake, we combine each of the appropriate ingredients (and no others). If we want to prove that someone broke the law, we prove each of the elements of the offense.

## B. Two Meanings of "Prima Facie Case"

The term "prima facie case" is ambiguous because it has two meanings. One meaning is stated above: the elements of a claim. The other meaning is the *evidence* that proves the elements of a claim. Let us call the first meaning (the elements of the claim) the **prima facie case in the first sense** or **prima facie-I**, and the second meaning (the evidence that proves the elements of the claim) the **prima facie case in the second sense** or **prima facie-II**.

The difference between the two meanings of "prima facie case" can be illustrated by extending the analogy between a prima facie case and a recipe. The basic recipe for white bread calls for several ingredients: wheat flour, sugar, salt, yeast, oil, and water. A cook who wishes to bake this recipe has several choices about ingredients. The cook may use Gold Medal bleached enriched wheat flour, store brand beet sugar, Morton's iodized salt, Mother's Favorite dry yeast, Planter's peanut oil, and tap water. Or the cook may use Robin Hood unbleached wheat flour, Holly's cane sugar, sea salt, Papa's Best cube yeast, Mazola corn oil, and Poland Springs water. Or the cook may use Hodgson Mills stone ground unbleached unenriched wheat flour, honey, kosher salt, Sister's Favorite yeast, Cora olive oil, and Perrier. And so forth. In spite of the subtle differences among these sets of ingredients, each set will produce a loaf of white bread. The recipe is like a prima facie case in the first sense; each set of ingredients is like a prima facie case in the second sense.

The tort of battery continues to provide a convenient illustration of these legal ideas. The prima facie case in the first sense of battery consists of the five elements listed above. Various prima facie cases in the second sense exist; that is, battery can be proved by various sets of evidence. For example—

### Proving Battery

#### PRIMA FACIE-II NO. 1

*W-1* testifies:

I saw *A* walk up behind *B* and poke *B* in the back.

And *B* testifies:

The blow hurt me grievously.

These evidentiary facts establish the elements of battery:

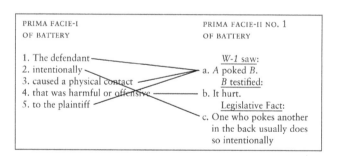

**Figure 17.1**

#### PRIMA FACIE-II NO. 2

*W-2* testifies:

I was walking my dog when I came upon a strange scene. *D* was lying on the ground, writhing and moaning, with his hand stretched around to his back. *C* was standing over *D* and saying, "I told you never to call me a wimp again. I said I would clobber you if you did."

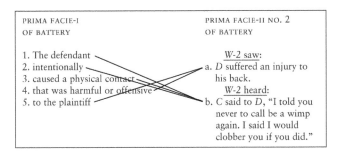

**Figure 17.2**

For any given legal claim, a single prima facie case in the first sense exists. That is, each legal claim consists of one, and only one, set of legally significant facts.[3] At the same time, an infinity of prima facie cases in the second sense exist, and each is different—different parties, different dates, different witnesses with different perspectives on the facts. Nonetheless, each prima facie-II, however it may differ from the others, proves the prima facie-I.

## II. Defenses

### A. DESTRUCTION OF THE PLAINTIFF'S PRIMA FACIE CASE

Two basic defensive strategies are available.[4] One strategy is to attack the plaintiff's prima facie case, that is, to attempt to convince the tribunal that the plaintiff has failed to prove one or more of the elements of the prima facie case. A defendant can pursue this strategy in two ways. One way is

---

3. This is not to say that the prima facie-I of a claim cannot change. A legislature or a tribunal has power to, and occasionally does, alter the elements of a claim. For example, it used to be necessary for a woman alleging rape to prove that she struggled vigorously to avoid it; today it suffices that she did not consent. But changes in a prima facie-I are infrequent and, for most purposes, one may assume that the prima facie-I is stable.

4. Other defensive strategies exist, such as a counterclaim, a cross-claim, and an interpleader. Although they are beyond the scope of this book, we may note that the principles in this section apply to them in large part.

to discredit the plaintiff's witnesses. For example, in the examples above, *A* might show that *W-1* is *B*'s spouse, or *C* might show *W-2* took a bribe from *D*. If the defendant convinces the tribunal that a witness lied or made a mistake, the facts to which that witness testified have not been proved and the prima facie case fails. The other way to pursue the strategy of attacking the prima facie case is to present witnesses who report different facts than the plaintiff's witnesses report. *W-4* might testify that *E* was in Pango Pango on the day that *F* was punched. If the tribunal believes the defendant's witnesses, or cannot decide whose witnesses to believe, once again the facts to which the plaintiff's witnesses testified have not been proved and the prima facie case fails.[5]

## B. AFFIRMATIVE DEFENSE

The other strategy for defending a case is to present an affirmative defense. An **affirmative defense** admits arguendo (for the sake of argument) that the prima facie-I is true, but offers a legitimate reason for what the defendant did. For example, one may consent to a physical contact, and so consent is an affirmative defense to battery: think of a boxing match.

Like the idea of a prima facie case, the idea of an affirmative defense is easily understood because it has a close analogue in everyday life. An affirmative defense is simply an excuse: the defendant did it, but had a good reason for doing it. Suppose Tommy's mother comes home and finds that half the cake she has baked for dessert is missing, and she accuses Tommy. "Yes," he admits, "I took it," and then he offers an excuse: "But I didn't eat it. I gave it to a poor homeless boy who knocked on the door and begged for food because he was starving to death." If Tommy's story is true (or, at least, if his mother believes it is true and he eats all his dinner and does not get a stomach ache), he will not be punished, even though he took the cake.

An affirmative defense is similar to a prima facie case in some regards. One similarity is that the term "affirmative defense" has two senses: **affirmative defense in the first sense** or **affirmative defense-I**, which is the legally significant facts of the defense, and **affirmative defense in the second sense** or **affirmative defense-II**, which is a set of evidentiary facts that

---

5. This strategy is also available to a plaintiff in regard to a defendant's affirmative defense, which is the next topic of discussion.

proves the legally significant facts. For example, an affirmative defense to battery is self-defense. The elements (the affirmative defense in the first sense) of self-defense are—

1. The plaintiff (who has sued the defendant for battery)
2. caused (e.g., pointed a pistol at)
3. the defendant
4. to form a belief that the plaintiff was about to injure the defendant;
5. the defendant's belief was reasonable under the circumstances; and
6. the defendant used no more than reasonable force to protect oneself.

### A Pinch at Pong

Hunk is a student at Working Man's Tech, and Wuss is a student at High Brow U. They occupy adjacent seats during the big ping-pong match between the schools. High Brow's player scores a point on a brilliant serve, and Wuss jumps to his feet and cheers. Hunk sets down his beer, stands, and says, "I see that you are a High Brow. For this you deserve a beating," and throws a punch that misses Wuss by an inch. As Hunk cocks his other arm, Wuss stomps on Hunk's big toe. Hunk sues Wuss for battery.

Hunk can prove a prima facie case of battery, as Wuss intentionally stomped on Hunk's toe. Wuss can prove the affirmative defense of self-defense.

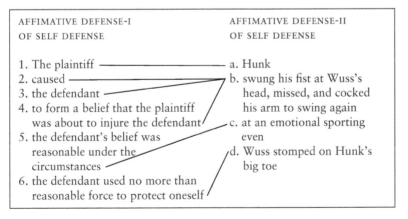

**Figure 17.3**

An affirmative defense implicitly concedes the truth of the prima facie case. Every excuse does. When Tommy said that he gave half of the cake to a homeless boy, Tommy admitted that he took the cake. Logically, then, a defendant should have to choose: either attack the prima facie case, or admit its truth and offer an excuse; and in the past the law required a defendant to make this choice. Today, however, a defendant need not choose between these defenses. That is, a defendant may attack the plaintiff's prima facie case *and* attempt to establish an affirmative defense. We are less logical today, but more practical.

A defendant who fails to prove an affirmative defense does not necessarily lose on that claim, for his attack on the prima facie case might be successful. For example, suppose the tribunal does not believe that Wuss had a reasonable fear of being socked by Hunk. In this event, Wuss's affirmative defense fails. But this failure does not dictate that Wuss lose the case, for his attack on the prima facie case might succeed. The tribunal might find that Wuss did not stomp on Hunk's toe intentionally.

By contrast, as noted above, a plaintiff who fails to prove a prima facie case must lose on that claim. If the tribunal finds that Wuss did not step on Hunk's toe intentionally, Hunk fails to prove an element of the prima facie case of battery and loses on that claim. But this failure does not dictate that Hunk lose the entire case, for he might allege and prove another claim as well. Although Hunk may fail to prove a case of battery, he might still prevail on a claim of negligence.

## III. Burden of Proof

Like the terms "prima facie case" and "affirmative defense," the term "burden of proof" is ambiguous because it has more than one meaning. It can mean the burden of production or the burden of persuasion.[6] Let us consider each meaning.

---

6. A burden of pleading also exists. It is the obligation of the plaintiff to state a claim in the complaint, or of the defendant to state a defense in the answer to the complaint. This obligation is an aspect of procedural law, which is generally beyond the scope of this book.

## A. BURDEN OF PERSUASION

**Burden of persuasion** refers to the obligation of a party to prove that a fact is true. This burden has three dimensions: who carries it, how heavy it is, and what happens if a party fails to carry it.

### 1. Who Carries the Burden of Persuasion?

Common sense tells us that if a party stands to gain from a tribunal's finding that a fact is true, that party (and not her adversary) should have the duty to convince the tribunal that the fact is true.[7] Tommy must prove that a homeless boy came begging for food; his mother need not prove that a homeless boy did not come to the door. In this regard, if not in others, the law follows common sense. The plaintiff has the burden of convincing the tribunal that the facts of the prima facie case are true; the defendant has the burden of convincing the tribunal that the facts of the affirmative defense are true.

### 2. How Heavy Is the Burden of Persuasion?

How firmly convinced must the trier of fact be in order to find that a fact is true? In most civil cases, the standard is **preponderance of the evidence**. This standard means that, in order for the party with the burden of persuasion to prevail, the evidence on that party's side must be stronger than the evidence on the other side. A little stronger is enough. Imagine a scale with the parties' evidence in the pans. It suffices that one pan is slightly lower than the other.[8]

Suppose the evidence is equally balanced—the tribunal cannot say which side is stronger, cannot decide which side to believe? In this event, the party with the burden of persuasion has failed to carry the burden. A tie base goes to the other guy.

### 3. What Happens If a Party Fails to Carry the Burden of Persuasion?

The consequence of failing to carry the burden of persuasion is losing on that issue. If Hunk fails to convince the tribunal that Wuss intentionally

---

7. Other bases for assigning the burden of persuasion exist, but they are far less common. An example is assigning the burden to the party with the better access to the evidence.

8. Another standard occasionally used in civil cases is **clear and convincing evidence**, which requires that the evidence of the party with the burden of persuasion be substantially stronger than the evidence of the other side. The standard **beyond reasonable doubt** is used only in criminal cases.

trod on Hunk's toe, Hunk loses on the claim of battery. If Wuss fails to convince the tribunal that he had a reasonable belief that he was about to be punched, he loses on the affirmative defense of self-defense. For this reason, the burden of persuasion is sometimes called the "risk of nonpersuasion." The plaintiff bears the risk of nonpersuasion with respect to the facts of the prima facie case; the defendant bears the risk of nonpersuasion with respect to the facts of an affirmative defense.

The burden of persuasion applies to facts, but the term is often used loosely in reference to issues or entire claims or defenses. The student may encounter a sentence such as, "The plaintiff failed to carry the burden of persuasion on the prima facie case." Analysis reveals, however, that the burden applies to facts. A plaintiff carries the burden of persuasion on an issue or a claim if and only if the plaintiff carries the burden on each legally significant fact of the claim. Likewise for a defendant and an affirmative defense. Thus, we would call it nonsense if a tribunal wrote, "The plaintiff has proved by preponderance of the evidence that the defendant intentionally inflicted a harmful contact on the plaintiff, but has failed to prove a prima facie case of battery." Such a statement can only mean that the plaintiff has failed to carry the burden of persuasion with respect to at least one element of the prima facie case. Accordingly, the student is advised to keep one's focus on the facts.

## B. BURDEN OF PRODUCTION

The second meaning of "burden of proof" is the **burden of production**. It tells the tribunal which party must *produce evidence* that a fact is true or false.

At the outset of a case, the burden of production follows the burden of persuasion. If a party has the burden of persuasion on a legally significant fact, that party also has the initial burden of production on that fact; that is, the party must offer evidence that tends to prove that the fact is true. If the plaintiff fails to carry the burden of production on an element of the prima facie case—offers no evidence tending to prove a legally significant fact—naturally the fact is not proved and the plaintiff must lose. Thus, in battery the plaintiff carries the burden of producing evidence that the contact was harmful or offensive. The burden might be carried, for example, by the nature of the physical contact (e.g., we may presume that a broken bone is harmful) or by the plaintiff's testifying, "It hurt like blazes!" Similarly, the defendant carries the burden of producing evidence on each element of an affirmative defense.

Unlike the burden of persuasion, which always stays with the same party, occasionally as a case progresses the burden of production may shift from one party to the other. The law of employment discrimination provides an example. In *McDonnell Douglas v. Green*, the Supreme Court held that a plaintiff alleging racial discrimination had established a prima facie case with evidence that he belonged to a racial minority, that he applied and was qualified for a job for which the employer was seeking applicants, and that he was rejected and the employer continued seeking applicants. Then the Court stated, "The burden then must shift to the employer to articulate some legitimate, nondiscriminatory reason for the [plaintiff's] rejection" (p. 802). Some lower courts erroneously interpreted this statement to mean that the burden of *persuasion* shifted to the employer, that is, that the employer had to convince the tribunal that the employer rejected the plaintiff for a nondiscriminatory reason. The Supreme Court subsequently corrected this error. In *Texas Department of Community Affairs v. Burdine*, the Court held that only the burden of *production* shifts. If a plaintiff proves a prima facie case as in *McDonnell Douglas*, the employer "must clearly set forth, through the introduction of admissible evidence, the reasons for the plaintiff's rejection" (p. 255); however, "the [employer] need not persuade the court that it was actually motivated by the proffered reasons" (p. 254). "The plaintiff retains the burden of persuasion" (p. 256). In other words, when a plaintiff proves a prima facie case, the burden of production shifts to the employer to challenge the plaintiff's evidence. The employer can carry this burden with evidence of a nondiscriminatory reason for rejecting the plaintiff. After the tribunal has heard from both parties, the burden of persuasion is on the plaintiff to convince the tribunal that his evidence is stronger.[9]

---

9. This paragraph should not be read to imply that the plaintiff in a trial presents all of one's evidence before the defendant presents any evidence. In fact, the defendant commonly uses the cross-examination of the plaintiff's witnesses to undermine their credibility, and even to elicit evidence that favors the defendant. In other words, the defendant can meet the burden of production via the testimony of the plaintiff's witnesses as well as via the testimony of the defendant's witnesses.

## IV. Prima Facie Case + Affirmative Defense = Rule of Law

The prima facie case and the affirmative defense together constitute a rule of law.[10] If one asks, "Should there be a law against battery?" one is in fact asking, "Should there be a law against intentionally inflicting a harmful or offensive contact on another person, absent consent, privilege, or the need for self-defense?" Whether a new prima facie case and affirmative defense should be recognized is an issue at a high level of abstraction. If a new nation were founded and all of its laws had to be declared, questions would arise whether there should be laws against battery, unfair labor practices, drinking alcohol under the age of twenty-one, making loud noises near your professor's home at night, and so forth. For each question answered yes, a prima facie case and, perhaps, affirmative defenses would have to be specified. If the new nation followed the Anglo-American tradition, this process could occur in the legislature, in the courts, and in administrative agencies.[11]

## V. Review

More than one answer to the following may be correct to questions 1–3.

1. The term "prima facie case" means—
   - ☐ (a) a recipe for disaster
   - ☐ (b) the facts that a party must prove in order for a tribunal to grant relief

---

10. Some prima facie cases have more than one affirmative defense; for example, the affirmative defenses to battery include self-defense, consent, and privilege. (An example of privilege is that a parent may restrain an unruly child.) And some prima facie cases admit of no affirmative defense; for example, if using explosives, however carefully, results in damage to neighboring property, the user will be liable.

11. Tribunals are more restricted in their ability to create new claims than are legislatures and administrative agencies. A plaintiff proposes that facts 6, 7, and 8 be recognized as a new claim. The tribunal may accept the plaintiff's proposal or reject it, but may not modify it or substitute another one. The reason is that a tribunal is restricted to deciding cases or controversies. The controversy between the plaintiff and the defendant is whether the defendant should be liable to the plaintiff for having performed facts 6, 7, and 8 (that is, whether facts 6, 7, and 8 should be the prima facie case of a new claim). The tribunal may decide this controversy, but may not use this case to decide that facts 6, 7, and 9 are a new claim. (If the tribunal did state that facts 6, 7, and 9 are a new claim, the statement would be labeled dictum and would not have the force of precedent.)

    ☐ (c) the exclusive right to extract minerals from a piece of land
    ☐ (d) the diagnosis of the disease from which the defendant suffers

2. The term "affirmative defense" means—
    ☐ (a) a defense presented by the plaintiff
    ☐ (b) an affirmation by the defendant that the defense is true
    ☐ (c) the opposite of a negative defense
    ☐ (d) a legal excuse

3. The term "burden of proof" means—
    ☐ (a) the duty to carry the judge's briefcase
    ☐ (b) the party who wins when the other party fails to prove certain facts
    ☐ (c) the duty to prove one or more facts are true
    ☐ (d) the wages of sin.

### Battery on a Barstool

π sued Δ for battery. π offered evidence that he and Δ were seated at a bar, watching a football game. π was rooting for the Doolittles and Δ was rooting for the Dingleberries, and π and Δ got into an argument over whether Killerback interfered with Stickyfinger's attempt to catch a pass. Words led to insults, after which, testified π, "Δ tweaked my nose, and it hurt." Δ testified that π had said that any fan of the Dingleberries was a low-down, no-account wroggler who deserved to be disregarded, disenfranchised, and discombobulated. π replied that he actually said, "The Dingleberries are performing poorly this season."

4. Δ's testimony was—
    ☐ (a) an element of the prima facie case
    ☐ (b) an attack on the prima facie case
    ☐ (c) an affirmative defense
    ☐ (d) a shift in the burden of proof.

5. What would have been the consequence if the tribunal believed Δ and did not believe π's reply?
    ☐ (a) π won the case.
    ☐ (b) Δ won the case.
    ☐ (c) π proved the prima facie case.

   ☐ (d) Δ proved an affirmative defense.
   ☐ (e) We can't know.

6. What would have been the consequence if the tribunal did not believe Δ's testimony?
   ☐ (a) π won the case.
   ☐ (b) Δ won the case.
   ☐ (c) π proved the prima facie case.
   ☐ (d) Δ proved an affirmative defense.
   ☐ (e) We can't know.

### The Two-Timer

Bloomberg testifies:

> I went to Zooey's home on the day in question because we had planned to go sailing together. It was a beautiful day for sailing, and Zooey loves to sail. But I found him lying in bed. He said he couldn't go with me because his back hurt because Franny had beat him up an hour earlier. Then I went to Franny's home; she was supposed to come along with Zooey and me on the boat. Franny was slouched in a chair, crying.
>
> I asked, "What's wrong?"
>
> She said, "I'm depressed because I just beat up Zooey. He's one of my best friends, but I had to stop him from two-timing my grandmother."

7. State why the testimony proves, or does not prove, each element of the prima facie case of battery. (Ignore the rule against hearsay as evidence.)

## VI. References

*McDonnell Douglas v. Green*, 411 U.S. 792 (1973).
*Texas Department of Community Affairs v. Burdine*, 450 U.S. 248 (1981).

# § 18

# APPLICATION OF LAW TO FACT

**Applying law to fact** and **application of law to fact** mean determining the legal consequences of a set of facts, in other words, determining what the governing rule of law requires of parties when those facts exist. Application of law to fact is the last of the four steps necessary to resolve an issue. The process of applying law to fact is the same for any decision maker—civilian, police officer, attorney, administrative agency, or tribunal. For convenience, the following discussion will speak of application of law to fact by a tribunal, but the principles are the same for anyone else.

The distinction between issues of law and issues of application of law to fact is primarily important for two purposes. First, when a case is tried to a jury, the judge resolves issues of law and the jury resolves issues of application of law to fact. Second, when the judgment of a trial court is appealed, the appellate court freely reviews rulings by the trial judge on issues of law, but is deferential to application of law to fact, whether by trial judge or jury.

## I. Application of Law to Fact Operates Issue by Issue

Each issue requires its own application of law to fact. If a single standard controls a case, and that standard has a single element, the case generates a single issue of application of law to fact, and resolving that issue decides the case. In many instances, however, the governing standard has several elements, and elements may have sub-elements. Each element (and sub-element) of the standard generates its own issue of application of law to fact. For example—

### The Raid

Unions in the past sometimes fought over their jurisdictions. Different unions claimed the right to represent the same unit of workers. If no union represented the unit at the time, it was acceptable for two (or more!) unions to compete for the right to represent the unit. However, if a union already represented the unit, it was disruptive to employer and workers alike for another union to try to interpose itself. Accordingly, in 1947 Congress added a new unfair labor practice to the Labor Act: if a union represents a unit of the workers of a company, it is illegal for another union to exert economic pressure on the company for the purpose of forcing it to bargain instead with the other union. Suppose union *A* has won a representation election among *ER*'s workers and the Board has certified *A* as the workers' bargaining agent. Union *B* wishes to represent those workers, and strikes *ER* for the purpose of forcing *ER* to bargain with *B* instead of *A*. The standard that governs this case has five elements, all of which must be satisfied, thereby generating five issues of application of law to fact. The Labor Board must resolve each of these issues in order to decide whether *B* broke the law.

### Table 18.1

| Element | Issue of application of law to fact |
| --- | --- |
| Both unions are labor organizations as defined in the Act. | Are *A* and *B* labor organizations as defined in the Act? |
| The employer is an employer as defined in the Act. | Is *ER* an employer as defined in the Act? |
| One of the unions presently represents a unit of workers of the employer. | Does *A* represent a unit of *ER*'s workers? |

| Element | Issue of application of law to fact |
|---|---|
| The other union applies economic pressure to the employer. | Did *B* strike *ER*? |
| The purpose of the other union is to force the employer to bargain with it instead of the union presently representing the workers. | Was *B*'s purpose to force *ER* to bargain with *B* instead of *A*? |

Each of these issues must be resolved in order to decide whether *B* broke the law. (*B* did.)

## II. Direct Application of Law to Fact

**Direct application of law to fact** occurs when a tribunal applies a legal standard to a set of facts and resolves the issue without invoking any other authority. *The Raid* illustrates direct application of law to fact. For example, one issue in the case was whether a union represented the workers of *ER*. The legal standard is that a union represents workers when the majority of them in an appropriate bargaining unit[1] desire the union to represent them. The facts were that *A* had won a representation election and the Board had certified *A* as the bargaining agent of the workers. To resolve the issue of whether a union represented *ER*'s workers, the Board applied the standard directly to the facts. No authority (other than the standard itself) had to be consulted before the Board could decide that *ER*'s workers were represented by *A*.[2]

### A. Direct Application of Law to Fact by Force of Logic

In many cases, the governing rule of law may be applied to the facts of the issue by means of a legal syllogism. Consider—

#### Caroline's Case

Caroline is five years old. The day is hot, and she wants a soda. She enters a convenience store, chooses her favorite brand, and walks to the cashier,

---

1. Appropriate bargaining units are discussed below in *Ben-El's Case* in this section.
2. Direct application of law to fact will become clearer to the student when it is contrasted below to mediated application of law to fact.

who scans the can and says, "That'll be a dollar thirty." Caroline opens her little purse and spills her savings on to the counter. The cashier counts the coins. "You only have 85 cents. I'm sorry, that's not enough." Caroline puts her money back into her purse and leaves without the soda.

The cashier's application of the "law" (the price of the soda) to the facts (Caroline's money) requires no judgment, and can be analyzed into sound legal syllogisms:

### QUASI SYLLOGISM

ISSUE

May Caroline purchase a soda?

MAJOR PREMISE (governing rule)

All persons who wish to purchase a soda must tender $1.30.

MINOR PREMISE (FACTS OF THE CASE)

Caroline tenders only 85¢.

CONCLUSION (application of law to fact)

∴ Because 85¢ is less than $1.30, Caroline may not purchase a soda.

### MODUS TOLLENS

ISSUE

May Caroline purchase a soda?

IF $p$, THEN $q$ (GOVERNING RULE)

If a person wishes to purchase a soda, one must tender $1.30

NOT q (FACTS OF THE CASE)

Caroline tenders only 85¢.

NOT $p$ (APPLICATION OF LAW TO FACT)

∴ Because 85¢ is less than $1.30, Caroline may not purchase a soda.

The cashier did not have to exercise judgment to conclude that Caroline lacked sufficient money to buy a soda. The conclusion followed from the premises by force of logic.

### Tommy's Case

Tommy is a typical thirteen-year-old boy. He overhears his nineteen-year-old brother talking with friends about a new theater in town that shows X-rated movies, and Tommy decides he wants to see one. The following Saturday afternoon, he goes to the theater and approaches the ticket booth.

The killjoy in the booth asks, "How old are you?"

"Sixteen," says Tommy.

"Sure," says the killjoy, "but the owner says you have to be at least eighteen to see this movie. Come back in about five years."

## Question

1. The killjoy applies law to fact directly without using judgment. Fit his reasoning into a legal syllogism.

## B. Direct Application of Law to Fact by Use of Judgment

In the preceding examples, application of law to fact called for no judgment on the part of the tribunal. The syllogisms operated by force of logic. In many other cases, judgment is necessary. Judgment resists analysis, but it can be illustrated. Let us begin with an example, from life outside the law, of application of law to fact that requires judgment.

### The Coach

Jackson is the coach of a basketball team. He is constantly deciding which players to put on the court and which to hold on the bench. Jackson ranks the players according to skills such as shooting, dribbling, passing, defense, and rebounding; but a player's rank alone does not determine whether one plays. Jackson also considers a player's "sense of the game," which includes deciding whether to shoot or pass, which type of shot to take, which player to pass to, and so on. And Jackson considers a host of other factors, such as match-ups against the players that the other team has on the court, how vigorous or fatigued a player appears to be, which team is ahead and by how many points and with how much time remaining in the game, when the next game is scheduled, whether that game is at home or away, who the players on that team are, and so forth. Jackson's standard is simple: play the players who will make the greatest contribution to winning this game and future games. Applying this standard requires human, indeed, super-human judgment.

Here is a legal example.

### Adora's Case

Adora's Adages are in great demand, and her company employs hundreds of adagers to produce and disseminate adages. Local 33 of the National Writers Union recently won a representation election among the adagers, after which Kiyoon, the president of the local, called Adora and requested a meeting for February 21 in order to begin collective bargaining. Adora replied,

"I'm not available on that date."
"How about the 22nd?" said Kiyoon.
"Not then either," answered Adora.
"The 23rd?"
"No."
"When are you available this month?"
"I don't have any time this month. Things are very busy. You know how it is."
"No, I don't," said Kiyoon. "When will you be available?"
"It looks like my first date is March 3."
"We can't wait that long."
"It's the best I can do."
"What time?"
"11:00 looks good."

Kiyoon waited. On March 1 Adora's secretary called him and said that Adora had another commitment and could not meet until March 5 at 3:00 p.m.

Kiyoon arrived at Adora's office on March 5 at 2:55. Adora's secretary said that she was busy at the moment, but would be with him shortly. At 4:15 the secretary said that Adora could see him. As he entered the room, Adora said,

> "This will have to be brief. I have a commitment at 4:30."
>
> "You can't be serious. I've waited two weeks for this meeting, and I've waited an hour and a half today. We can't do anything in fifteen minutes."
>
> "Well, if you'd rather postpone—"
>
> "No way," said Kiyoon, and he handed her a list of the union's demands.
>
> "I'll look it over and get back to you," said Adora as she walked out the door.

Two more weeks passed, and Kiyoon heard nothing from Adora. He called her office several times, but the secretary always said that Adora was on another line or in a meeting. Finally, on April 13 Kiyoon stationed himself outside of Adora's office and waited until she emerged.

> "Are our demands acceptable?" he asked.
>
> "No," she answered as she walked toward the exit.
>
> "None of them?"
>
> "None."
>
> "Well, what do you propose?"
>
> "I think things are fine as they are now."
>
> "We have to sit down and talk about this."
>
> "Schedule something with my secretary," said Adora over her shoulder as she left the building.

Kiyoon consulted with the national union's attorney, who sent a letter to Adora, saying that he intended to file an unfair labor practice charge against her unless she began bargaining forthwith.

Adora's secretary called Kiyoon to say that Adora had reserved the afternoon of March 31 for bargaining, and she and Kiyoon met at 1:00.

> "The adagers haven't had a pay raise in three years, and you've upped our monthly quota by 30 percent," complained Kiyoon.
>
> "You should be glad that demand for adages is increasing."

"I am, but we need a raise—25 percent at least."

"That's impossible."

"Nothing's impossible."

"The competition is very stiff."

"How about 20 percent?"

"No way."

"Bottom line: 10 percent."

"I'll give you 2."

"I'll take it to the members. So let's talk about the speedup."

"What speedup?"

"Over the last nine months you've increased our monthly quota by thirty percent."

"It's not a quota. It's a goal."

"Whatever it is, it's too high. We're burning out. People are getting sick."

"I'm sorry to hear that, but we need the goal in order to turn around orders quickly. People who want an adage want it fast. If we can't meet their demand, they'll go somewhere else, and you know there's plenty of places they can go."

"Can't you cut back a little, say to fifteen percent?"

"Truly, I am sorry it's so hard on the adagers. It's hard on all of us. But there's no way I can reduce production."

"Twenty percent."

"You're wasting your breath. There's no point in talking about this."

"So let's talk about vacations."

"What about them?"

"We need two weeks of paid vacation."

"You think I'm made of money?"

"I think you're making a lot of money."

"You'd be surprised."

"How much are you making?"

"Let's stick to business."

"We need a paid vacation. Everybody gets paid vacations. It increases productivity."

"One week after ten years of service."

"Nobody works here ten years."

"Now they'll have a reason to."

"One week after one year."

"Sorry, no can do."

"I'll take it to the members. Now, about the production quota—"

"You're not listening to me. I said no, and I meant it. Don't mention this again."

"We need to discuss seniority."

"Why?"

"Protection against layoffs, shift preferences."

"We prefer to base our personnel decisions on productivity."

"Loyal workers deserve protection. It's good for morale."

"It's not good to tie our hands like that."

"Then let's discuss the production quota."

"Didn't you hear what I said? I am not going to discuss the production goal. When you're ready to listen to me, we can talk again. Please go now."

"It's only 2:00. We scheduled the whole afternoon."

"What's the point? You're not listening to me. Good afternoon."

Kiyoon reported to the union's lawyer what happened at this meeting.

"She's not bargaining in good faith," said the lawyer. "I think we should file a charge with the Board."

"Go ahead," Kiyoon said. "We've got nothing to lose."

The lawyer filed a charge of refusal to bargain with the regional office of the Labor Board. Section 8(a)(5) makes it an unfair labor practice for an employer "to refuse to bargain collectively" with a union, and § 8(d) defines collective bargaining as "the performance of the mutual obligation . . . to meet at reasonable times and confer in good faith with respect to wages, hours, and other terms and conditions of employment, or the negotiation of an agreement . . . ." Ali, a field examiner in the regional office, investigated the charge, confirmed the facts above, and then spoke with the regional director.

"I think," said Ali, "this is an easy 8(a)(5). Adora wouldn't meet at reasonable times. She gave up next to nothing in bargaining. She refused to discuss the production quota and seniority. It's a slam dunk."

The regional director replied, "I disagree about meeting at reasonable times. We have to look at the norms in this area. Kiyoon asked for a meeting for February 21 and got one on March 5. That's not expeditious, but it was only two weeks and she's talking now. I'm not going to issue a complaint on that basis."

"But what about the way Adora treated him? She cancelled the first meeting and kept him waiting an hour and a half for the second meeting. Then she cut that one short after less than fifteen minutes, and she didn't respond to the union's demands for more than two weeks. And then she threw him out after an hour when they'd scheduled the whole afternoon."

"That's certainly not respectful; but they did meet for a substantial period of time on March 31. They made some progress, and she said they would talk again."

"She's not bargaining in good faith: a measly two percent raise after three years without a raise; nothing on seniority; ten years before a vacation, which is a joke; the union can't even talk about the speedup—I wouldn't call that bargaining. I don't think she has any desire to reach an agreement with the union."

"You have to keep in mind that 8(d) specifically says that a party doesn't have to agree to a proposal or make a concession. They went back and forth on the raise, and they're probably not finished bargaining over vacations and seniority. You might have a point about the speedup, however. It sounds like she refused even to discuss the issue, which would definitely be a refusal to bargain. Overall, I'd say she's a pretty tough bargainer, but that's legal. They'll probably reach an agreement, which the union won't be happy with—or maybe it'll strike, who knows? Right now, except for the speedup, I don't think we could make a charge stick. Let's give them some more time. I don't want to give Adora the phony excuse that she doesn't have to bargain while the matter is before the Board. Call the union and let them withdraw the charge and, if things get worse, they can file it again."

Let us focus on the duty to bargain "in good faith."[3] Good faith and bad faith are states of mind; therefore, this aspect of the duty to bargain is judged by a subjective standard. Trying to read someone's mind is problematic. The evidence in *Adora's Case* was conflicting. On the one hand, Adora's disrespectful behavior suggests bad faith. So does a pattern of failures to make concessions, or trivial concessions that are virtually insults. On the other hand, failure to make concessions is not unlawful, and Adora offered a two percent raise, which is not insubstantial, and

---

3. The regional director actually applied two standards to *Adora's Case*. The first was whether Adora was willing to meet at reasonable times. Reasonableness is an objective standard, and Adora was within the norm. The second standard was the duty to bargain in good faith.

proposed a one-week vacation after ten years of service. This evidence led one reasonable person, Ali, to one conclusion, and another reasonable person, the regional director, to the opposite conclusion. That reasonable persons can differ over the resolution of an issue is a mark of a standard that requires judgment.[4]

*Adora's Case* illustrates application of a subjective standard using judgment. Perhaps judgment is always required in applying a subjective standard. Objective standards may also require judgment. Here is an example that would never happen in real life:

### Amanda's Case

Amanda rents a house near the campus. She throws a party on the Saturday night before classes begin, and many of her friends attend. The guests drink various beverages and play music at a high volume through large speakers. At 10:00 p.m. the man living in the house next door approaches Amanda.

"The music is keeping my children awake. Please turn it down."

"It doesn't seem too loud to me," Amanda replies.

The neighbor calls the police. An officer arrives and informs Amanda that Municipal Ordinance 1.16 states, "No resident shall make unreasonably loud noise. The term 'resident' includes a resident's guest. The penalty for making unreasonably loud noise is a fine of one hundred dollars for the first offense and five hundred dollars for any further offenses."

"It's not so loud," Amanda protests.

The officer responds, "It is unreasonably loud. Your neighbors can't sleep. If you don't turn it down, I'll have to cite you. And while I'm at it, I'd probably have to check some IDs."

Amanda reduces the volume.

The student may be thinking that the standard of unreasonable loudness is subjective. Perhaps it is subjective as that word is used in ordinary English today, but the student will recall from § 15 SUBJECTIVE AND OBJECTIVE STANDARDS that in law "subjective" means depending on the

---

4. The regional director exercised judgment in another way as well. Although the issue concerning the speedup did not call for judgment—it is always a refusal to bargain to decline to discuss a mandatory subject—nonetheless, the regional director exercised judgment in deciding not to pursue that violation at the present time.

state of mind of a party. The student may reply, isn't reasonableness a state of mind? Of course, reasonableness is a state of mind, but not the state of mind of any particular party. Reasonableness is a community standard, a social judgment. For this reason, the standard of unreasonable loudness was an objective standard. Nonetheless, the police officer used judgment in applying the standard. Although he believed that Amanda's music violated the municipal ordinance and, therefore, he could have cited her, he used judgment in giving her the opportunity to reduce the volume. Not every law needs to be enforced to the letter.

An example under the Labor Act of an objective standard, the application of which requires judgment, is a standard with several sub-elements, as in—

### Ben-El's Case

Ben-El's sells automobile parts and accessories; it also sells, installs, and repairs tires. The parts and accessories division is called the "store"; the tires division is called the "tire shop." The store and the tire shop are located side by side in the same building; viewed from the entrance, the store is on the left and the tire shop is on the right. The front of the store displays automobile accessories; the back of the store contains shelves of automobile parts. The front and back of the store are separated by a counter with computers and cash registers on it. The front of the tire shop displays tires; the back of the shop contains pneumatic lifts and other equipment for installing and repairing tires. The front and back of the tire shop are separated by a wall with a door. A wall without a door separates the back of the store from the back of the tire shop. No barrier separates the front of the store from the front of the shop.

Jobs in Ben-El's are divided into three categories. One category is "store clerk," of whom there are ten on each shift. They stock the shelves of the store, both in front and in back, and serve customers (answer questions, fetch parts from the back of the store, receive payments for merchandise). Store clerks are paid wages of $12 per hour. A second category of jobs is "tire seller," of whom there are two on each shift. Their primary duty is selling tires in the front of the tire shop. Tire sellers are paid a commission on each sale. The third category of jobs is "technician," of whom there are eight on each shift; they install and repair tires. Technicians are paid wages of $15 per hour.

Ben-El's is open from 6:00 a.m. to 10:00 p.m. Half of the workers in each category of job are on the morning shift, half on the afternoon shift.

A single manager is responsible for all operations. The manager typically arrives for work at 9:00 a.m. and leaves at 6:00 or 7:00 p.m.

Local 22 of the United Food and Commercial Workers has been trying to organize Ben-El's for a few weeks, and has persuaded four store clerks, six technicians, and two tire sellers to join the union or to sign cards authorizing the union to represent them in bargaining. Twelve is less than a majority of Ben-El's workers, but the Board will hold a representation if a union can demonstrate a "showing of interest" among the workers. Cards from at least 30 percent of the workers constitute a showing of interest. In Ben-El's case, the union needs cards from (40 x 0.3 =) 12 workers. Based on the twelve cards it has, the union petitions the Board to hold an election.

A petition for an election must specify the "bargaining unit" which the union desires to represent. The employer may object to the petition on various grounds, one of which is that the bargaining unit in the union's petition is not appropriate.

What is an appropriate bargaining unit? A labor union does not have a legal right to represent a group of workers for collective bargaining merely because a majority of the workers in the group desire union representation. Rather, a union may represent a group of workers only if their jobs share a "community of interest," which is to say that the jobs are similar enough that collective bargaining has a good chance of success regarding the terms and conditions of employment that apply to those jobs. The reason is that workers who hold jobs that share a community of interest will have similar goals in collective bargaining, whereas workers who hold jobs that lack a community of interest will have dissimilar goals, and that the more similar the goals which a union pursues, the more likely that collective bargaining will succeed. Jobs that share a community of interest constitute an appropriate bargaining unit.

The Labor Board has a great deal of experience deciding whether a bargaining unit is appropriate. Based on that experience, the Board has created a list of factors or criteria that indicate whether a particular group of jobs is an appropriate bargaining unit. The criteria include similarity of job duties, similarity of skills, extent of shared working areas, commonality of supervision, similarity of methods of compensation, degree of interchange of duties among jobs, and the list goes on. In any given case, the issue of application of law to fact is whether a particular bargaining unit is appropriate. It is unusual for all of the criteria to point in the same direction. When some criteria indicate one result (this unit is appropriate) and some criteria indicate the opposite result (this unit is not appropriate), they rarely point with equal force: thus, criterion α might indicate unequivocally the appropriateness of the unit whereas criterion β indicates the opposite but is a close call; and a particular criterion might be more important in one case than in another.

Local 22 files a petition for an election. The petition specifies a bargaining unit comprising all the jobs in the store and the tire shop, excluding the manager. Ben-El's objects on the ground that the three categories of jobs in the store and the tire shop are so different that successful bargaining about them would be impossible. The Board holds a hearing on Ben-El's objection, presided over by hearing officer Juanita, and the parties present their evidence. The overall issue of application of law to fact is whether the jobs share a community of interest, but each of the criteria (similarity of skills, commonality of supervision, etc.) generates a separate issue of application of law to fact. The facts stated above are introduced as evidence.

After the conclusion of the hearing, Juanita evaluates the evidence. She applies law to fact regarding each of the criteria for a community of interest. For example, she reasons—

## SIMILARITY OF SKILLS

### ISSUE

Do the jobs of store clerk, tire seller, and technician require similar skills?

### MAJOR PREMISE

Similarity of skills means similarity of the ability to use knowledge for a purpose.

### MINOR PREMISE

Store clerks have considerable knowledge of automobile parts. Tire sellers are skilled in persuasion. Technicians have the narrow skill of mounting and dismounting tires and patching them.

CONCLUSION

∴ The jobs of store clerk, tire seller, and technician do not require similar skills.

## Commonality of Supervision

ISSUE

Do the categories of jobs have common supervision?

MAJOR PREMISE

Commonality of supervision means having the same supervisors.

MINOR PREMISE

All categories of worker in Ben-El's are supervised by the same manager.

CONCLUSION

∴ The jobs have common supervision.

## Working Areas

ISSUE

Are jobs performed in the same area?

MAJOR PREMISE

Area refers to the physical space in which workers perform tasks.

MINOR PREMISE

All categories of worker perform tasks in the same building. No barrier separates the store from the front of the tire shop, but store clerks perform no tasks in the tire shop and tire sellers perform no tasks in the store. Technicians work in an enclosed space separated from the front of the tire shop and from the store.

CONCLUSION

∴ All tasks are performed in the same building but in different parts of it.

After applying all of the criteria of appropriate bargaining units to the facts of the case, Juanita finds that some criteria (e.g., common supervision) point toward a community of interest, other criteria (e.g., similarity of skills) point toward the absence of a community of interest, and still other criteria (e.g., shared working areas) do not point one way or the other. Then she writes a report to the regional director, who puts all of the criteria into an imaginary scale in his mind and weighs the criteria that indicate a community of interest against the criteria that indicate the absence of a community of interest. He concludes that the former are weightier and approves the bargaining unit requested by the union.

The regional director uses judgment as he weighs objective criteria against one another. He concludes that the workers share a community of interest, but another reasonable person might reach the opposite conclusion.

In addition to weighing various criteria against one another, balancing competing interests is a common example of an objective standard that requires judgment to apply. The right of political protesters to freedom of speech is balanced against the need for order in a community. The interest of a lumber company in harvesting timber is balanced against the risk to endangered species in a forest. The right of an employer to manage one's business is balanced against the right of a union to recruit and represent workers.

## III. Application of Law to Fact Using Precedent

In direct application of law to fact, the tribunal resolves the issue using only the standard being applied. In **application of law to fact using precedent,** the tribunal consults previous decisions of tribunals that have dealt with this issue. If a tribunal has previously decided the same issue, stare decisis may bind the present tribunal to resolve the issue in the same way. If a tribunal has previously decided an issue that is similar, but not exactly the same, the previous decision may guide the present tribunal or restrict its discretion.

## A. Application of Law to Fact Using Binding Precedents

When a tribunal confronts an issue of application of law to fact which has been resolved in a previous case, the latter case sets a precedent for the case at bar. Consider—

### The Honor Society Cases

Section 123 of the by-laws of the honor society λΘλ pertains to admission. The section states that, to be invited to join the society, a student must have a cumulative grade point average of at least 3.8 and be a leader on campus. The admissions committee is considering the applications of Candace and Peter. Candace's average is 4.0, and she is the captain of the debating team. Peter's average is 4.0, and he is vice-president of the campus poker society. The committee offers admission to Candace. As for Peter, a senior on the committee remembers that last year the committee declined to admit Sandy. Her grades were good, but her leadership was inadequate. She had been the vice-president of the spelunking club, and the committee felt that the vice-presidency of a group is an insignificant office. The committee rejects Peter's application.

The issue in Peter's case is the same as the issue in Sandy's case, namely, is the vice-presidency of a group evidence of leadership? The committee has previously resolved this issue in Sandy's case, and it follows its precedent in Peter's case.

Consider now a legal example—

### Harry the Harrier

Local 99 of the International Brotherhood of Harriers represents the harriers who are employed by Harquebus, Inc. Production is organized into departments; for example, stocks are made in the Stock Department, and barrels, in the Barrel Department. Each department has its own ladder of progression. The jobs are organized so that each higher step on a ladder is less physically demanding, more mentally demanding, and better paid than the step below. Thus, promotion up a ladder is desirable. Section II.A of the labor contract between Local 99 and Harquebus provides that when a vacancy occurs in a department, the company will promote the most senior worker on the next lower step of the ladder, provided that the worker is willing and able to do the job.

The ladder of progression in the Trigger Department has four steps. Harry and three other harriers occupy step 3. Hilda is the most senior harrier on this step; Harry is the second most senior, David is third, and Robert is last. Recently, a vacancy occurred in step 4 when a harrier retired. Adhering to the contract, the company offered the job to Hilda, but she declined it. Then the company offered the job to David. Harry, being more senior than David, filed a grievance with the union.

The contract establishes a grievance procedure. It begins with a meeting between the shop steward, who is an employee of the company as well as an officer of the union, and the supervisor of the department. If the grievance is not resolved at this step, the union may request a meeting with the superintendent of the plant. If the grievance is not resolved at the second step, the union may demand arbitration before an arbitrator approved by the American Arbitration Association. Arbitration is an informal trial. The decision of the arbitrator is binding on the company and the union.

Upon receiving Harry's grievance, the shop steward requests a meeting with the supervisor of the Trigger Department. At the meeting, the supervisor points out that the contract does not address the case in which a worker declines a promotion. Therefore, the supervisor argues, after Hilda declined promotion, the company was free to fill the vacancy with anyone the company chose. The superintendent takes the same position in the second step.

In the Harriers' Union, the decision on whether to take a grievance to arbitration is made by an elected grievance committee. The steward reports the company's argument to this committee, which decides not to demand arbitration because it appears that the company is right.

Harry hires a lawyer, who sues the union for breach of the duty of fair representation. As its name implies, this duty requires a union to represent workers fairly. The lawyer contends that the union was unfair to Harry because it should have taken his case to arbitration, in which it should have argued that the contract implicitly requires the company to honor seniority in all promotions in a department; and, therefore, assuming that Harry is able to do the work (and no one says otherwise), the company should have promoted him. The union moves to dismiss the case. Judge Janus writes:

> This case involves the union's administration or enforcement of its contract with the employer, in particular, grievance handling. The duty of fair representation requires the union to represent workers "without hostile discrimination, fairly, impartially, and in good faith." *Steele v. Louisville & Nashville RR.* at 204. The duty applies to the administration, as well as to the negotiation, of a labor contract. *Conley v. Gibson.* An individual worker does not have a right to have one's grievance taken to arbitration. *Vaca v. Sipes.* Mere negligence on the part of the union, albeit regrettable, does not breach the duty. *United Steelworkers of America v. Rawson.*
>
> The complaint contains no allegation that the union's decision not to pursue arbitration of Harry's grievance resulted from discrimination of any sort, personal hostility to him, or any other illicit motive. The complaint alleges that the grievance committee simply did not think of a particular argument that might have helped Harry. Even if we assume that the argument would have been obvious to any labor lawyer, and would have convinced any arbitrator, the union's failure to think of this argument was at most negligent.
>
> We take guidance from *Cannon v. Consolidated Freightways Corp.*, in which an employer discharged a driver after a crash because he refused to take a sobriety test. The driver filed a grievance, and the union took the matter to arbitration. The panel of arbitrators denied the grievance on the basis of its informal rule that refusing to take a sobriety test generates a presumption of drunkenness. The driver sued the union for breach of the duty of fair representation on the theory that, in the arbitration, the union did not challenge the sobriety rule for being informal and improperly promulgated. The court wrote, "At most, the failure to raise the defense was an act of neglect or the product of a mistake in judgment. However, 'proof that the union may have acted negligently or exercised poor judgment is not enough to support a claim of unfair representation.' *Bazarte v. United Transportation Union* at 872." *Cannon* at 294.
>
> The motion to dismiss is granted.

Judge Janus had to address four conceptually prior issues of law before he could apply law to fact. All of those issues had previously been decided, and he was bound by those precedents. Those issues, the precedents, and the resolutions were—

Table 18.2

| Issue | Precedent and resolution |
|---|---|
| 1. What is the standard in a fair representation case? | 1. Per *Steele v. Louisville & Nashville RR.*, a union must represent workers "without hostile discrimination, fairly, impartially, and in good faith." |
| 2. Does the duty of fair representation apply to administration of a labor contract? | 2. Per *Conley v. Gibson*, yes. |
| 3. Does a worker have a right to have one's grievance taken to arbitration? | 3. Per *Vaca v. Sipes,* no. |
| 4. Does negligence by a union violate the duty of fair representation? | 4. Per *United Steelworkers of America v. Rawson*, no. |

With these issues resolved, the judge could apply the law to the facts of the case at bar. His research revealed that previous tribunals had addressed the same issue, and their decisions were binding on him:

| Issue | Precedent and Resolution |
|---|---|
| 5. Did the union breach the duty of fair representation in handling Harry's grievance? | 5. Per *Cannon v. Consolidated Freightways Corp.*, which followed *Bazarte v. United Transportation Union*, the union was at worst negligent and, therefore, did not breach the duty. |

The judge's application of law to fact can be analyzed into a legal syllogism, the minor premise of which is an analogy.

ISSUE

Did the union breach the duty of fair representation?

MAJOR PREMISE (RULE OF LAW)

Negligence does not violate the duty.

MINOR PREMISE (APPLICATION OF LAW TO FACT)

Analogy to *Cannon v. Consolidated Freightways*

ISSUE

Was it negligent for a union to fail to present to an arbitrator an argument that might have won the case for the grievant?

PRECEDENT *Cannon v. Consolidated Freightways*

Facts of the precedent

In presenting a case to a panel of arbitrators, the union failed to argue that an informal rule on which the arbitrators relied had not been promulgated properly.

Rationale of the precedent

The union's failure was merely an act of neglect or a mistake of judgment.

Result of the precedent

The union did not breach the duty of fair representation.

CASE AT BAR *Harry the Harrier*

Facts of the case at bar and their similarity to the facts of the precedent

In the case at bar, the union dropped Harry's grievance because it did not think of the argument that the labor contract implicitly required the company to honor seniority in all promotions in a department. Similarly, the union in *Consolidated Freightways* did not argue that a rule on which the arbitrators relied had not been promulgated properly.

Argument that the rationale of the precedent applies to the facts of the case at bar

In both cases, the union may have been negligent, but negligence does not violate the duty of fair representation.

CLAIM

*Consolidated Freightways* controls the outcome of the case at bar.

CONCLUSION

∴ The union did not violate the duty of fair representation.

The *Honor Society Cases* and the *Harry the Harrier* exemplify application of law to fact using precedent that is binding on the tribunal. The following case exemplifies application of law to fact using precedent that is not binding, but provides guidance to the tribunal.

## B. Application of Law to Fact Using Guiding Precedents

In other cases, precedent guides or limits, but does not determine, a tribunal's application of law to fact. Consider again the *Honor Society Cases*, but suppose that Peter was the treasurer instead of the vice-president of the poker society. The admissions committee might have taken guidance from Sandy's case: offices below the presidency are often merely résumé builders. But the committee would not have been bound by the precedent of Sandy's case, for the committee might have reasoned that, whereas a vice-president typically does nothing, a treasurer handles money and money is especially important in a poker club.

Consider now a legal example in which precedent guided application of law to fact:

### The Battle of the Sexes

The Loyal Order of the Albatross represents a unit composed of forty workers, twenty-five of whom are men and fifteen of whom are women. After negotiating for several weeks, the bargaining committee of the union and the employer agree that compensation will increase by a dollar per hour. The employer is indifferent as to how this increase is allocated across wages and fringe benefits. The union committee decides to put 60 cents into wages, and the issue becomes how to allocate the remaining 40 cents. Female members often miss work, and lose wages, because a child is too sick to go to school and too young to stay home alone; they want to use the 40 cents to fund a job in the plant for a full-time provider of care for sick children. Male workers prefer to use the 40 cents to fund extension of the annual paid vacation by four days. The committee decides to extend vacations. The women sue the union in Judge Devorah's court.

The governing rule is that the union's decision must be reasonable. Judge Devorah looks for precedents to inform her discretion, and she finds the decision of Judge Janus in the *Pension Case*. In that case, the Tattlers' Union represented a bargaining unit of employees of Shauna & Co. The unit was composed of one hundred workers, sixty-five of whom were over fifty years of age and thirty-five of whom were under fifty. Prior to opening negotiations toward a new contract, the bargaining committee of the union estimated that Shauna would agree to increase total compensation by half a dollar. Then the committee considered the question, how should the increase be allocated between wages and contributions to the workers' pension accounts? The younger workers, who had financial obligations resulting from mortgages and growing families, argued that most of the increase should go into wages. The older workers, whose mortgages were paid off and whose children had left home, argued that most of the increase should go into their pension accounts. After lengthy deliberation, the committee decided to propose that 30 cents go into pensions and 20 cents into wages. Shauna accepted the proposal.

A younger worker sued the union in Judge Janus's court. The judge wrote that the governing rule of law was the duty of fair representation. In the context of negotiating a collective bargaining agreement, the Supreme Court held in *Ford Motor Company v. Huffman* that the duty allows a union to adjust the interests of workers within "a wide range of reasonableness" (p. 338). The issue, therefore, was whether the decision of the bargaining committee was within the range of reasonableness. The choice to increase pension contributions more than wages favored 65 percent of the bargaining unit (the older workers), but also benefitted the remaining 35 percent (the younger workers). Judge Janus held that the committee's decision was reasonable.

With this precedent in mind, Judge Devorah wrote:

> In the case at bar, extending paid vacations primarily favors the male workers. The precise percentages cannot be established because some men might benefit from care for sick children (e.g., if the men are single parents or their wives also work), and some women might not benefit from it (e.g., if they have no young children or a grandmother is handy). On the assumption that all such variables are distributed evenly across the classes of men and women, the bargaining committee's decision

primarily favors (25 ÷ 40 =) 62.5 percent of the bargaining unit, approximately the same percentage as primarily benefitted in the *Pension Case* (65 percent). Also as in the *Pension Case*, the interests of the other workers were not neglected. In the *Pension Case*, all workers, old and young alike, enjoyed a 20-cent increase in wages and a 30-cent increase in pension contributions. In the case at bar, all workers, women and men alike, receive a 60-cent increase in wages and four additional days of paid vacation. Accordingly, this court holds that the bargaining committee's decision was reasonable and did not violate the duty of fair representation.

Precedent helped Judge Devorah decide whether the union's decision was reasonable. If favoring 65 percent of the workers in the *Pension Case* was reasonable, favoring 62.5 percent in the *Battle of the Sexes* was probably reasonable as well; and in both cases the less favored group received substantial benefits. Judge Devorah's discretion was not controlled by Judge Janus's decision, but was guided by it.

## IV. Review

### *Dipaboli's Case*

Dipaboli got the job of the ticket seller for the roller coaster at the fair. The owner trained her on Monday, and she observed the following events.

Cassie sought to buy a ticket.

"How old are you?" asked the owner.

"Twelve," Cassie answered.

"Is anyone going to ride with you?" he asked.

"No."

"Can you walk under this bar without ducking?" He pointed to a horizontal bar that was five feet off the ground.

Cassie walked under it.

"I'm sorry," the owner said, "you can't ride."

Devon sought to buy a ticket.

"How old are you?" asked the owner.

"Fourteen," answered Devon.

"Are you going to ride alone?"

"Yes."

"Can you walk under this bar without ducking?"

Devon bumped his head against the bar.

"That'll be five dollars."

Rhea sought to buy a ticket.

"How old are you?" asked the owner.

"Eighteen."

"That'll be five dollars."

Dylan sought to buy a ticket.

"How old are you?" asked the owner.

"Fourteen," answered Dylan.

"Can you walk under this bar?" asked the owner.

Dylan walked under it.

"Are you going to ride alone?"

"No," said Siri, who was standing behind Dylan. "I'm his mother, and I'll ride with him."

"That'll be ten dollars," said the owner.

On Tuesday Dipaboli worked alone. Samuel sought to buy a ticket.

"How old are you?" asked Dipaboli.

"Fifteen," answered Samuel.

"Are you going to ride alone?" she asked.

"Yes," he answered.

"Can you walk under this bar?" she asked.

Samuel walked under the bar.

"I'm sorry," said Dipaboli, "I can't sell you a ticket."

(1) What was the issue of application of law to fact in *Samuel's Case?*

(2) State each precedent that was binding on Dipaboli, and indicate how it affected her decision.

Hint: Dipaboli followed four precedents, not merely three.

## V. References

*Bazarte v. United Transportation Union*, 429 F.2d 868 (3d Cir., 1970).

*Cannon v. Consolidated Freightways Corp.*, 524 F.2d 290 (7th Cir., 1975).

*Conley v. Gibson*, 355 U.S. 41 (1957).
*Ford Motor Co. v. Huffman*, 345 U.S. 330 (1953).
*Steele v. Louisville & Nashville RR.*, 323 U.S. 192 (1944).
*United Steelworkers of America v. Rawson*, 495 U.S. 362 (1990).
*Vaca v. Sipes*, 386 U.S. 171 (1967).

# § 19

# A Model of Legal Argument

## I. Neither a Quasi Syllogism nor a Statistical Syllogism Can Capture a Legal Argument

Can legal argument be analyzed into the form of a syllogism? Consider a typical example:

### Shimul's Case

C. W. Bumpkin, the justice of the peace in the Village of Backwater in the State of Confusion, presides in cases of minor traffic violations. Shimul appears in court in answer to a citation issued by Officer Quota for driving 44 miles per hour on Route 79. After hearing the testimony of the officer and Shimul, Justice Bumpkin gives the following opinion.

Section 123.456(a)(1)Bl) of the Motor Vehicle Code of this state provides that the speed limit on Route 79 is 55 miles per hour except where a lower limit is posted. Section 1 of the Code provides that no one shall operate a vehicle in a manner that is not reasonable and safe under the conditions of the weather and the road. Officer Quota testified that Shimul was driving southbound on Route 79 one mile north of Backwater at 10:28 a.m. on December 6, 2016. The posted speed limit at that place is 55 miles per hour. Quota's speed gun showed that Shimul's rate of speed was 44 miles per hour. Quota also testified that heavy snow had begun to fall shortly after 9:00 a.m., that at least two inches of snow lay on the road, and that the road had not yet been salted. In his opinion, the greatest speed at which a vehicle could safely travel under those conditions was 20 or 25 miles per hour. Shimul testified that her vehicle was equipped with all-wheel drive and electronic stability control, that it had snow tires on each wheel, that she grew up in rural Maine, and that she was fully in control of the vehicle.

I credit Officer Quota's judgment that the reasonable and safe speed limit under the conditions was no more than 25 miles per hour. I reject Shimul's argument that she should be excused because she was in control of her vehicle. Given the conditions, she might have lost control at any moment, probably destroying property and perhaps injuring or killing herself or other persons. Therefore, I find her guilty and fine her the amount prescribed by law.

We can analyze Justice Bumpkin's opinion into the following elements:

1. The posted speed limit was 55 miles per hour.
2. Weather and road conditions can reduce the speed limit.
3. Because of the weather, the reasonable and safe speed limit at the place and time was 25 miles per hour.
4. Shimul was traveling at 44 miles per hour.
5. That Shimul was in control of her vehicle was not an excuse.
6. Shimul violated the speed limit.

Elements 3, 4, and 6 can be fitted into a quasi syllogism:

MAJOR PREMISE

The reasonable and safe speed limit under the conditions was 25 miles per hour.

MINOR PREMISE

Shimul was traveling at 44 miles per hour.

CONCLUSION

Shimul violated the speed limit.

The other elements, however, do not fit into a quasi syllogism, yet they are important parts of the justice's argument. It is evident, therefore, that a quasi syllogism does not capture a legal argument.

Also, the major premise of a quasi syllogism does not allow for the possibility that the law may be uncertain. For example, Shimul and Officer Quota disagreed over the reasonable and safe speed under the conditions, and the justice could (at least in theory!) have sided with either one of them; but the quasi syllogism does not reflect this uncertainty.

By contrast, a *statistical* syllogism can capture uncertainty. Could a statistical syllogism capture the justice's argument? An observer in the courtroom might think, "There's a 99 percent chance that Justice Bumpkin will agree with Officer Quota and a 1 percent chance that the justice will agree with Shimul." This observation might be accurate, and it would be appropriate as a premise in a statistical syllogism if our purpose were to predict who will win the case.[1] But the purpose of Justice Bumpkin's argument was not to predict the outcome of the case that he himself was deciding. His purpose was to present a reasoned argument that identified and interpreted the law, applied it to the facts of the case before him, and responded to Shimul's argument. A statistical syllogism can capture only a part of such an argument.

---

1.

MAJOR PREMISE

In ninety-nine cases out of one hundred, a town justice will accept a police officer's judgment of the reasonable and safe speed under the conditions.

MINOR PREMISE

Officer Quota says the reasonable and safe speed was 25 miles per hour, and Shimul says it was at least 44 miles per hour.

CONCLUSION

Justice Bumpkin will find that 25 miles per hour was the reasonable and safe speed.

## II. A Model of Legal Argument

### A. TOULMIN'S MODEL

For hundreds of years, scholars and lawyers analyzed legal reasoning into deduction and analogy. Induction was thought to apply only to evidence, that is, to the way facts were proved.

In the mid-twentieth century, Stephen Toulmin published *The Uses of Argument*, in which he pointed out that legal argument, though it often incorporates deductive reasoning, is fundamentally probabilistic and, therefore, a form of induction. Drawing on appropriate sources and following the rules of legal argument, an advocate, who could be an attorney or a judge, argues that the correct law is α β γ. Also drawing on appropriate sources and following the rules, another advocate, who could be an opposing attorney or a dissenting judge, argues that the correct law is χ Ψ π. In this sense, the advocates' arguments are probabilistic. Neither advocate's argument is analytic; neither must be accepted by every rational person. Rather, each argument has a certain probability of success, and this statement is true even though the arguments may be expressed in the form of a syllogism.

For example, in *United Steelworkers of America v. Weber*, a cause célèbre of the 1970s, an employer and a labor union created a training program for unskilled workers so that a limited number of them could qualify for skilled jobs. Due to a history of discrimination against African-Americans, the employer and the union adopted an affirmative action plan under which at least half of the workers admitted to the training program were African-Americans. Although applicants were accepted to the program on the basis of their seniority in the plant, in effect the plan created two seniority rosters, one for each race. The first person admitted to the program was the most senior African-American; the second person admitted was the most senior European-American; the third person admitted was the second most senior African-American, and so on. Because of discrimination in the past, most African-American workers had been hired only recently. As a result, even the most senior African-American who was admitted to the program had less seniority than some European-Americans who were not admitted. One of those European-Americans, Brian Weber, sued under Title VII of the Civil Rights Act of 1964, claiming that he had been discriminated against because of his race. Sections 703(a) and (d) of this statute make it illegal "to discriminate against any individual . . . because of such individual's race."

Weber relied on the text of the statute to argue that it outlawed the affirmative action plan. The employer and the union argued that the purpose and legislative history of the statute demonstrate argue that Congress intended to increase employment opportunities for African-Americans and women. The plan in the case at bar was not unfair to white workers because it awarded them half of the spots in the training programs. Accordingly, the statute permitted the plan. Weber replied that purpose and legislative history cannot change the meaning of the perfectly clear text of the statute. The employer and the union responded that purpose and legislative history indicate what the meaning of the text is. All arguments were plausible; they followed the rules of legal argumentation, and the judges were free to choose between the competing arguments. The outcome of the arguments, therefore, was probabilistic.[2]

Here is Toulmin's model of legal argument:

DATUM $\rightarrow$ CLAIM

    ^         QUALIFIER?

WARRANT

    ^         REBUTTAL?

BACKING

DATUM, which is the singular of "data," is a fact (or set of facts) that leads one to make a claim.

CLAIM is the result the advocate desires.

WARRANT is the rule that governs the issue. If the warrant is accepted, it leads to the claim.

BACKING is the argument that justifies using this warrant to settle the issue. The justification may be grounded on authority, such as a statute or an analogy to a precedent, or on public policy.

QUALIFIER responds to an objection to the datum, claim, warrant, or backing. A qualifier accepts the objection and works around it by indicating the limit of the claim (i.e., the claim goes this far, but no farther). We place a question mark after this element because it is not a part of every argument.

REBUTTAL responds to an objection to the datum, claim, warrant, or backing. A rebuttal denies the objection and rebuts it. We place a question mark after this element because it is not a part of every argument.

---

2. The majority of the Supreme Court found the plan to be lawful.

Toulmin's model has been called a syllogism on its side, and this appellation is fair. The WARRANT in Toulmin's model is the major premise in a quasi syllogism; the DATUM is the minor premise; and the CLAIM is like the conclusion.

DATUM →              CLAIM              QUALIFIER?
(minor premise)      (conclusion)

∧

WARRANT                                 REBUTTAL?
(major premise)

∧

BACKING

## B. Our Revision of Toulmin's Model

Toulmin has influenced our thinking about legal reasoning, and we are happy to acknowledge our debt to him. Nonetheless, we feel the need to revise the model in minor ways. First, we add an element that is implied in the model. Legal arguments always address issues. Toulmin's model does not explicitly state the issue that the argument addresses. The model does imply the issue because the claim, expressed as a question, is the issue. For example, if the claim is, all men are created equal, the issue is, are all men created equal? Good advocacy includes an explicit statement of the issue. At least for the beginning student, therefore, we think it best to modify the model by adding ISSUE as an element of the model.

Second, lawyers usually speak of "facts," not "data" (except in certain technical contexts). Thus, we change DATUM to FACTS.

Third, for lawyers "warrant" refers to an order of a court, such as an arrest warrant. Accordingly, we change WARRANT to GOVERNING RULE, which we think captures Toulmin's meaning in ordinary English.

Fourth, we rename BACKING, calling it RATIONALE. Although lawyers would understand the word "backing," they more commonly use the word "rationale." (They use the word "argument" to refer to all of the elements in the model taken together.) The rationale consists of reasons for adopting the claim. Because claims vary in nature, rationales also vary. On an issue of law, the claim is the rule of law that should govern the case, and the rationale is the reason(s) for the tribunal to adopt that rule. On an issue of fact, the claim is that a fact is true, and the rationale is the reason(s) for the tribunal to believe that the fact is true. On an issue of application of law to fact, the claim is the result that the tribunal should reach after applying the governing rule to the facts of the case, and the rationale is the reason(s) for the tribunal to apply the governing rule so as to reach that result.

Fifth, qualifiers and rebuttals are responses to objections. Although the objection may usually be inferred from the QUALIFIER or REBUTTAL, we think it best to state the objection explicitly.

Sixth, we move CLAIM so that it follows immediately after ISSUE. Our reason is that one can more easily understand an argument when one knows where it is going.[3]

Finally, we stand the model upright. As Toulmin presented it, the model is a fine visual representation of a legal argument, but we are accustomed to reading on the standard page, which is longer than it is wide.

Here is Toulmin's model of legal argument with our revisions:

ISSUE

CLAIM

FACTS (TOULMIN'S DATUM)

GOVERNING RULE (TOULMIN'S WARRANT)

RATIONALE (TOULMIN'S BACKING)

OBJECTION/QUALIFIER?

OBJECTION/REBUTTAL?

A complete argument contains all of the necessary elements of this model except that, as we mentioned above, the elements OBJECTION/QUALIFIER and OBJECTION/REBUTTAL are sometimes unnecessary. Also, an argument may be complete even though a necessary element is not expressly stated. A skilled advocate often implies, rather than states, one or more of the elements of a complete argument; the reason may be a belief that the elements that are omitted are obvious to an informed reader, or a desire to emphasize the elements that are stated. The beginning student, of course, should leave nothing to implication.

As the student learned in § 7 ARGUMENTS CLASSIFIED BY FUNCTION, a legal argument can be used to specify the issue, to prove the facts, to determine the law, or to apply law to fact. The revised model of legal argument captures each of these uses.

---

3. Nonetheless, the order of the elements of the model is not rigid. Sometimes changing the order of the elements makes an argument more forcible.

### 1. *Issues as to the Issue*

Arguments on the question, "What is the issue in this case?" fit into the revised model of legal argument. For example—

#### Janus v. American Federation of State, County, and Municipal Employees

The intersection of three principles has resulted in as many uneasy compromises in labor law. The first principle is majority rule. The majority of workers in a bargaining unit decide whether or not the unit will be represented by a union. Carried to its extreme, this principle would mean that if the majority chose a union, everyone in the unit would have to join the union. The second principle is freedom of association. The government may not force a person to join a club, a party, or any other group. Carried to its extreme, this principle would mean that a union could not represent workers who do not wish representation, even if the majority of workers in the unit do. The first compromise is that if the majority of workers in a unit choose to unionize, the union will *represent* all of the workers in the unit, and the collective bargaining agreement will cover everyone; but no worker may be required to *join* the union. It is not uncommon that a substantial fraction of workers who are represented by a union refuse to join it.

This compromise has led to (what some call) an inequity. A union provides services for the workers whom it represents: it bargains contracts for them, presents their grievances to their employer, and represents them in arbitrations. These services cost money. Members of the union pay dues to cover this cost. Workers who refuse to join the union (let us call them "refusers") receive the same services as members, but pay no dues. Accordingly, a second compromise has been fashioned. An employer and a union may agree that refusers must pay for their share of the services that the union provides. A workplace covered by such an agreement is called an "agency shop," and refusers' share is called an "agency fee."

How much should refusers pay? At this point, the third principle becomes relevant, namely, freedom of speech. The government may not force a person to support a cause or candidate that the person does not wish to support. Support includes paying money, for example, contributing funds to a political party or to a candidate for public office. Unions often use members' dues to engage in political activity.

Members agree to such use. Refusers do not. The third compromise is that the agency fee may not include the cost of unions' political activity, but may include the cost of negotiating and enforcing collective agreements.

The agency shop has been legal in the private sector of the economy for many years,[4] and was legalized in the public sector by the Supreme Court's decision in *Abood v. Detroit Board of Education* in 1977. Recently, however, refusers revived their attack on the agency shop in the public sector. Their principal argument was that when unions negotiate with the government, public policy is affected. For example, when a union of a city's employees succeeds in negotiating a raise in wages, the city may need to raise taxes; and taxation is public policy par excellence. If a refuser is required to pay an agency fee that includes one's share of the cost of negotiating such a contract, the refuser is, in effect, being required against one's will to support a particular public policy—a violation, argues the refuser, of freedom of speech.

The constitutionality of the agency shop came before the Supreme Court recently in *Janus v. American Federation of State, County, and Municipal Employees*. But what was the issue in the case? The refusers said the issue was, does an agency shop in the public sector infringe on a refuser's right to freedom of speech? The unions said the issue was, should the Supreme Court overrule the precedent set in *Abood*? The parties' arguments as to the issue in the case can be expressed in the revised model of legal argument. Here (in simplified form) is the union's argument—

ISSUE

What is the issue in *Janus v. American Federation of State, County, and Municipal Employees*?

CLAIM

The issue is, should the Supreme Court overrule the precedent set in *Abood v. Detroit Board of Education*?

---

4. Approximately half the states in America have "right-to-work" laws, under which a refuser may not be required to pay an agency fee.

FACTS

The Supreme Court upheld the constitutionality of the agency shop in the public sector in *Abood v. Detroit Board of Education*.

GOVERNING RULE

A precedent should be followed except in extraordinary circumstances.

RATIONALE[5]

Stability in the law is an important value in a legal system; instability in the law inspires disrespect for it. A precedent should not be overruled merely because judges change their mind on an issue. Only extraordinary circumstances justify overruling a precedent. Therefore, the issue in the case at bar is whether *Abood* should be overruled due to extraordinary circumstances.

### Exercise 1

Fit into the revised model the refusers' argument as to the issue in the case.

### 2. *Issues of Fact*

This book has generally not addressed proof of issues of fact. Nevertheless, because most students have an intuitive understanding of how facts are proved, we will offer here an example of how the revised model of legal argument captures arguments about issues of fact.

In § 5 INDUCTION we presented part of a conversation created by Prof. Corbett. Here is his entire example with an addition of our own—

α:   O'Malley is probably Catholic.
β:   Why do you say that?
α:   He is Irish and was born in southern Ireland.
β:   So what?

---

5. An issue as to the issue in a case is an issue of law. Accordingly, the rationale will be the reasons for the tribunal to frame the issue as in the claim. The governing rule in this argument is that a precedent should be followed except in extraordinary circumstances. Accordingly, the rationale in this argument consists of reasons for following precedents.

α: Most such people are Catholic.

β: How do you know that?

α: The *Times* said 93 percent are.

β: I don't trust the *Times*.

α: It was quoting official census data.

β: Even so, O'Malley could be one of the 7 percent, or he might have lapsed.

α: That's why I said "probably."

Prof. Corbett designed, and we have added to, this conversation in order to illustrate Toulmin's model of legal argument. We can fit the conversation into the revised model—

ISSUE

Is O'Malley Catholic?

CLAIM

α: O'Malley is probably Catholic.

FACTS

α: He is Irish and was born in southern Ireland.

GOVERNING RULE

β: So what?

α: Most such people are Catholic.

RATIONALE[6]

β: How do you know that?

α: The *Times* said 93 percent are.

OBJECTION/REBUTTAL

β: I don't trust the *Times*.

α: It was quoting official census data.

---

6. On an issue of fact, the rationale will be the reasons for the tribunal to believe the fact is true. In Prof. Corbett's example, the rationale consists of the reason for believing that most Irish born in southern Ireland are Catholic.

OBJECTION/QUALIFIER

> β:  Even so, O'Malley could be one of the 7 percent, or he might
> have lapsed.
>
> α:  That's why I said "probably."[7]

### 3. Issues of Law

The revised model of legal argument captures arguments on what the law
is or should be.[8] Sometimes the issue and its resolution affect many persons and situations (operate at a high level of abstraction). For example, when a union represents a unit of workers, should it be illegal for the
employer or the union to lie to the other party? Other times the issue and
its resolution affect only a few persons and situations (operate at a lower
level of abstraction). For example, should it be an unfair labor practice
for an employer to threaten to close the business if the workers vote to
unionize? Whether the issue operates at a high level of abstraction, a low
level, or in between, the authority on which the tribunal relies to resolve
the issue can be a public policy, a constitution or statute, or a precedent.
Arguments on any issue of law fit into the revised model.

Consider the issue at a high level of abstraction mentioned in the preceding paragraph. An opponent of a rule against lying might argue that
it can be difficult to draw a line between a lie and the truth (is an exaggeration a lie? is failing to state a relevant fact a lie?) and equally difficult

---

7. We noted above that the model is a quasi syllogism in which the governing rule is the
major premise, the facts are the minor premise, and the claim is the conclusion. Thus, the
quasi syllogism in the conversation between α and β is—

MAJOR PREMISE (GOVERNING RULE)

Most Irish born in southern Ireland are Catholic.

MINOR PREMISE (FACTS)

O'Malley is Irish and was born in southern Ireland.

CLAIM (CLAIM)

O'Malley is probably Catholic.

8. When no law indisputably governs a situation, a question of legal philosophy arises:
does the law or governing rule already exist, but we are unaware of it and the tribunal must
find it, or does the tribunal make a new law? We take no position on this issue, though we
believe that the modern view is that tribunals make law.

to distinguish between petty lies that should be overlooked and serious lies that should be rectified. A proponent of a rule against lying might argue that §§ 8(a)(5), 8(b)(3), and 8(d) of the Labor Act require parties to bargain in good faith, and a lie cannot be considered an act in good faith; also that it is unfair for a party to gain through lying an advantage in bargaining, such as a concession from the other party, which the latter would not otherwise have allowed. The opponent might reply that bargaining in good faith means only bargaining with a sincere desire to reach an agreement; also, that everybody lies in bargaining, and both sides know it and adjust to it. Let us fit the opponent's argument into the revised model of legal argument—

ISSUE

Should it be an unfair labor practice for an employer or a union to lie to the other party?

CLAIM

No. Lying should not be considered an unfair labor practice.

FACTS

Employers and unions sometimes lie to one another.

GOVERNING RULE

Sections 8(a)(5), 8(a)(3), and 8(d), read together, require parties to deal with one another in good faith, but good faith is not synonymous with total honesty.

RATIONALE[9]

The line between truth and lie is difficult to draw. For example, when does an exaggeration become a lie? When is omission of a relevant fact a lie? The Board would be hard pressed to answer these questions. Further, the Board would be swamped if it could be called upon to adjudicate every claim of a lie. Inevitably, the Board would

---

9. On an issue of law, the rationale will be the reasons that the tribunal should adopt the governing rule in the claim, in this example that lying should not be an unfair labor practice.

need to distinguish between serious lies, which should be rectified, and petty lies, which should be ignored; but any such distinction would be difficult to make on a principled basis and with consistency across cases. Therefore, the Board should ignore lies during organizing campaigns.

OBJECTION/REBUTTAL

Proponent argues that the Act requires parties to deal with one another in good faith, and lying is the opposite of dealing in good faith. This argument is specious because the good faith to which the statute refers is the sincere desire to reach an agreement. A party who lies may well hope that the lie will facilitate an agreement.

OBJECTION/REBUTTAL

Proponent argues that it is unfair for a party to gain an advantage in bargaining by lying. In fact, however, lying rarely yields an advantage. Both sides lie in bargaining with some frequency; and they know it, and they adjust to it.

## Exercise 2

Fit into the revised model the argument of proponents that lying is an unfair labor practice.

Now consider the issue that operates at a lower level of abstraction: should it be an unfair labor practice for an employer to threaten to close the business if workers unionize? In support of a rule against threats to close a business if the workers vote to unionize, a proponent might argue that the Labor Act prohibits employers from coercing workers, and a threat to close the business is coercive because workers would fear losing their jobs. An opponent of such a rule might reply that workers are rational adults who know that an employer might make a rash statement in the heat of an election campaign, but would be unlikely to liquidate a profitable business rather than deal with a union. The proponent might respond that one's job is so important to a worker that even the slight possibility of losing it could influence one's vote. Let us fit the proponent's argument into the revised model of legal argument—

ISSUE

> Should it be an unfair labor practice for an employer to threaten to close the business if the workers vote to unionize?

CLAIM

> Yes. Threatening to close a business if workers vote to unionize should be an unfair labor practice.

FACTS

> Employers sometimes threaten to close a business if the workers vote to unionize.

GOVERNING RULE

> Section 8(a)(1) of the Labor Act makes it illegal for an employer to interfere with, restrain, or coerce workers in the exercise of their rights under the Act.

RATIONALE

> A threat to close a business if the workers unionize is coercive because it makes them believe that they will suffer a penalty (lose their jobs) if they exercise their legal right to unionize.

OBJECTION/REBUTTAL

> Opponent argues that workers will discount a threat to close the business, that they are rational adults who know that rash statements are sometimes made in the heat of battle, and that an employer would be unlikely to give up a profitable business rather than deal with a union. This argument is mistaken, however, because jobs are important to workers and even a small chance that unionizing would cost them their jobs could influence them to vote against their true wishes.

## Exercise 3

Fit into the revised model the argument of the opponent that threatening to close the business if the workers vote to unionize is not an unfair labor practice.

## 4. Issues of Application of Law to Fact

The definition of "application of law to fact" is determining the legal consequences of a set of facts. Thus, the process of applying law to fact assumes that the law is already known, in other words, that the law which applies to the facts, as well as the meaning or interpretation of that law, have already been determined.

In *Shimul's Case*, the governing rule was that no one shall operate a vehicle in a manner that is not reasonable and safe under the conditions of the weather and the road. This rule generated an issue of fact and an issue of application of law to fact. (1) The issue of fact was, what was the reasonable and safe speed under the conditions of the weather and the road? (2) The issue of application of law to fact was, did Shimul exceed the reasonable and safe speed? Let us fit Judge Bumpkin's reasoning on these issues into the revised model—

**(1)**

ISSUE

> What was the reasonable and safe speed under the conditions of the weather and the road?

CLAIM

> The reasonable and safe speed was no more than 25 miles per hour.

FACTS

> Two inches of snow lay on the road, which had not yet been salted. Officer Quota, an expert, testified that the maximum safe speed in his opinion was 20 or 25 miles per hour.

GOVERNING RULE

> The opinion of an expert as to a fact within the expert's expertise is strong evidence of the truth of the fact.

RATIONALE

> In the opinion of Officer Quota, an expert, the reasonable and safe speed was 20 or 25 miles per hour.

OBJECTION/REBUTTAL

Shimul argues that she was experienced in driving in wintery conditions, that her vehicle was appropriately equipped, and that she was in control of it at all times. This argument is unavailing because she might have lost control of her vehicle at any time, endangering lives and property.

After Judge Bumpkin had determined the relevant facts, including the reasonable and safe speed, he applied law to fact and reached a conclusion. As the student learned in § 18 APPLICATION OF LAW TO FACT, application of law to fact often reduces to a simple syllogism in which the governing rule is the major premise, the facts are the minor premise, and the claim is the conclusion.[10] Thus, in *Shimul's Case* the syllogism was—

MAJOR PREMISE

The reasonable and safe speed limit under the conditions was 25 miles per hour.

MINOR PREMISE

Shimul was traveling at 44 miles per hour.

CONCLUSION

Shimul violated the speed limit.

Judge Bumpkin's application of law to fact fits into the revised model of legal argument, which incorporates the elements of the foregoing syllogism—

(2)

ISSUE

Did Shimul violate the speed limit?

CLAIM

Yes. Shimul violated the speed limit.

---

10. This is the more common form taken by application of law to fact. A less common form cannot be reduced to a syllogism and is discussed in § 18 Application of Law to Fact.

FACTS

The posted speed limit on Rt. 79 was 55 miles per hour, but snow was falling and two inches of it lay on the road, which had not been salted. Shimul was traveling on this road at 44 miles per hour. The reasonable and safe speed under these conditions was no more than 25 miles per hour.

GOVERNING RULE

The reasonable and safe speed was 25 miles per hour.

RATIONALE[11]

Section 1 of the Motor Vehicle Code provides that no one shall operate a vehicle faster than is reasonable and safe under the conditions of the weather and the road. In the judgment of Officer Quota, an expert, the reasonable and safe speed under the conditions was 25 miles per hour. Shimul's vehicle was moving at 44 miles per hour, which exceeded the speed limit under the prevailing conditions.

OBJECTION/REBUTTAL

Shimul argues that she is experienced in driving in wintery conditions, that her vehicle was appropriately equipped, and that she was in control of it. Even if so, these facts are not an excuse because she might have lost control of her vehicle at any moment.

### Exercise 4

Fit into the revised model Shimul's argument that she did not violate the speed limit.

## III. The Value of the Model

The foregoing discussion makes evident that the revised model of legal argument accomplishes everything that a syllogism does—and more: for

---

11. On an issue of application of law to fact, the rationale of the argument will consist of reasons why the tribunal should apply the governing rule so as to sustain the claim, in this example that Shimul exceeded the speed limit under the conditions of the weather and the road.

the model incorporates the quality of soundness. As the student learned in § 4 DEDUCTION, a syllogism proves only that an argument is valid, which means that the form of the argument is correct. A syllogism does not prove that the argument is sound or true.[12] But most reasoning in life, including in the law, aims at sound arguments, not merely valid ones. Truth matters. Thus, the GOVERNING RULE must be correct. If the GOVERNING RULE in a legal argument were, "No American may criticize the government without the president's permission," we would call the argument absurd. The element RATIONALE provides proof that the GOVERNING RULE is appropriate for resolving this dispute. Indeed, the student will find that the principal focus of a dispute often lies in the RATIONALE. Also, a syllogism that follows the rules is necessarily valid, and so it need not include any qualifications or rebut any counterarguments. In life and in law, the limits of an argument are important, as is rebutting counterarguments. The revised model incorporates these functions in QUALIFIER and REBUTTAL. Finally, a syllogism was valid 2,500 years ago when Aristotle named it, is valid today, and will be valid 2,500 years from now. No argument in real life is that strong. The revised model recognizes that the strength of an argument is important.

## IV. Review

### Exercise 5

Fit into the revised model (a) Brian Weber's argument that the affirmative action plan in *United Steelworkers of America v. Weber* violated Title VII of the Civil Rights Act of 1964, and (b) the employer and union's argument that the plan did not violate the statute.

---

12. An example of a valid syllogism that is untrue:

MAJOR PREMISE

   All men are bananas.

MINOR PREMISE

   Socrates is a man.

CONCLUSION

   Socrates is a banana.

## Exercise 6

"The Bible tells me that all humans are created by God, and so each of us has a piece of the divine in us. God is the only thing of value in the universe, and, therefore, the only thing of value in humans is the piece of the divine that God gives us. It follows that all humans are equal. Only a heathen or a minion of Satan would deny this. Of course, some of us succumb to temptation from the devil and go astray, but most of us find our way."

Fit the foregoing argument into the revised model of legal argument. Label each element (issue, governing rule, etc.). If an element is not stated, write "Not stated" after its label.

## V. References

*Abood v. Detroit Board of Education*, 431 U.S. 209 (1977).

*Janus v. American Federation of State, County, and Municipal Employees*, https://www.supremecourt.gov/opinions/17pdf/16-1466_2b3j.pdf (2018).

*United Steelworkers of America v. Weber*, 443 U.S. 193 (1979).

# Answers

## § 1. Issues

1. All except a.
2. d
3. a, b, c, d.
4. c
5. All except i and k.
6. (a) Do the bylaws apply to a new member who has not read them? (b) Is a rally an athletic contest within the meaning of the bylaws? (We do not include the issue, what is the appropriate punishment for Sally? because the facts do not include any disagreement over this issue.)
7. (a) Did one student copy from the other? (b) Did the students write their papers together?

## § 2. Identifying the Governing Rule of Law

The holding of *Medo Photo* is the governing rule of law for *Exchange Parts* because the facts of the cases are analogous. In each of them, an employer offered workers an inducement to reject their union (wage increases in *Medo Photo*, new holiday and overtime benefits in *Exchange Parts*). Such an offer interferes with the workers' right freely to decide whether or not to be represented by a union.

## § 3. Levels of Abstraction

1. False. The more persons and transactions, the *higher* the level of abstraction.

2. True

3. High

4. Low

5. All are correct.

6. a, c

7. b, d

8. *Mary's Case*

8(a). Here are two examples. Other adjudicative facts and arguments may be correct.

ADJUDICATIVE FACT: Mary said, "I have no money." ARGUMENT: Mary was concerned that, lacking money, she could not afford the costs of carrying, delivering, and rearing a child. She would not incur these costs if she aborted.

ADJUDICATIVE FACT: Mary said, "how could I finish high school" and "everyone would know I was pregnant and not married." ARGUMENT: Mary wanted to finish high school, and she did not want the embarrassment of others' knowing she was pregnant and unmarried. She could achieve both of these goals by aborting.

8(b). Here are two examples. Other adjudicative facts and arguments may be correct.

ADJUDICATIVE FACT: Mary is sixteen years old. ARGUMENT: Some girls aged 16 are not familiar with the early signs of pregnancy. If Mary did not know that she was pregnant, she could not have intentionally aborted.

ADJUDICATIVE FACT: Mary's sister Magda is a nurse. ARGUMENT: Mary trusted her sister and had no reason to suspect that the pill was an abortifacient.

8(c). Here are two examples. Other legislative facts and arguments may be correct.

LEGISLATIVE FACTS: Some women are injured by abortions, and some women who abort have deep regrets afterwards and become seriously depressed. ARGUMENT: Abortion is dangerous, and prohibiting it would promote public health.

8(d). Here are two examples. Other legislative facts and arguments may be correct.

LEGISLATIVE FACT: In the past, many women who could not obtain legal abortions were injured or killed when they resorted to back-alley abortions by incompetent practitioners. ARGUMENT: Outlawing abortions will cost the health and lives of many women.

9. *Wimp v. Bully*

9(a). ADJUDICATIVE FACTS: Wimp said he had been working thirty hours a week in Labor Law. Bully replied that people like Wimp made life miserable for everyone else. LEGISLATIVE FACTS: When *A* feels that his life is miserable because of *B*'s behavior, *A* often seeks revenge against *B*. ARGUMENT: Bully desired revenge against Wimp for busting the curve in Labor Law and deliberately thrust his elbow into Wimp's face.

9(b). ADJUDICATIVE FACTS: Bully and Wimp were classmates in Professor King's course on Labor Law. As Bully and Wimp were walking, discussing the course, Professor King appeared nearby, and Bully pointed to him. LEGISLATIVE FACT: When *A* and *B* are companions and *A* notices *C*, who is known to both *A* and *B*, it is common for *A* to point in the direction of *C*. ARGUMENT: The blow to Wimp's face was accidental. Bully was merely pointing out the presence of Professor King.

10. *H* seeks to win an argument by moving to a higher level of abstraction. *W* speaks of the present incident. *H* raises the level of abstraction from this one incident to an entire relationship.

Both are "right." *W* may well be too busy to talk to *H* at this moment. *H* may not in general pay enough attention to *W*, and *W* may rightfully complain about *H*'s inattention; and those complaints are inconsistent with *W*'s rejection of *H*'s attention at this moment.

## § 4. Deduction

1. The minor premise is missing: α is a polygon with three sides.

2(a). The major premise is missing: All watermelons are juicy.

2(b).

MAJOR PREMISE

All watermelons are juicy.

MINOR PREMISE

This fruit is juicy.

INVALID CONCLUSION

∴ This fruit is a watermelon. (Fallacy of the undistributed middle. Other fruits are also juicy.)

3(a). The major premise is missing: All puppies are adorable.

3(b).

MAJOR PREMISE

All puppies are adorable.

MINOR PREMISE

This beast is not adorable.

CONCLUSION

This beast is not a puppy.

4(a). The conclusion is missing: Annika Sörenstam did not train hard.

MAJOR PREMISE

All Olympic athletes train hard.

MINOR PREMISE

Annika Sörenstam was not an Olympic athlete.

INVALID CONCLUSION

∴ Annika Sörenstam did not train hard. (Fallacy of the illicit major. Sörenstam trained hard in golf, which was not then an Olympic sport.)

5(a). The major premise is missing: If the stock market goes up, I can get rich.

MAJOR PREMISE

If the stock market goes up, I will get rich.

MINOR PREMISE

The stock market is not going up.

INVALID CONCLUSION

∴ I won't get rich. (Fallacy of denying the antecedent. There are other ways to get rich.)

6. The major premise is the missing element: If the university had increased tuition, some students would have transferred to other schools.

7(a). If the Greeks hold a party, the dorms will be empty.

7(b).

MAJOR PREMISE

If the Greeks hold a party, the dorms will be empty.

MINOR PREMISE

The dorms are empty.

INVALID CONCLUSION

∴ The Greeks are holding a party. (Fallacy of affirming the consequent. The dorms could be empty for another reason.)

8. All persons who knowingly use in a game a football that is not inflated to a pressure of 12.5–13.5 psi violate a rule of the league.

9. All persons who take property that they do not own, with the intent of making it their own, without the owner's consent, are guilty of theft.

10.(a). A valid quasi syllogism:

MAJOR PREMISE

All members of ΔβT who serve alcohol to a guest under age twenty-one violate a rule of the fraternity

MINOR PREMISE

Senior, a member of ΔβT, served beer to a guest, Freshone, who was aged nineteen.

CONCLUSION

∴ Senior violated a rule of the fraternity.

10(b). A valid modus ponens.

MAJOR PREMISE

IF *p*, THEN *q*.

If a member of ΔβT serves alcohol to guest under age twenty-one, the member violates a rule of the fraternity.

MINOR PREMISE

*p*

Senior, a member of ΔβT, served beer to a guest, Freshone, who was nineteen.

CONCLUSION

*q*

∴ Senior violated the rule.

11. b (Valid but unsound. The minor premise is false because no creature is half man and half bull.)

12. d (Even if the syllogism were valid, it would be unsound because the minor premise (goats do not nourish their kids with milk) is false.)

13. d Fallacy of denying the antecedent.

(If *p*, then *q*.) If I were the last man on earth, you wouldn't go out with me.

(Not *p*.) I'm not the last man on earth.

(∴ Not *q*.) You will go to the dance with me.

14. d (Unsound because some students who are tired have not studied enough.)

(All *A*'s are *B*'s.) All students who are tired have studied enough to pass the test.

(*C* is a *B*.) You are tired.

(*C* is an *A*.) You have studied enough to pass the test.

## § 5. Induction

### 1.

PARTICULARS

That which is greater was previously less, and that which is less was previously greater. That which is weaker was previously stronger, and that which is stronger was previously weaker. And the same for better/worse, more just/less just, hotter/cooler, sleep/waking.

GENERALIZATION

All things that have opposites are generated out of their opposites.

INFERENCE

Life and death are opposites, and so one is generated from the other.

ARGUMENT

If life is generated from death, the soul does not die. If generation were a straight line instead of a circle, all things would reach the same state and there would be no generation. For example, when we sleep, we would never awaken; and when something dies, it would stay dead.

### 2.

MAJOR PREMISE

Most Irish who are born in southern Ireland are Catholic.

MINOR PREMISE

O'Malley is Irish and was born in southern Ireland.

CONCLUSION

∴ O'Malley is (probably) Catholic.

3(a). Cops cite only 1 percent of people who text while driving.

3(b).

MAJOR PREMISE

Cops cite only 1 percent of people for texting while driving.

MINOR PREMISE

Bea is texting while driving.

CONCLUSION

∴ Bea is unlikely to be cited (or, Bea has a 1 percent chance of being cited).

## § 6. Arguments in General

1. b, c, d
2. a, b, c, d
3. a, c, d

## § 7. Arguments Classified by Function

The issue in *Jefferson Standard* was whether concerted activity, which is protected by the Labor Act, includes behavior that is disloyal or indefensible. This issue operated at a high level of abstraction, and was an issue of law, because the resolution of the issue would affect many persons in many situations. The function of the arguments in the case was to resolve the issue of law.

## § 9. Policy Arguments

1. b, c, d
2(a). (i) Gissel's lawyer: (1) A document signed under social pressure should not be taken to represent the true will of the signer. (2) One who signs a document and changes one's mind should not be bound by the document.

2(a). (ii) Union's lawyer: (1) Employers should not intimidate workers. (2) A wrongdoer should not benefit from one's own wrongdoing.

2(b). (i) Gissel's lawyer: (1) The cards do not reflect the workers' true will. (2) The effect of an employer's intimidation of workers will diminish over time.

2(b). (ii) Union's lawyer: (1) The cards reflect the workers' true desires. (2) Gissel would use the additional time before a rerun election to campaign against the union.

2(c). (i) The normative claim is that workers should be considered adults who can withstand social pressure. (ii) The argument regarding social pressure can be analyzed thus—

ISSUE

Do authorization cards signed under social pressure express the true will of the signers?

MAJOR PREMISE

If an adult signs a document under social pressure, the document nonetheless expresses the will of the adult.

MINOR PREMISE

Workers are adults who sign authorization cards under social pressure.

CONCLUSION

Authorization cards express the will of the signers.

(iii) This modus ponens is valid. Is it sound? The major premise is a statement of fact. It is relevant to the issue of whether authorization cards express the will of workers. Whether the statement is true is open to question; expert opinion should be used to evaluate the truth of the statement. If it is true, it operates at the appropriate level of abstraction because both the issue and the statement apply to all workers. The minor premise is also a statement of fact. It is relevant to the issue because the statement is the very fact that generates the issue. The union appears to concede that the statement is true. It operates at the level of abstraction of all workers, which is the same level as the issue.

## § 10. Doctrinal Arguments

1. a, b, e

2(a).

Issue 1

Are undocumented workers employees as defined in the Labor Act?

2(b).

### EMPLOYER'S ARGUMENTS AND THEIR CLASSIFICATIONS

Argument 1

Undocumented workers take jobs illegally, and Congress could not have meant to give them rights under the Labor Act.

Function

To interpret the Labor Act

Basis

The intent of the Labor Act

Argument 2

Protecting undocumented workers would be inconsistent with the Immigration Act because they would be encouraged to sneak into America.

Function

To interpret the Labor Act in light of the Immigration Act

Basis

The purpose of the Labor Act and the Immigration Act.

2(c).

### LABOR BOARD'S ARGUMENTS AND THEIR CLASSIFICATIONS

Argument 1

The Act defines "employee" to include all employees except specifically excluded classes of workers; undocumented workers are not specifically excluded.

Function

To interpret the Labor Act

Basis

The text of the Labor Act (its definition of "employee")

Argument 2

The Act was intended to promote collective bargaining to improve workers' wages and working conditions, which would deteriorate from competition with undocumented workers who could not unionize.

Function

To interpret the Labor Act

Basis

The purpose of the Labor Act

Argument 3

Protecting undocumented workers would not be inconsistent with the Immigration Act because that statute does not make it a crime for an employer to hire an undocumented worker or for an undocumented worker to take a job.

Function

To interpret the Labor Act in light of the Immigration Act.

Basis

The purpose of the Immigration Act

3(a).

Issue 2

Did the employer commit an unfair labor practice by writing to the INS?

3(b).

### EMPLOYER'S ARGUMENT AND ITS CLASSIFICATION

Argument

> To count as discrimination, an employer's act must be the proximate cause of the worker's disadvantage; but the workers' illegal status, not the employer's letter, caused their deportation.

> Function

>> To apply law to fact to determine whether the letter violated § 8(a)(3).

> Basis

>> The text of § 8(a)(3), which implies that the employer's act must be the cause of the disadvantage to the workers

3(c).

### LABOR BOARD'S ARGUMENT AND ITS CLASSIFICATION

Argument

> The employer's letter to the INS was the cause of the workers' disadvantage because, but for the letter, the INS would not have investigated them.

> Function

>> To apply law to fact to determine whether the employer violated § 8(a)(3).

> Source

>> The text of the section, which implies that the employer's act must be the cause of the disadvantage to the workers

The Supreme Court agreed with the Labor Board, holding that undocumented workers are employees under the Labor and that the employer committed an unfair labor practice by reporting them to the INS.

## § 11. Analogies and Precedents

1. Burns: antecedent: "my luve," consequents: "red rose" and "melodie."
*As You Like It*: antecedent: "the world," consequent "a stage"; antecedent: "men and women," consequent: "players." *Macbeth*: antecedent: "life," consequents: "walking shadow" and "a poor player."

2. At least one problem with Aspasia's analogies is that a husband and a wife make a commitment to one another that one does not make to one's possessions.

3. THE CAPTAIN'S ANALOGY

ISSUE

Should the general of an army have absolute authority over all persons and objects in or that might affect the army?

PRECEDENT The captain of a ship

Facts of the precedent

The captain of a ship is responsible for everything that happens on and to the ship.

Rationale of the precedent

One who may be held responsible for events should have the power to influence them.

Result of the precedent

The captain has absolute authority over all persons and objects on a ship.

CASE AT BAR The general of an army

Facts of the case at bar and their similarity to the facts of the precedent

The general of an army is also responsible for everything that is done by and happens to the army.

Argument that the rationale of the precedent applies to the facts of the case at bar

The rationale of the Captain's Analogy is that one who may be held responsible for all events should have the power to control them. This rationale applies with equal force to the general of an army because the general is also responsible for everything.

CLAIM

The general must have absolute authority over all soldiers, other persons, and objects in, affected by, or able to affect the army.

4. *THE CASE OF THE SECOND BITE*

ISSUE

Is Δ liable to π due to Brutal's biting π?

PRECEDENT: *Fershing v. Norlander*

Facts of the precedent

Norlander's dog Terror bit Turayhi without provocation, thereby putting Norlander on notice of the dog's tendency to bite. Then Terror bit Fershing without provocation.

Rationale of the precedent

The owner of a dog that has bitten a person is aware of the dog's tendency and has a duty to control it.

Result of the precedent

Norlander was liable to Fershing for damages.

CASE AT BAR: *π v. Δ*

Facts of the case at bar and their similarity to the facts of the precedent

Like Norlander's dog Terror, Δ's dog Brutal bit a person without provocation. In both cases, the dog had previously bitten without provocation, and so the owners knew they had to control their dogs.

Argument that the rationale of the precedent applies to the facts of the case at bar

Norlander was responsible for her dog's second bite because she knew of its tendency to bite and failed to control it.

Likewise, Δ knew of his dog's tendency to bite and failed to control it.

CLAIM

Δ is liable to π for damages.

5. The judge omitted the name and facts of the precedent and its result; the facts of the case at bar and their similarity to the facts of the precedent; and the argument that the rationale of the precedent applies to the facts of the case at bar.

6. *THE FINE PRINT CASES*

ANALOGY BETWEEN *DAVID v. GOLIATH* AND *DANIEL v. DROP-YOUR-CALL*

(a). Analysis

ISSUE

Should Judge Devorah adopt the rule that a party is not bound by a clause in a contract that a person of ordinary education and intelligence could not understand?

PRECEDENT: *David v. Goliath*

Facts of the precedent

David's lease with Goliath Rentals contained clauses about occupancy and rent that a person of ordinary education and intelligence could not understand.

Rationale of the precedent

(Not stated) Although we should usually be held to the contracts we enter, fairness requires that one understand the obligations one is assuming. It is unfair to hold a consumer dealing with a corporation to a clause written in legalese that a person of ordinary education and intelligence could not understand.

Result of the precedent

The court adopted the rule that a person will not be held to a clause in a contract written in legalese that a person of ordinary education and intelligence could not understand.

CASE AT BAR: *Daniel v. Drop-Your-Call*

Facts of the case at bar and their similarity to the facts of the precedent

> Clause *Z* of Daniel's contract with Drop-Your-Call provided that the law of the State of Decay would govern any disputes under the contract. The contract was written in legalese and printed in fine print. These facts are similar to the facts of *David v. Goliath*, which contained clauses about occupancy and rent that were written in lawyer speak.

Argument that the rationale of the precedent applies to the facts of the case at bar

> The rationale of *David v. Goliath* was that it is unfair to hold a consumer dealing with a corporation to a clause in a contract that a person of ordinary education and intelligence could not understand. This rationale applies equally to *Daniel v. Drop-Your-Call* because David was and Daniel is a consumer dealing with a corporation.

CLAIM

> Judge Devorah should adopt the rule from the State of Oblivion that a consumer who signs a contract is not bound to any clause that a person of ordinary education and intelligence could not understand.

(b). Function of the Issue

This is an issue of law.

(c). Use of the Analogy

The analogy is used to choose the governing rule of law.

(d). Evaluation of the Analogy

The precedent from the State of Oblivion appears to be authoritative. It is not binding in the State of Grace, but may have persuasive force. The facts of the precedent and of the case at bar are analogous. In both cases, a consumer was dealing with a corporation, and the contracts were written in legalese that an ordinary consumer could not understand. The analogy is relevant because the precedent and the case at bar deal with the same issue, namely, whether a party should be bound by a clause in a contract that a person of ordinary education and intelligence could not understand. No more convincing analogy comes to mind.

### ANALOGY BETWEEN *FAR v. AWAY* AND *DANIEL v. DROP-YOUR-CALL*

(a). Analysis

ISSUE

> Could a person of ordinary education and intelligence understand clause Z?

PRECEDENT: *Far v. Away*

> Facts of the precedent

>> Doris had a credit card issued by Usurious Bank. Clause Y of her application for the card contained a clause that was similar to clause Z of Daniel's contract with Drop-Your-Call. When a dispute arose between Doris and the bank, the latter asserted that the dispute was governed by the law of the State of Decay.

> Rationale of the precedent

>> (Not stated) An ordinary consumer cannot understand legalese.

> Result of the precedent

>> Doris was not bound by clause Y.

CASE AT BAR: *Daniel v. Drop-Your-Call*

> Facts of the case at bar and their similarity to the facts of the precedent

>> Clause Z of Daniel's contract was nearly identical to clause Y of Doris's application.

> Argument that the rationale of the precedent applies to the facts of the case at bar

>> Both clauses were written in legalese, which an ordinary consumer cannot understand.

CLAIM

> Judge Devorah should hold that a person of ordinary education and intelligence could not understand clause Z and, therefore, that the dispute between Daniel and Drop-Your-Call should be governed by the law of the State of Grace and not by the law of the State of Decay.

(b). Function of the Issue

This is an issue of application of law to fact. The court had to determine the legal consequences of the facts of the case.

(c). Use of the Analogy

The analogy is used to apply law to fact, that is, to determine whether clause Z could be understood by a person of ordinary education and intelligence.

(d). Evaluation of the Analogy

The cases are analogous because clauses Y and Z are nearly identical. The issues are the same (could an ordinary person understand the clause?) and no better analogy comes to mind.


## § 12. Distinctions

### 1. *THE CASE OF THE SUPERVISOR'S QUESTIONS*
The union's advocate may argue:

> It is true that the *War between the Unions* allowed supervisors to question workers about which union they supported, but the rationale of that case does not apply to the case at bar. The employer in
> 1 the *War between the Unions* was confronted with two unions' competing claims of majority support. The employer had to know which claim was true in order to know with which union to bargain. To be sure, a risk did arise that the employer, knowing who supported which union, might have retaliated against workers, but this risk was outweighed by the employer's interest in obeying the

law. For this reason, the Board held that the supervisors' questions about the workers' allegiance were permissible. Obviously, this reasoning has no bearing on the case at bar. In this case, only one union is involved. It is still trying to organize the workers and has not claimed to have attained majority support. Therefore, the employer has no legitimate reason to question the workers about their union allegiance, and nothing outweighs the risk that the employer will use the information to retaliate against workers.

## 2. YOUNG TOM'S CASE

### MOTHER DRAWS AN ANALOGY, AND TOM DISTINGUISHES IT

MOTHER'S ANALOGY

Facts of the precedent

X takes money without permission.

Rationale of the precedent

To deprive of possession without permission is to steal.

Result of the precedent

X stole the money

CASE AT BAR: TOM'S CASE

Similarity of the facts of the precedent and the facts of the case at bar

Like X, Tom took money without permission.

Rationale of the precedent applies to the case at bar

Tom deprived Mom of her money without permission.

Result of the case at bar

Tom stole the money.

TOM'S DISTINCTION

Difference of fact between the precedent and the case at bar

Tom intended to repay the money whereas X did not.

Importance of the difference of fact

Mother would regain the use of her money when Tom repaid it.

Conclusion

X's case is not a precedent for Tom's case.

### TOM DRAWS AN ANALOGY, AND MOTHER DISTINGUISHES IT

#### THE ADVERSARY'S PRECEDENT: TOM'S ANALOGY

Facts of the precedent

Dad took money from the drawer for pizza without permission, but with intent to return it.

Rationale of the precedent

It's not stealing if you intend to return the money.

Result of the precedent

Dad did not steal the money.

#### CASE AT BAR

Similarity of the facts of the precedent and the case at bar

Both Tom and Dad intended to return the money.

Rationale of the precedent applies to the case at bar

Tom intended to return the money, so he did not steal it.

Result of the case at bar

Tom did not steal the money.

#### MOTHER'S DISTINCTION

Difference of fact between the precedent and the case at bar

Dad took the money to buy dinner for the family—an authorized use. Tom took the money for a video game—an unauthorized use.

Importance of the difference of fact

> Taking property for an authorized use is tantamount to taking it with permission, whereas taking property for an unauthorized use is taking it without permission.

Conclusion

> Dad's case is not a precedent for Tom.

### TOM DRAWS A DISANALOGY, AND MOTHER REFUTES IT

TOM'S DISANALOGY

Facts of the other case

> At least Tom did not say that Ashley took it.

Rationale of the other case

> It is a capital crime to accuse your sister of something that you know she did not do.

Result of the other case

> What Tom did was not so bad after all.

Mother's refutation

> It is irrelevant that you did not falsely accuse Ashley.

> or

> What matters is that you did not ask permission.

3. *THE DISTINCTION BETWEEN* OVER v. OUT *AND* DANIEL v. DROP-YOUR-CALL

### DROP-YOUR-CALL'S ANALOGY OF THE CASE AT BAR TO *OVER v. OUT*

ISSUE

Could a person of ordinary intelligence understand clause $Z$?

PRECEDENT: *Over v. Out*

Facts of the precedent

> The contract between Cable Television and Nightly News contained clause $X$, which provided that disputes under the

contract would be decided according to the law of the State of Decay.

Rationale of the precedent

(Not stated) The parties were able to understand clause $X$.

Result of the precedent

The dispute between Cable Television and Nightly News was governed by the law of the State of Decay.

CASE AT BAR: *Daniel v. Drop-Your-Call*

Facts of the case at bar and their similarity to the facts of the precedent

Clause $X$ of the contract between the parties was similar to clause $Z$ of David's contract.

Argument that the rationale of the precedent applies to the facts of the case at bar

If Cable Television and Nightly News could understand clause $X$, David could understand clause $Z$.

CLAIM

Judge Devorah should hold that David could understand clause $Z$ and, therefore, that the dispute between Daniel and Drop-Your-Call should be governed by the law of the State of Decay.

JUDGE DEVORAH'S DISTINCTION OF *OVER v. OUT FROM THE CASE AT BAR*

DIFFERENCE(S) OF FACT BETWEEN THE PRECEDENT AND THE CASE AT BAR

Cable Television and Nightly News were big companies with lawyers to write and review their contracts. Drop-Your-Call is a big company, but David is a consumer.

IMPORTANCE OF THE DIFFERENCE(S) OF FACT

Big companies have experience with contracts and understand them; the companies also have easy access to legal advice. Thus, it is likely that Cable Television and Nightly News both understood clause $X$.

But an individual consumer has little experience with contracts, may not understand legalistic clauses like clause Z, and cannot afford legal advice for every contract. A rule of law that is fair for contracts between big companies can be unfair for a contract between a big company and a consumer.

RESULT OF THE CASE AT BAR

Clause Z should be void because an ordinary person could not understand it.

## § 14. Reductios ad Absurdum

1. Aristotle argued that the *Paradox of the Arrow* rests on the false assumption that time is composed of indivisible moments. In other words, Zeno assumed that time is an infinite series of separate and indivisible moments (like points on a line), but time is in fact something else (perhaps a continuum). Other resolutions have been proposed as well.

2. As the student learned in mathematics, a problem that is difficult to solve in one form can sometimes be solved by converting it into another form. The *Paradox of Achilles and the Tortoise* is substantially the same as the *Dichotomy Paradox*, which Aristotle describes thus: "that which is in locomotion must arrive at the half-way stage before it arrives at the goal." In this paradox, the tortoise does not move. In order for Achilles to reach it, he must reach point M-1, which is midway between himself and the tortoise. Achilles arrives at point M-1. Now before he can reach the tortoise, he must reach point M-2, which is midway between point M-1 and the tortoise. But once he reaches point M-2, he still must reach point M-3, which is midway between point M-2 and the tortoise. Because the number of points on a line is infinite, and the number of midpoints is also infinite, Achilles cannot traverse them in a finite period of time (such as his life). Therefore, he will never reach the tortoise—or any other destination, and so motion is impossible.

Here is another way to express Zeno's argument:

PROPOSITION I

Achilles must first traverse an infinite number of divisions in order to reach the tortoise.

PROPOSITION 2

It is impossible for Achilles to traverse an infinite number of divisions.

CONCLUSION

∴ Achilles can never surpass the tortoise.

Archimedes resolved the paradox in this form by proving that a finite number can be the sum of an infinite number of terms that get progressively smaller (½ + ¼ + ⅛ + . . . = 1). Modern calculus reaches the same conclusion. Also, as the *Paradox of the Arrow* may rest on the false assumption that time is composed of an infinite number of indivisible moments, so the *Paradox of Achilles and the Tortoise* and the *Dichotomy Paradox* may rest on the false assumption that a line is composed of an infinite number of points. This assumption is appropriate in geometry, but in practice a line is composed of discrete points with no midway points between them. If so, Achilles could progress from one point to another until he reached the tortoise.

3(a).

PROPOSITION

An increase in the minimum wage will improve the lives of low-paid workers.

ABSURDITY

An increase in the minimum wage will worsen the lives of low-paid workers.

ARGUMENT

If the minimum wage increases, a business will demand more output from its workers. The business will accomplish this end by some combination of speedups, reduced hours, and substitution of capital for labor. The burden of such measures will fall on the workers whose wages have just risen due to the increase in the minimum wage. Therefore, the increase will worsen the lives of the very workers it was meant to improve.

CONCLUSION

The minimum wage should not be increased.

3(b). Liberal economists argue that the increased wage bill may be offset in various ways. Productivity may increase because higher-paid workers will be more motivated or because higher pay will attract better workers. Revenue may increase because consumers will have more income to spend due to the increase in the minimum wage. Or the increased cost of labor may be taken from profits, or the business may raise prices.

Which side is right? The results of empirical studies appear to be mixed.

4(a).

PROPOSITION

Augustus is a god.

ABSURDITY

Augustus is not a god.

ARGUMENT

August has a birthday; therefore, he was born. But gods are eternal. If Augustus was born, he is not eternal, and so he is not a god.

CONCLUSION

Augustus is not a god.

4(b). The error is that the gods of Olympus were born and so had birthdays.

5. One possible answer: A court enforces obligations that arise before the lawsuit began. Before the lawsuit, Euanthlus had not won his first case; therefore, per his contract with Protagoras, Euanthlus does not owe the fee. The contract between them did not contemplate that they would be opposing parties in a lawsuit; therefore, the contract did not create any obligations in such a case.

## § 15. Subjective and Objective Standards

1. Many answers are possible. For example, "Everything in moderation."

2. Many answers are possible. For example, an old man gives candy to a child. If his motive is kindness, the act is praiseworthy. If his motive pederasty, the act is criminal.

3. Many answers are possible. Graded scale: who has the highest grade point average in the class? Binary scale: is Tom the oldest man in the world?

4(a). On a subjective standard, the issue would be, did Atreus in his mind agree to exchange his kingdom for a golden lamb? On an objective standard, the issue would be, would a reasonable person in Thyestes's place have believed that Atreus agreed to exchange his kingdom for a golden lamb?

4(b). On a subjective standard, the issue would be, did Thyestes in his mind agree to return the kingdom to Atreus if the sun moved backwards in the sky? On an objective standard, the issue would be, would a reasonable person in Atreus's place have believed that Thyestes agreed to return the kingdom to Atreus if the sun moved backwards?

## § 17. Prima Facie Case, Affirmative Defense, Burden of Proof

1. b

2. d

3. b, c

4. c because Δ claims that he was provoked by π.

5. e If the tribunal believed Δ and disbelieved π, the question became, did the provocation justify the tweak? From the facts given, we cannot know what the tribunal's answer would have been.

6. e If the tribunal disbelieved Δ's testimony, his affirmative defense failed. But failing to prove an affirmative defense does not mean that Δ lost the case. π still had to prove the prima facie case. The facts do not indicate how the tribunal felt about π's prima facie case and, therefore, we cannot know who won the case.

7.

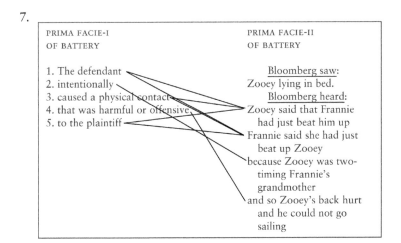

PRIMA FACIE-I
OF BATTERY

1. The defendant
2. intentionally
3. caused a physical contact
4. that was harmful or offensive
5. to the plaintiff

PRIMA FACIE-II
OF BATTERY

Bloomberg saw:
Zooey lying in bed.
Bloomberg heard:
Zooey said that Frannie
  had just beat him up
Frannie said she had just
  beat up Zooey
because Zooey was two-
  timing Frannie's
  grandmother
and so Zooey's back hurt
  and he could not go
  sailing

# § 18. Application of Law to Fact

## 1. *Tommy's Case*

### QUASI SYLLOGISM

ISSUE

May Tommy see the movie?

MAJOR PREMISE (GOVERNING RULE)

One must be at least eighteen years old to see the movie.

MINOR PREMISE (FACTS OF THE CASE)

Tommy is younger than eighteen.

CONCLUSION (APPLICATION OF LAW TO FACT)

∴ Tommy may not see the movie.

### MODUS TOLLENS

ISSUE

May Tommy see the movie?

IF P, THEN Q (GOVERNING RULE)

If a person wishes to see the movie, one must be at least eighteen years old.

NOT *q* (FACTS OF THE CASE)

Tommy is younger than eighteen.

NOT *p* (APPLICATION OF LAW TO FACT)

∴ Tommy may not see the movie.

## 2. *Dipaboli's Case*

2(a). The issue of application of law to fact regarding Samuel was, may Samuel ride the roller coaster?

2(b).

| THE PRECEDENT | WHAT DIPABOLI LEARNED FROM IT |
|---|---|
| 1. Rhea | One who is eighteen may ride without regard to height or companion. |
| 2. Cassie | One who is under eighteen, less than five feet tall, and unaccompanied may not ride. |
| 3. Devon | One who is five feet tall may ride without regard to age or companion. |
| 4. Dylan | One with an adult companion may ride without regard to age or height. |

2(c).

### QUASI SYLLOGISM

ISSUE

May Samuel ride the roller coaster?

MAJOR PREMISE (GOVERNING RULE)

In order to ride, one must satisfy at least one of three criteria: be at least eighteen years old, be accompanied by an adult, or stand at least five feet tall.

MINOR PREMISE (FACTS OF THE CASE)

Samuel is younger than eighteen, less than five feet tall, and unaccompanied.

CONCLUSION (APPLICATION OF LAW TO FACT)

∴ Samuel may not ride.

MODUS TOLLENS

ISSUE

May Samuel ride the roller coaster?

IF *p*, THEN *q* (GOVERNING RULE)

If one is not eighteen years old, is not accompanied by an adult, and does not stand at least five feet tall, one may not ride.

NOT *q* (FACTS OF THE CASE)

Samuel is younger than eighteen, unaccompanied, and less than five feet tall.

NOT *p* (APPLICATION OF LAW TO FACT)

∴ Samuel may not ride.

## § 19. A Model of Legal Argument

1. ARGUMENT OF REFUSERS AS TO THE ISSUE IN *JANUS v. AFSCME*

ISSUE

What is the issue in *Janus v. American Federation of State, County, and Municipal Employees*?

CLAIM

The issue is, does an agency shop in the public sector infringe on a refuser's freedom of speech?

FACTS

The labor contract between a public employer and a union contains an agency shop clause, which requires refusers to pay their fair share of the cost of the union's negotiating and enforcing the contract.

GOVERNING RULE

Freedom of speech prohibits the government from compelling a person to support a cause or candidate.

RATIONALE

Public policy is inevitably affected when unions negotiate with the government. If a refuser is compelled to pay one's fair share of the cost of negotiating a labor contract, the refuser is effectively required to support a particular policy. For example, if the union negotiates a raise in pay, taxes must be increased or some other program be decreased. If a refuser must pay the cost of negotiating a raise, the refuser is willy-nilly supporting an increase in taxes or a decrease in another program.

The Supreme Court accepted the refusers' formulation of the issue, overruled *Abood*, and held that the agency shop is unconstitutional in the public sector.

2. ARGUMENT OF PROPONENTS THAT LYING IS AN UNFAIR LABOR PRACTICE.

ISSUE

Should it be an unfair labor practice for an employer or a union to lie to the other party?

CLAIM

Yes, lying should be considered an unfair labor practice.

FACTS

Employers and unions sometimes lie to one another.

GOVERNING RULE

Sections 8(a)(5), 8(a)(3), and 8(d), read together, require parties to deal with one another in good faith.

RATIONALE

A lie cannot be considered good-faith bargaining. It is fundamentally unfair for a party to obtain a concession from the other party based on a lie.

OBJECTION/REBUTTAL

Opponents argue that it is difficult to draw a line between a lie and the truth and to distinguish petty lies from serious ones, also that the Board would be swamped with cases about lying. But making such determinations is the job of the Labor Board, which is staffed by experienced professionals in the field. Honesty leads to trust, which leads to successful bargaining, which it is the duty of the Board to promote.

**3.** ARGUMENT OF THE OPPONENT THAT THREATENING TO CLOSE THE BUSINESS IF THE WORKERS VOTE TO UNIONIZE IS NOT AN UNFAIR LABOR PRACTICE

ISSUE

Should it be an unfair labor practice for an employer to threaten to close the business if the workers vote to unionize?

CLAIM

No, threatening to close the business if the workers vote to unionize should not be considered an unfair labor practice.

FACTS

Employers sometimes threaten to close the business if the workers vote to unionize.

GOVERNING RULE

Section 8(a)(1) makes it illegal for an employer to interfere with, restrain, or coerce workers in the exercise of their rights under the Act.

RATIONALE

Workers are rational adults who know that an employer might make a rash statement in the heat of an election campaign, but would be unlikely to liquidate a profitable business rather than deal with a union.

**4.** SHIMUL'S ARGUMENT THAT SHE DID NOT VIOLATE THE SPEED LIMIT

ISSUE

Did Shimul exceed the reasonable and safe speed under the conditions?

CLAIM

No, Shimul did not exceed the reasonable and safe speed.

FACTS

The posted speed limit was 55 miles per hour. Shimul was traveling 44 miles per hour. Although snow was on the road, she grew up in rural Maine and was experienced in driving in wintery conditions. In addition, her vehicle was equipped with all-wheel drive and electronic stability control, and had snow tires on the wheels. She was in control of the vehicle at all times.

### GOVERNING RULE

No one shall operate a vehicle in a manner that is not reasonable and safe under the conditions of the weather and the road.

### RATIONALE

In determining the reasonable and safe speed, one must take into account not only the conditions of the weather and the road, but also the skill and experience of the driver, the equipment of the vehicle, and the performance of the driver. Imagine someone from Florida driving on Route 79 in upstate New York on December 6, 2016 at 10:28 a.m. The vehicle lacks all-wheel drive, electronic stability control, and snow tires, and is fishtailing down the road. For this driver in this vehicle under these conditions, the reasonable and safe speed might have been 10 miles per hour, or 5—or even zero! By contrast, Shimul was experienced in driving on snow-covered roads; her vehicle was well equipped for winter, and she was in full control at all times. She did not exceed the reasonable and safe speed.

### OBJECTION/REBUTTAL

Officer Quota judged that the reasonable and safe speed was 25 miles per hour, but at the time he cited Shimul, he must have based his judgment on the average driver and vehicle, not on Shimul and her vehicle. He could not have known about her experience in wintery conditions or about the equipment on her vehicle. In addition, the officer evidently did not take into account that Shimul was fully in control of her vehicle. She had not lost control of it, and this fact, together with her experience and well-equipped vehicle, prove that she was not likely to lose control of it and, therefore, that she did not exceed the reasonable and safe speed.

**5.** (A) WEBER'S ARGUMENT THAT THE AFFIRMATIVE ACTION PLAN IN *STEEL-WORKERS v. WEBER* VIOLATED TITLE VII

ISSUE

Did the affirmative action plan violate Title VII?

CLAIM

Yes, the affirmative action plan violated Title VII.

FACTS

An employer and a union agreed to operate a program that would train unskilled workers for skilled jobs. Admission to the plan was based on seniority within a worker's race. The most senior African American applicant was admitted; then the most senior European American applicant was admitted; then the second most senior African American was admitted; then the second most senior European American, and so on. Brian Weber was denied admission to the program although African Americans who had less seniority in the plant than he had were admitted.

GOVERNING RULE

Sections 703(a) and (d) make it illegal "to discriminate against any individual . . . because of such individual's race."

RATIONALE

"To discriminate against any individual . . . because of such individual's race" is to deny that individual an employment opportunity that he would have received if he belonged to another race. With his seniority in the plant, Weber would have been admitted to the training program if he were an African American. He was a victim of "reverse discrimination" and, therefore, the company and the union discriminated against him because of his race.

OBJECTION/REBUTTAL

The employer and union argue that the purpose and legislative history of the statute permit reverse discrimination by affirmative action plans. This argument is erroneous. The text of the statute is perfectly clear, and purpose and legislative history cannot override clear text.

## 5. (B) THE EMPLOYER AND UNION'S ARGUMENT THAT THE PLAN DID NOT VIOLATE TITLE VII

### ISSUE

Did the affirmative action plan violate Title VII?

### CLAIM

No, the affirmative action plan did not violate Title VII.

### FACTS

An employer and a union agreed to operate a program that would train unskilled workers for skilled jobs. Admission to the plan was based on seniority within a worker's race. The most senior African American applicant was admitted; then the most senior European American applicant was admitted; then the second most senior African-American was admitted; then the second most senior European American, and so on. Brian Weber was denied admission to the program although African Americans who had less seniority in the plant than he had were admitted.

### GOVERNING RULE

Sections 703(a) and (d) make it illegal "to discriminate against any individual . . . because of such individual's race."

### RATIONALE

The purpose and legislative history of the statute demonstrate that Congress intended to increase employment opportunities for African Americans and women. The plan in the case at bar served this objective without being unfair to white workers, who received half of the spots in the training program.

### OBJECTION/REBUTTAL

The words of the statute can be read to outlaw the plan in the case at bar, but words are ambiguous. The purpose and legislative history of a statute clarify the meaning of its words, showing that Congress did not intend to outlaw reasonable affirmative action plans that promote opportunities for African Americans and women without ignoring the interests of white workers.

### 6. THE BIBLE TELLS ME SO

ISSUE

Are all humans equal in value?

CLAIM

Yes, all humans are equal in value.

FACTS

God is the only thing of value in the universe. God creates and gives each of us a piece of the divine.

GOVERNING AUTHORITY

The Bible tells me so.

RATIONALE

(1)

MAJOR PREMISE

God is the only thing of value in the universe.

MINOR PREMISE

God creates and gives each of us a piece of the divine.

CONCLUSION

The only thing of value in us is the piece of the divine that God gives us.

(2)

MAJOR PREMISE

Equality means being of equal value.

MINOR PREMISE

The only thing of value in us is the piece of the divine that God gives us.

CONCLUSION

We are equal because we all have the only thing that is valuable.

OBJECTION/QUALIFIER

Some of us succumb to Satan and go astray, but most of us find our way.

OBJECTION/REBUTTAL

Some deny this reasoning, but they are heathens or minions of Satan.

CPSIA information can be obtained
at www.ICGtesting.com
Printed in the USA
LVHW04s0220300918
591802LV00001BA/63/P